CUSTOMIZE YOUR CROSS-STITCH

— FRIENDS AND FAMILY —

Learn to customize, prepare, stitch, and finish your very own personalized cross-stitch creations

Lizzy Dabczynski-Bean

STITCH PEOPLE.

Walter Foster

Quarto.com • WalterFoster.com

First published in 2023 by Walter Foster Publishing,
an imprint of The Quarto Group,
100 Cummings Center, Suite 265D, Beverly, MA 01915, USA.
T (978) 282-9590 F (978) 283-2742

27 26 25 24 23 1 2 3 4 5

ISBN: 978-0-7603-8535-7

Design and Page Layout: Samantha J. Bednarek, samanthabednarek.com
Author Illustrations: Eden Tinney

Printed in China

THIS BOOK IS DEDICATED TO THE EVER-SUPPORTIVE AND WONDERFULLY CREATIVE STITCH PEOPLE COMMUNITY:

the people who are stitched, the people who do the stitching, and the hearts we stitch together in the process.

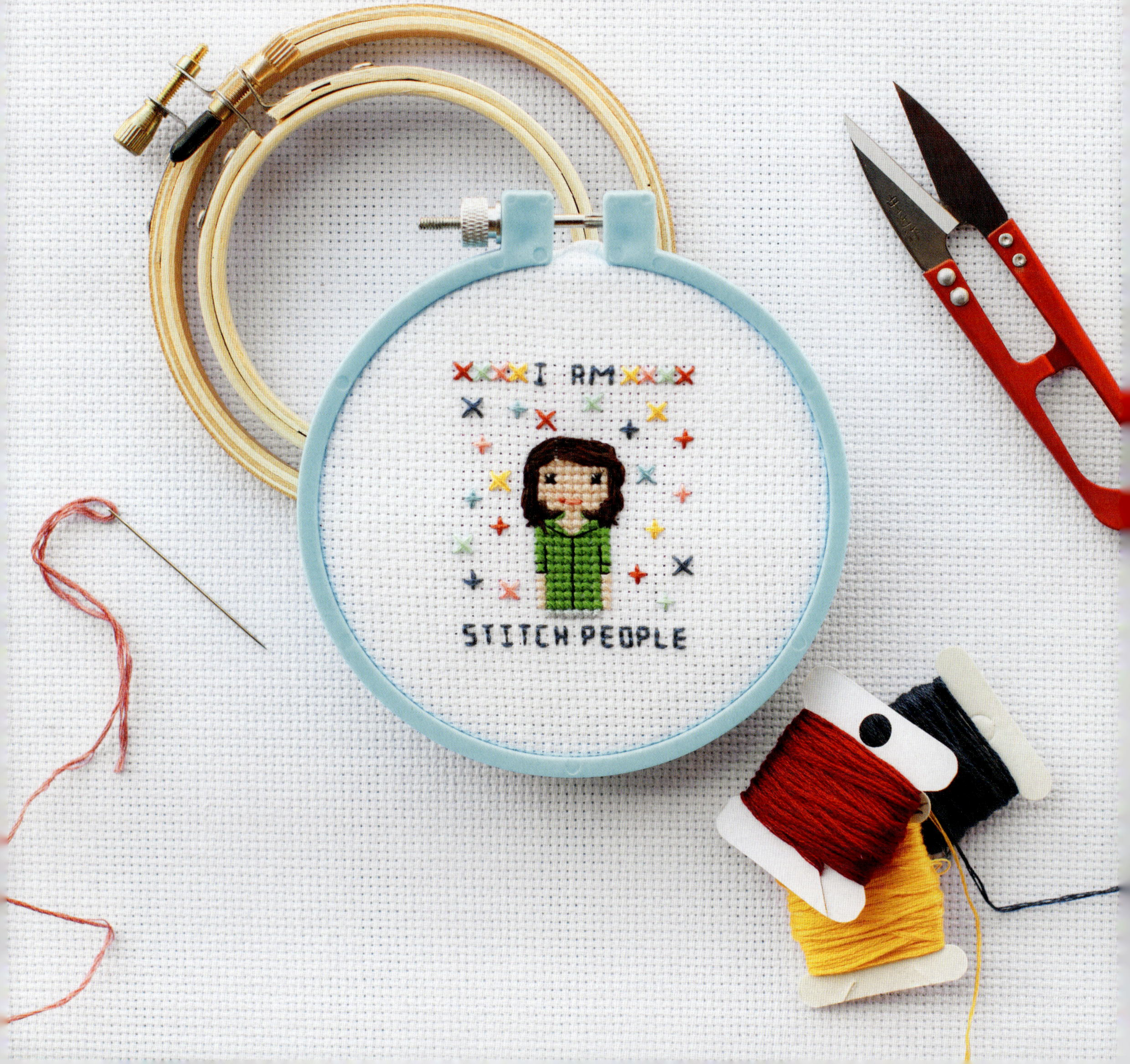

table of contents

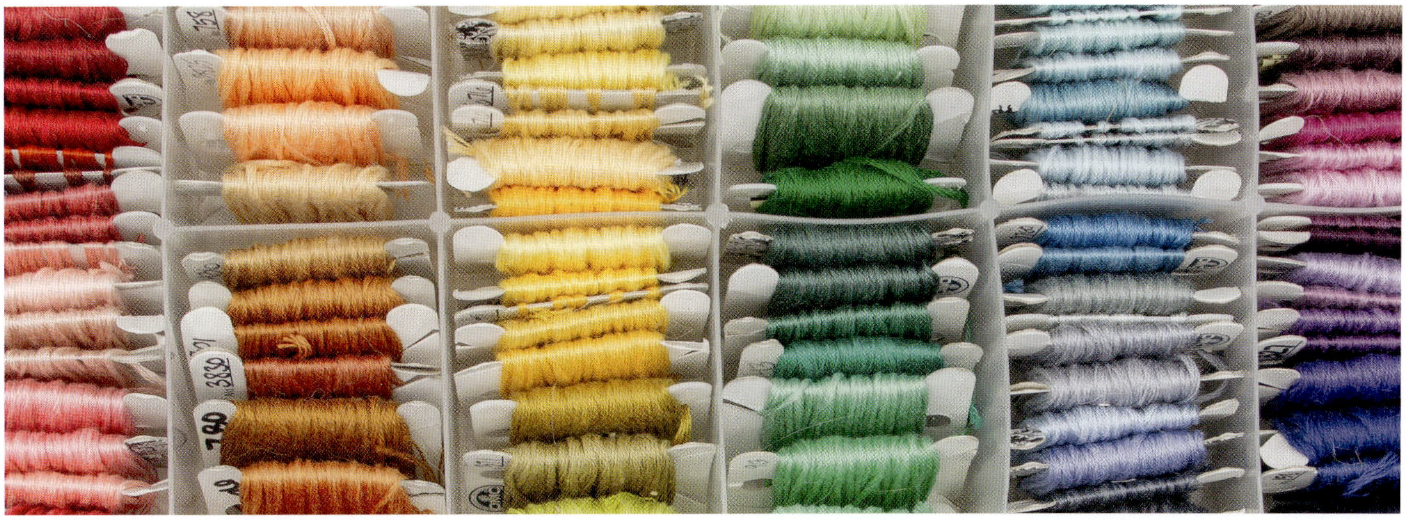

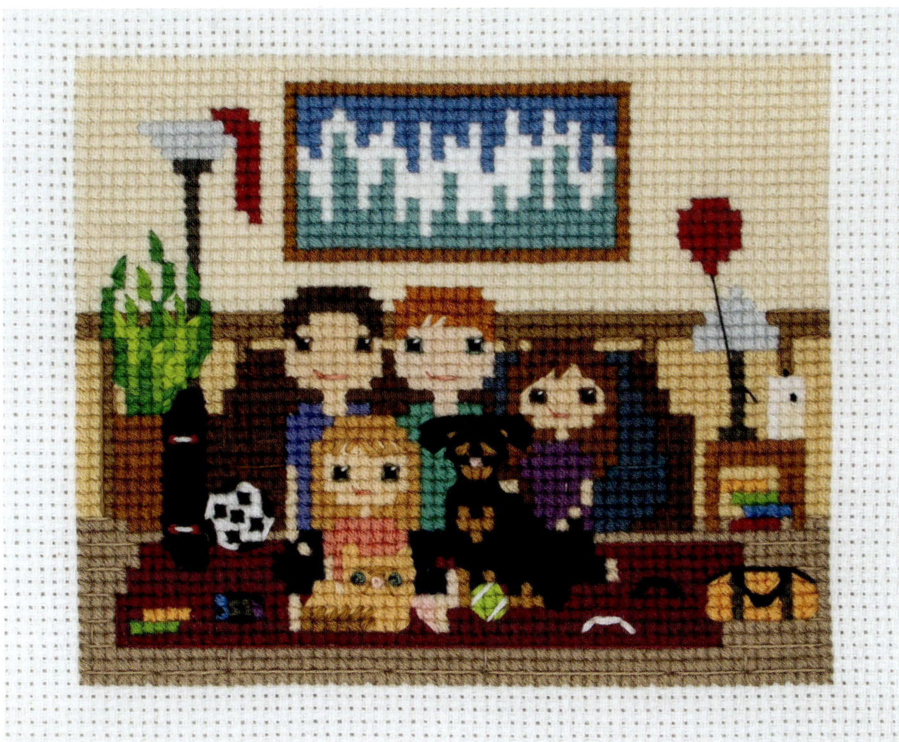

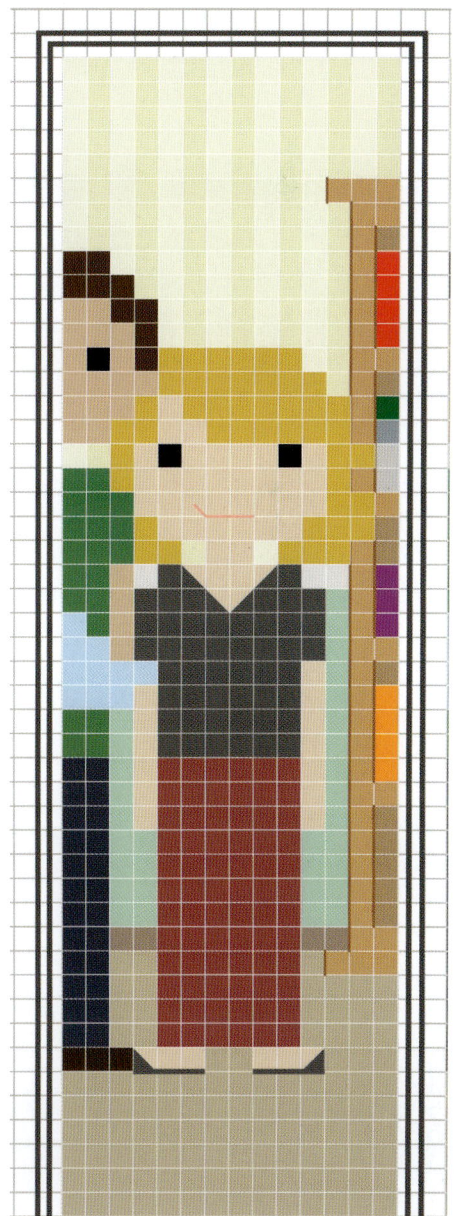

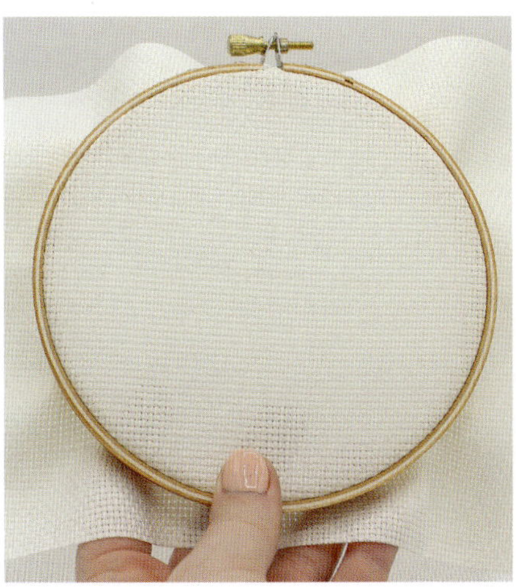

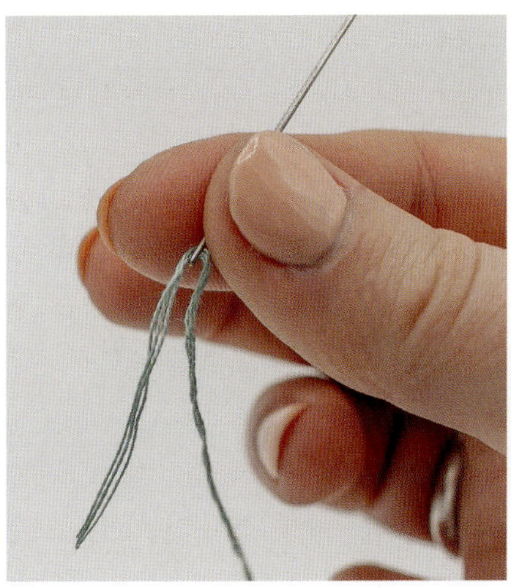

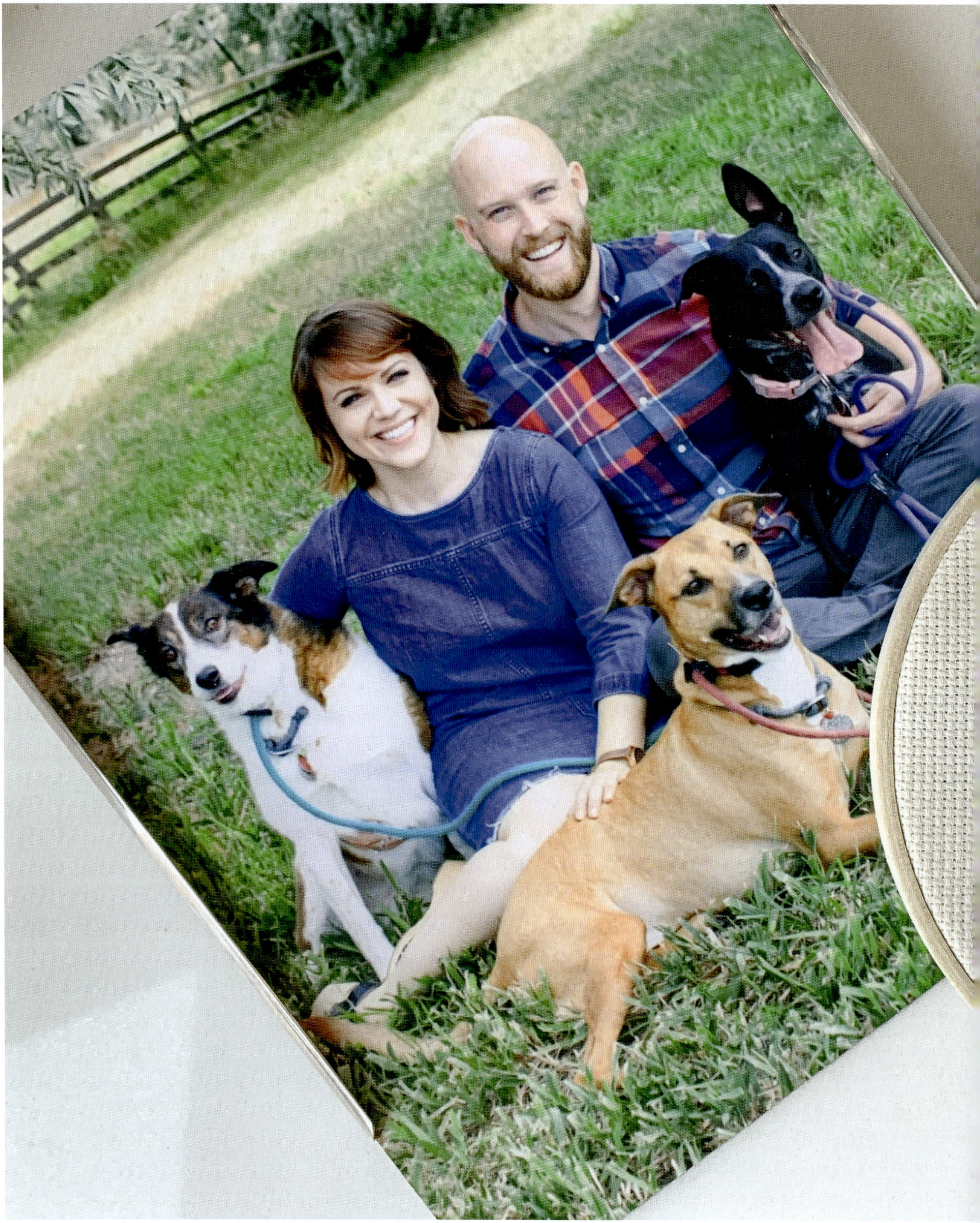

welcome!

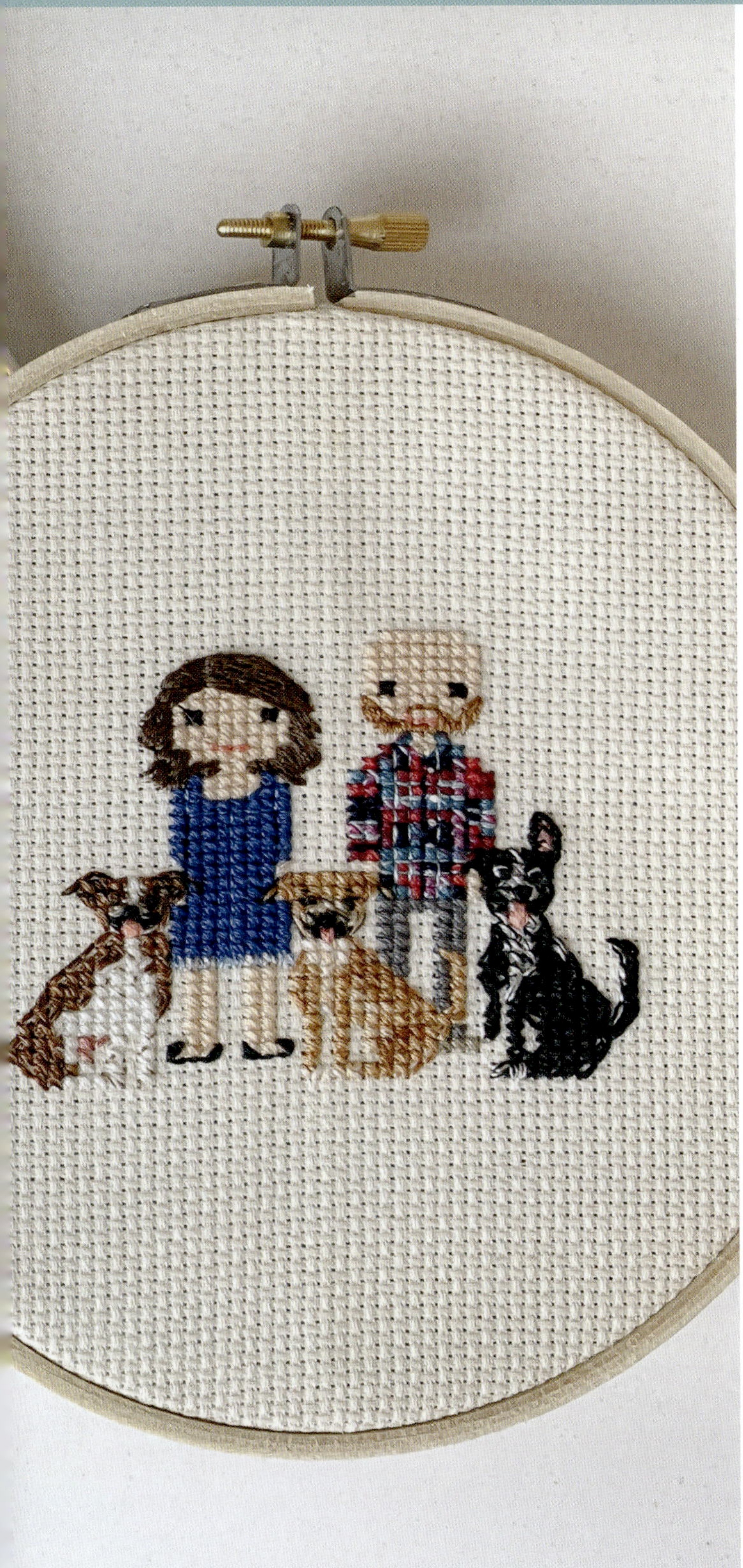

HI THERE! I'M LIZZY BEAN, THE FOUNDER OF STITCH PEOPLE.

I started Stitch People in 2011 with my husband, Spencer, after I created some cross-stitched family portraits for my family members as Christmas gifts. "Why don't you sell these online," he suggested. And (long story short) I did!

It wasn't long before we saw reposts and feedback all over the Internet from fellow crafters and cross-stitchers who expressed interest in learning how to create their own, fully customized cross-stitched family portraits. That's what led us from primarily creating finished, handmade portraits, to creating patterns for stitchers like *you*!

The majority of our offerings up to this point have been collections of mix-and-match patterns for stitchers to create their own cross-stitched family portrait patterns completely from scratch. But that can be a very overwhelming prospect! That's where this book comes in. We've taken out even more of the guesswork for you to be able to jump right into creating your own, customized cross-stitched portraits.

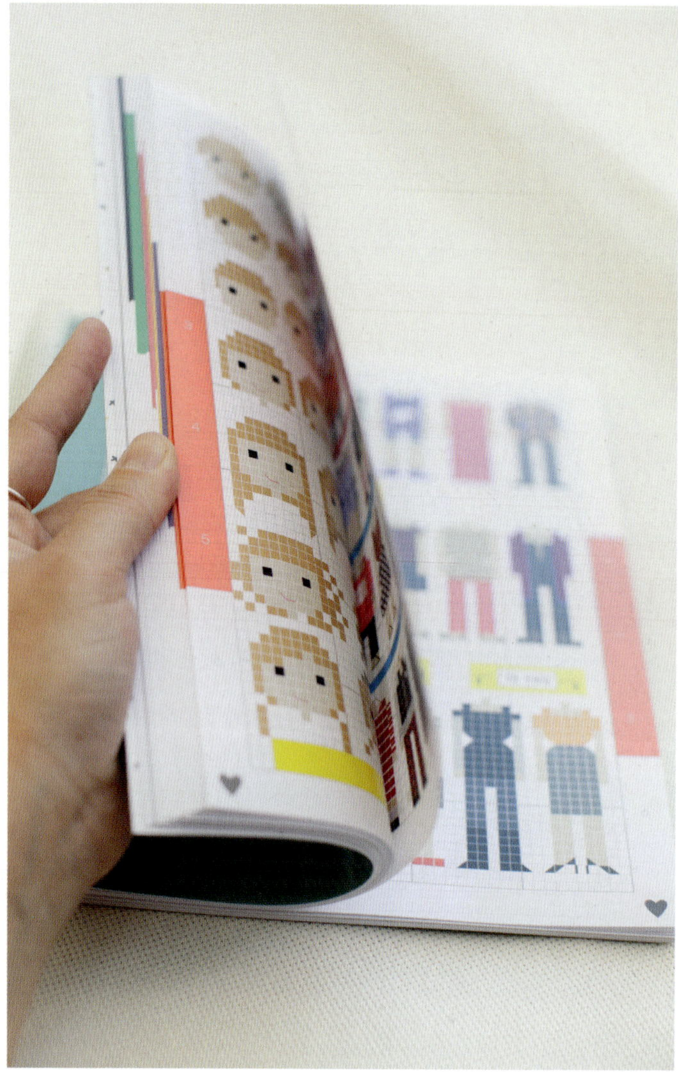

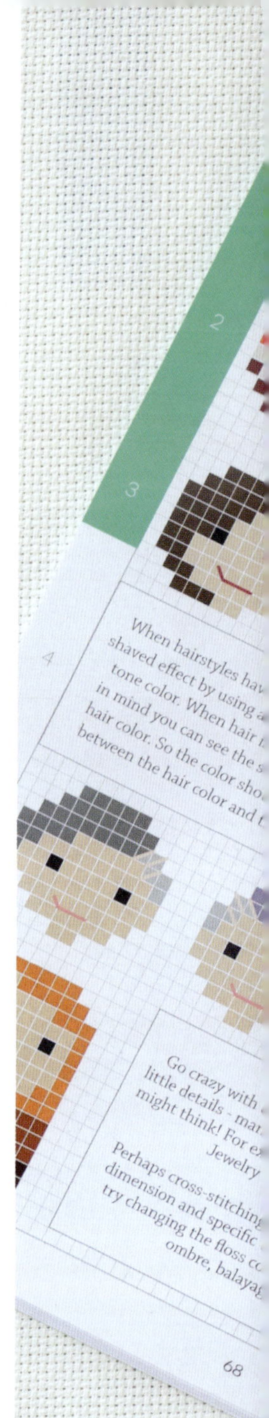

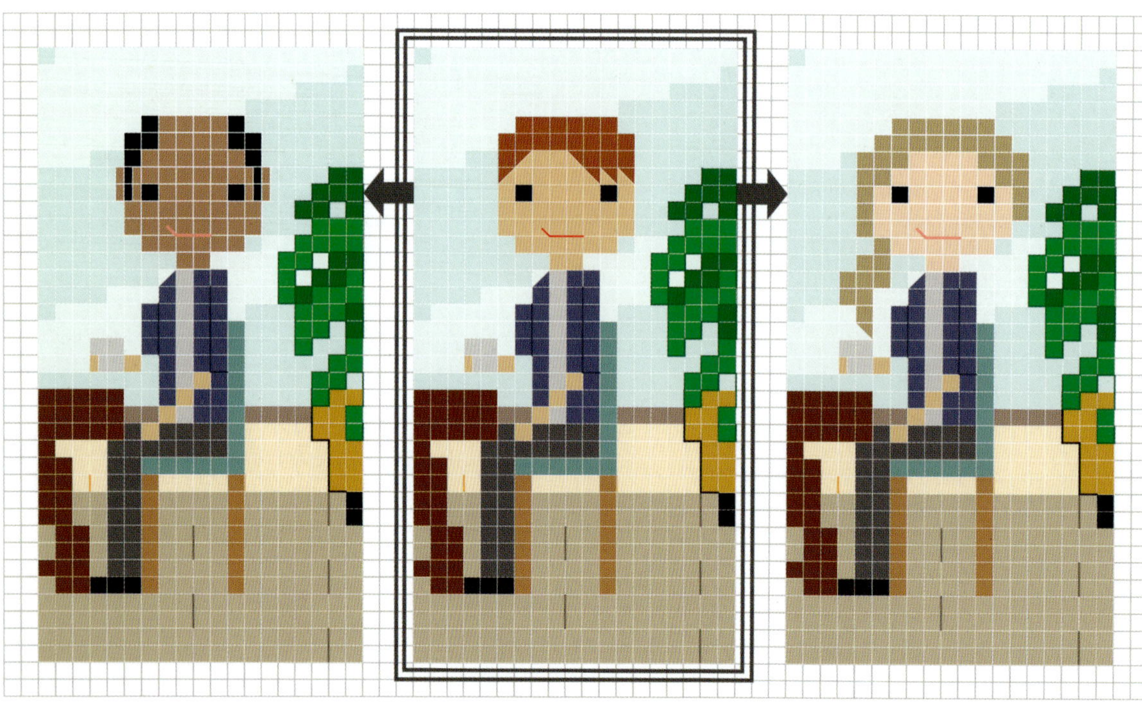

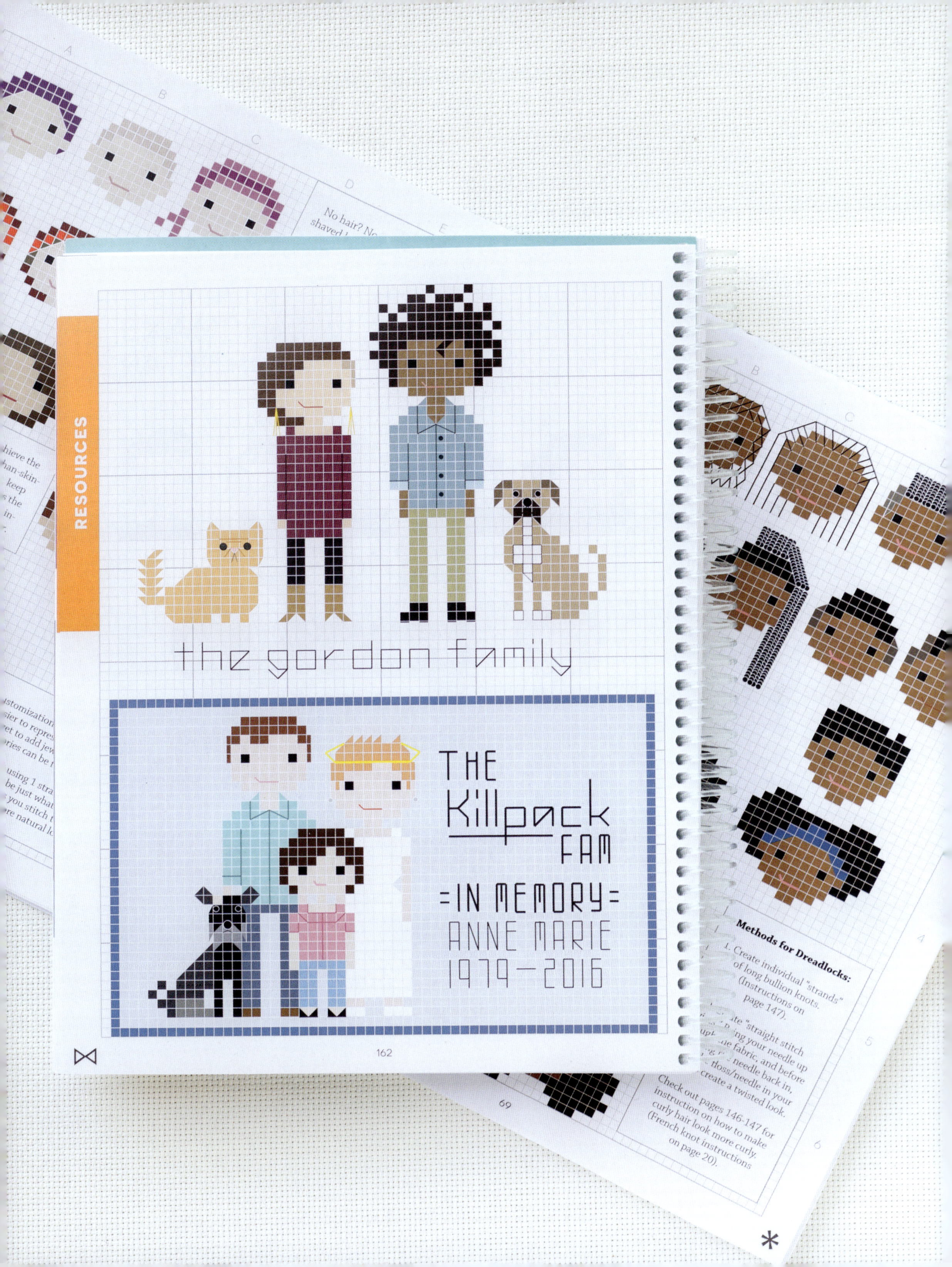
RESOURCES
the gordon family
THE
Killpack
FAM
=IN MEMORY=
ANNE MARIE
1979–2016
162
Methods for Dreadlocks:
1. Create individual "strands" of long bullion knots. (Instructions on page 147).
Check out pages 146-147 for instruction on how to make curly hair look more curly. (French knot instructions on page 20).
69

about the book

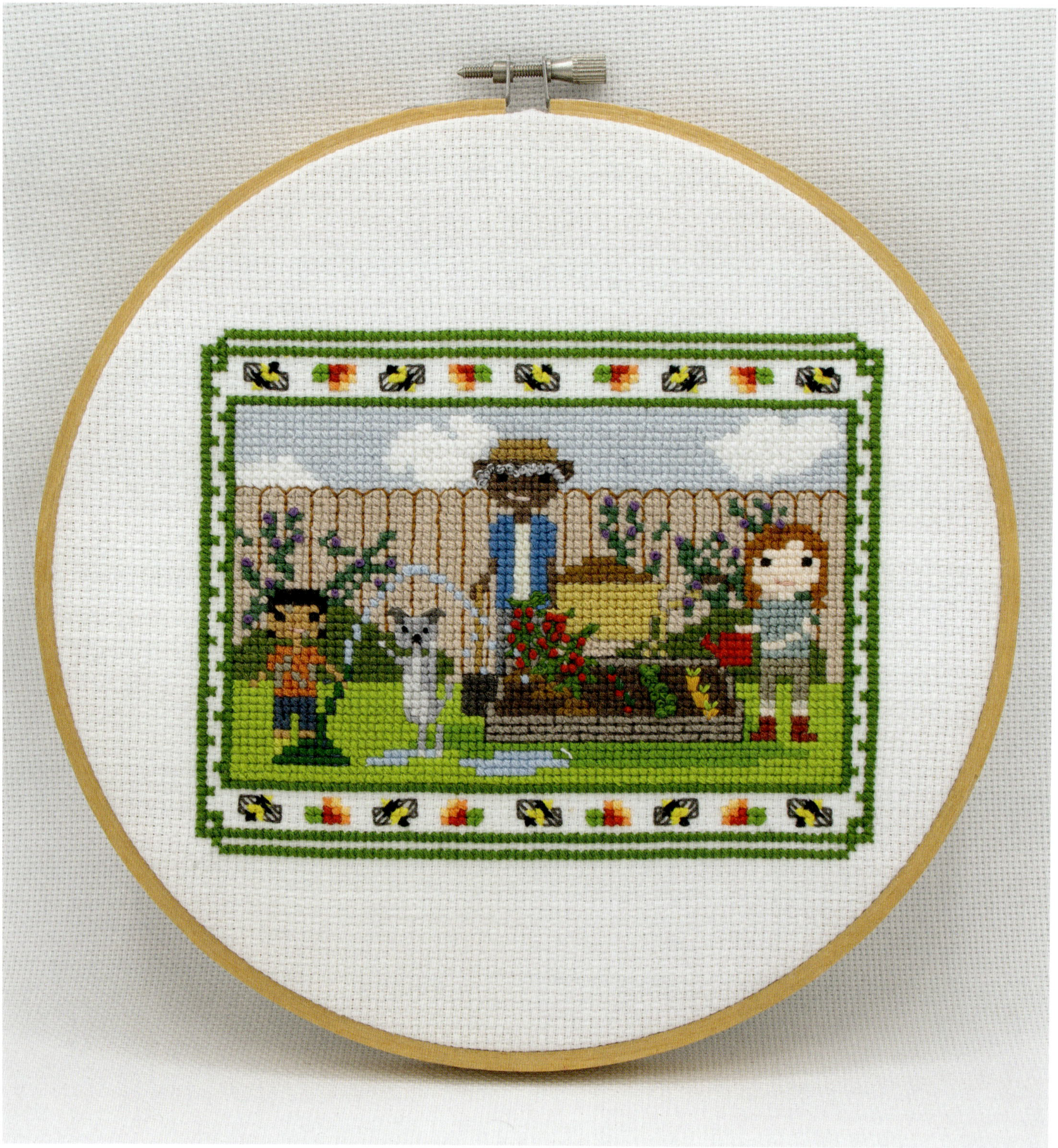

CROSS-STITCHED FAMILIES

You'll likely soon realize that it would be impossible to create patterns that match every family or friend group on the planet. From age gaps, to physical differences and beyond, each and every family unit or bunch of friends is entirely unique. That's why Stitch People patterns are all about customization.

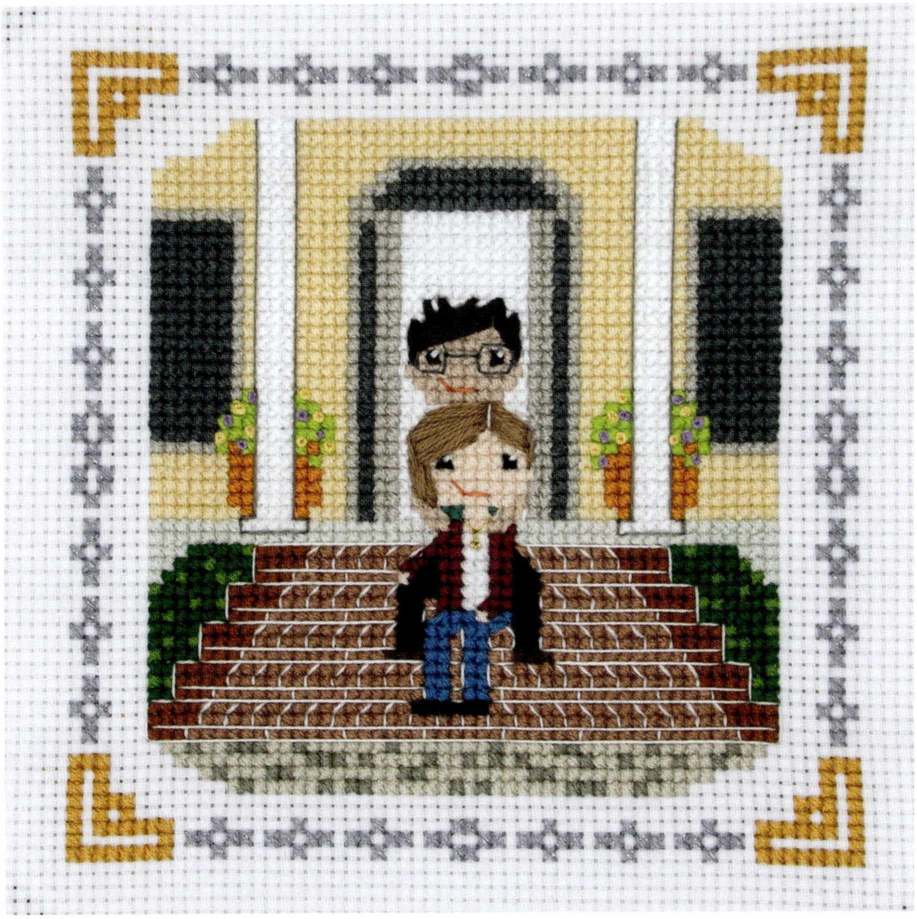

In this particular collection of patterns, you'll find ready-made scenes of friend and family groups doing all sorts of friendly and family-ish activities! "But these characters don't look like me and my family!" you may think. Never fear! I'll show you what to do to make customizations to the patterns in this book to accommodate your unique circumstances.

LEAN INTO YOUR CREATIVITY

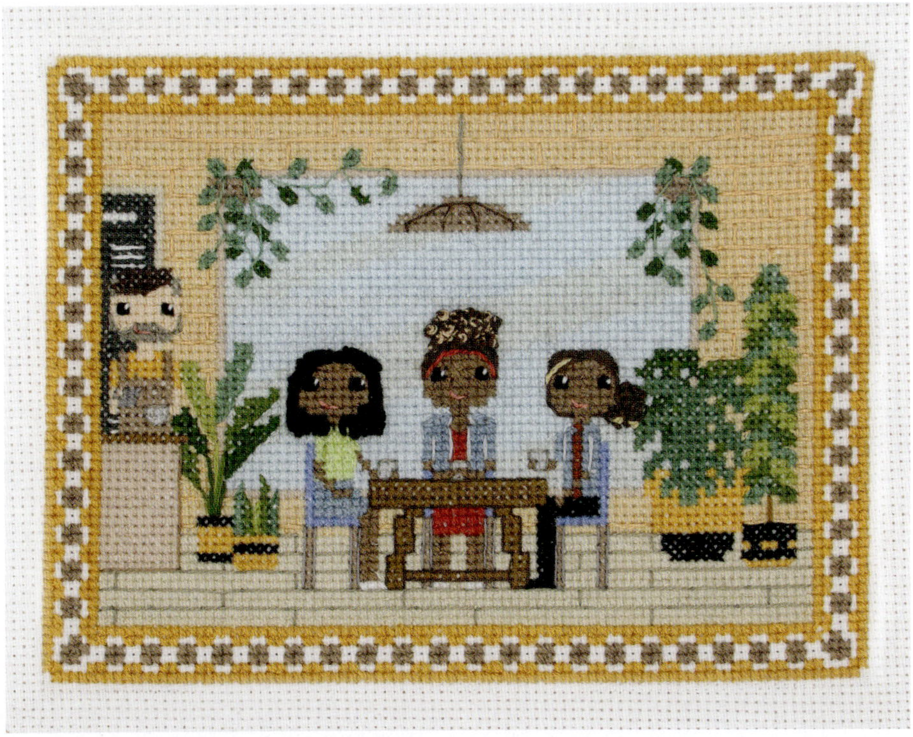

Stitch People is all about igniting your personal creativity. It's important to remember to follow your creative heart and lean into your creative autonomy. At the end of the day, cross-stitching is just drawing and coloring with thread instead of crayons, and fabric instead of paper. There's no "wrong" way to draw or paint, so

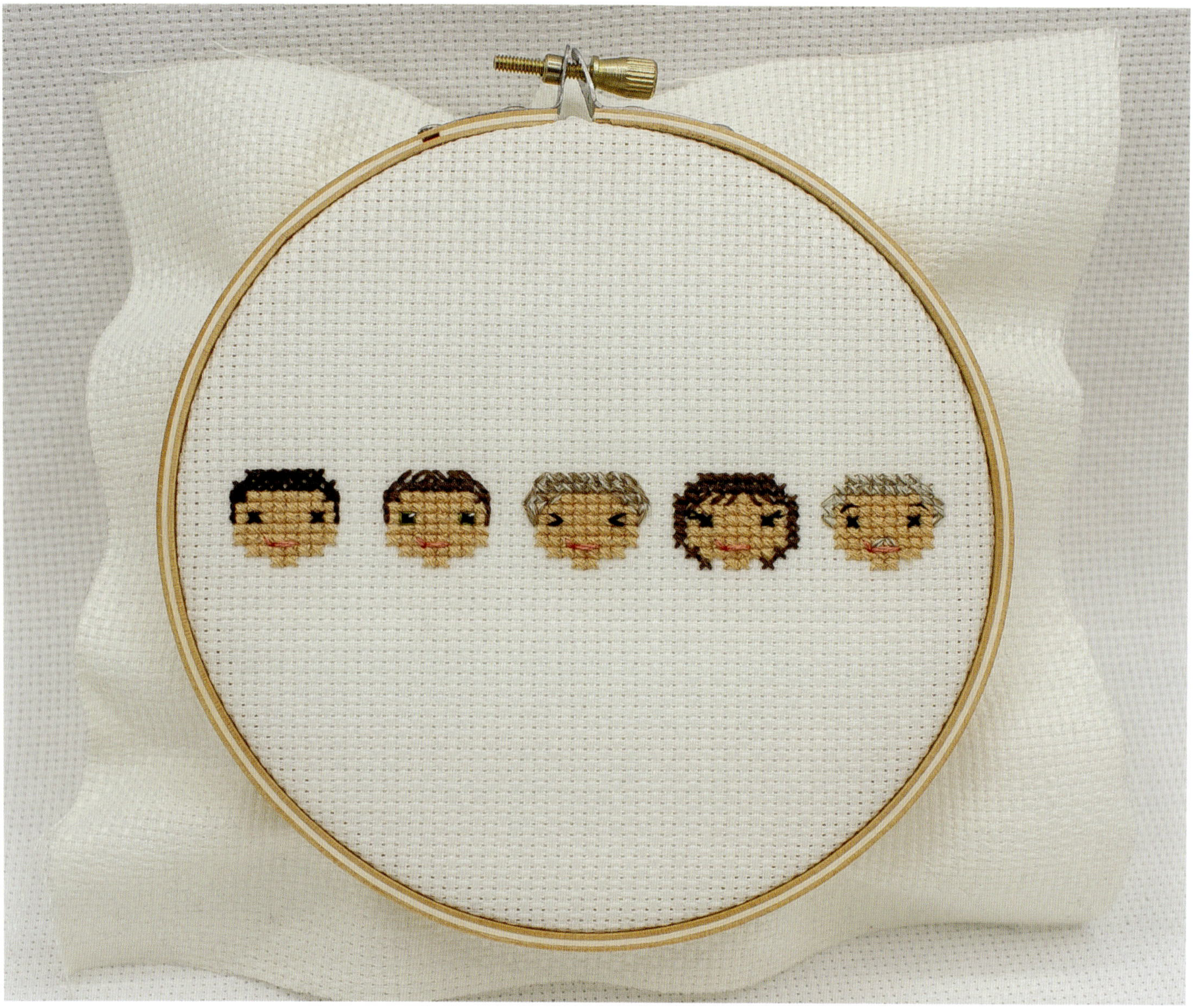

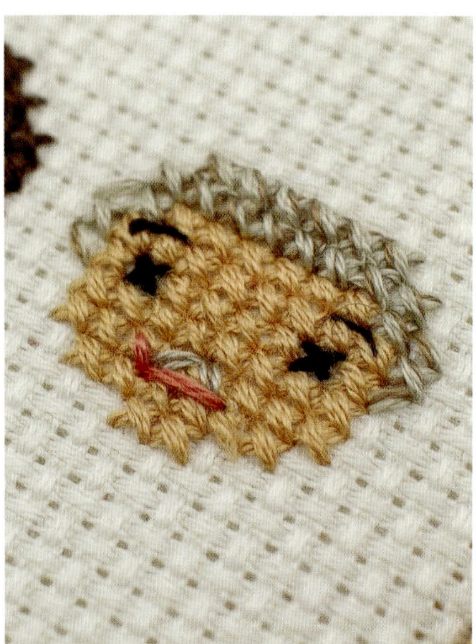

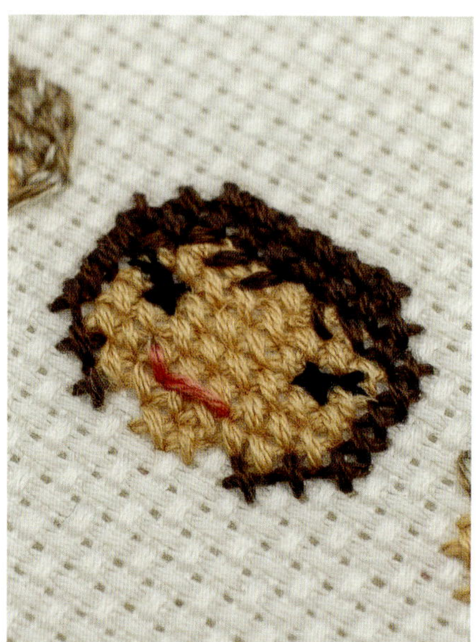

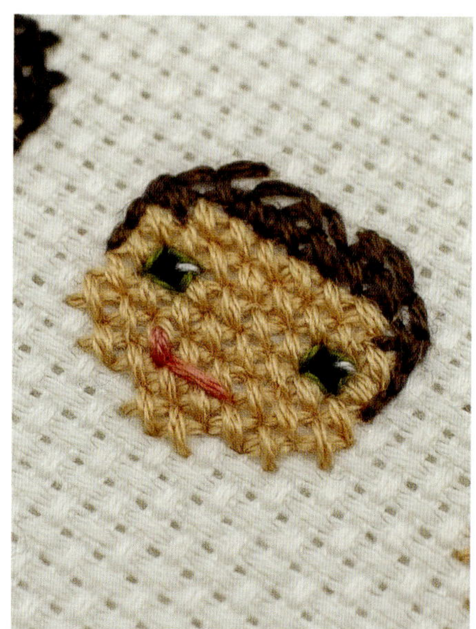

likewise, there's no "wrong" way to stitch. Sure, there are some surefire tips and tricks developed over the ages (cross-stitching is a centuries-old handmaking tradition, after all), but I would like to encourage you to take a deep breath, smile, and enjoy the journey.

We have a saying at Stitch People: "There's no such thing as a cross-stitch emergency." It serves as a reminder not only that cross-stitching is meant to be fun and not a high-stress activity, but also that cross-stitching is a nonessential, creative hobby. It's certainly not a life-or-death situation. Therefore, no matter how many "mistakes" you make, or how many imperfections you may perceive within your final work...it really is okay! (You're probably the only one who notices the flaws, anyway!)

STITCH PEOPLE'S DESIGN STYLE

The story behind how and why Stitch People came about is lengthy, but suffice it to say that one of the primary drivers behind the design style of Stitch People was simplicity. Thus, I was inspired by the precedent of template-style character designs in other genres. If you think about LEGO® characters, Funko POP figurines, Disney's Tsum Tsums or Vinylmations, or even American Girl® Dolls, you'll understand what I mean.

Since cross-stitching takes place on such a small scale, it becomes difficult to customize every single feature of a person. So characters remain "templated" and consistent from person-to person for simplicity's sake, merely as a stylistic choice. Clothing, hair color, and skin color (like American Girl Dolls or other examples mentioned) become the primary ways to distinguish characters. We do have instructions for adjusting character height and width if desired.

YOU CAN DO IT!

We live in a world that teaches us to color inside the lines. And if you think about it, we're very used to someone else providing those lines for us! So it's very natural to feel cautious about customizing your own patterns. I promise you can do it, whether you're brand new to cross-stitching or have been a stitcher for decades.

I know you're ready, and I can't wait to start stitching with you, so let's go!

tools + materials

CROSS-STITCHING MATERIALS ARE FAIRLY CONSISTENT FROM PROJECT TO PROJECT, WHICH MAKES IT VERY EASY TO COLLECT WHAT YOU NEED FROM CRAFT STORES AND ONLINE RETAILERS. YOU MAY EVEN HAVE A FEW HELPFUL TOOLS AND MATERIALS LYING AROUND YOUR HOUSE ALREADY!

FABRIC

While cross-stitching can technically be done on any fabric, the primary type of fabric used for cross-stitching is called Aida fabric, pronounced AY-duh (where AY rhymes with pay). Aida fabric is woven into a grid with holes throughout, convenient for creating cross-stitches. The size of Aida fabric is identified by a number equal to the number of squares or stitches that will fit within an inch (2.5 cm) of space on that fabric. For example, a size 14 Aida fabric can accommodate 14 cross-stitches per inch (2.5 cm). Size 14 is the most common size of Aida fabric, and is what I recommend using for Stitch People-style portraits.

Aida fabric comes in many different colors! White, off-white, and natural or oatmeal finish fabrics are most common, but you can add a great level of artistic flair to any portrait by choosing a different color. Remember—there's no wrong way!

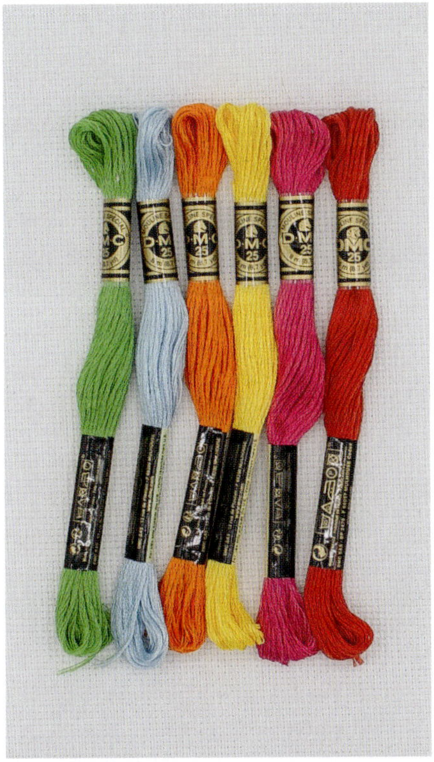

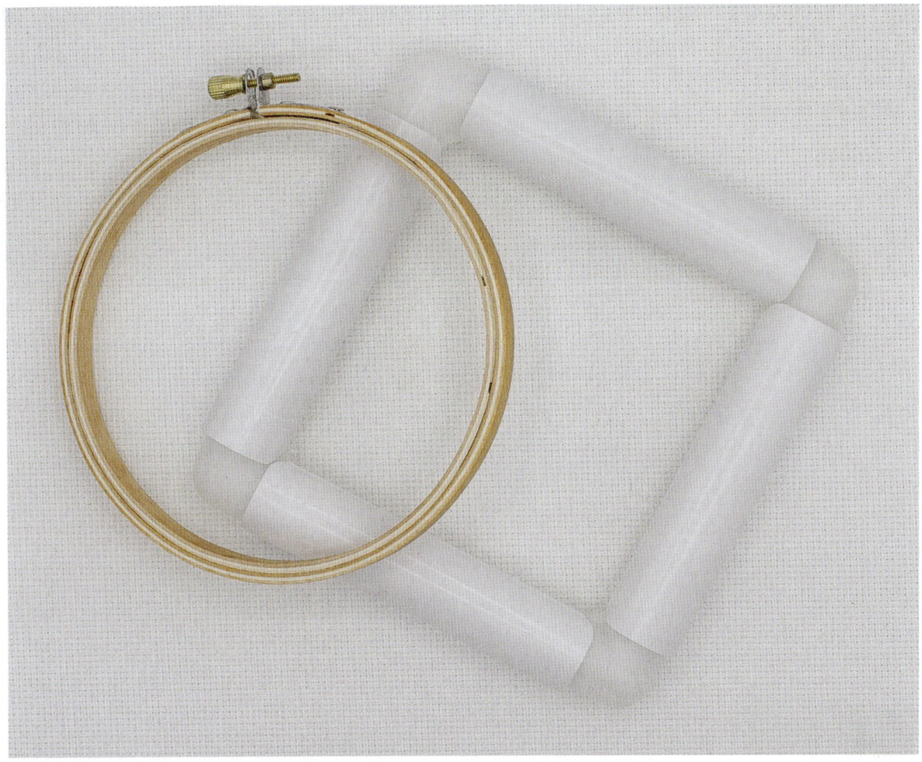

FLOSS

The type of thread used for cross-stitching is called embroidery floss. Though there are many different brands that make floss, I will be referencing DMC® floss colors, as DMC is the most commonly available, and has hundreds of colors perfect for cross-stitched portraits.

Embroidery floss comes in a skein, pronounced skEEN, and consists of 6 individual threads gently twisted together. It is common for cross-stitch and embroidery projects to require or suggest dividing the 6 threads, depending on the use and the project.

For the project in this book, I generally recommend using 3 threads of floss for cross-stitching on size 14 Aida fabric.

HOOP, FRAME, OR STAND

It's very difficult to cross-stitch on floppy, unsecured fabric. Most people cross-stitch with their Aida fabric secured in an embroidery hoop. These are commonly made of wood or bamboo, and come in various sizes.

You may also like to use a plastic Q-Snap™, or a different style of embroidery stand to secure your work. Some fit in your lap, clamp to a desk, or stand from the floor. This is entirely up to your personal preference!

For the projects in this book, I recommend using an 8-inch (20 cm) embroidery hoop.

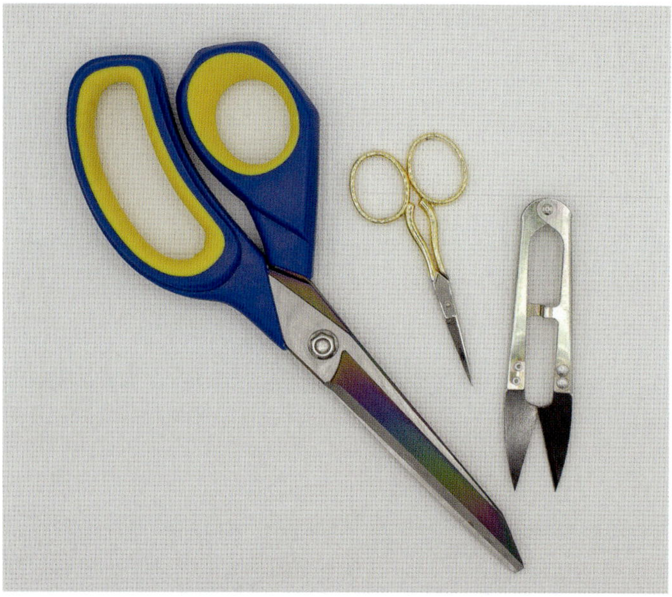

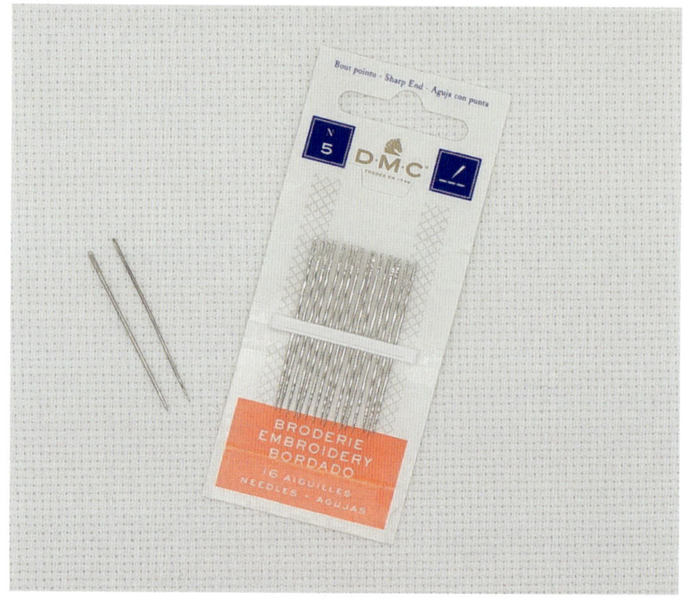

SCISSORS

I recommend having two pairs of scissors on hand: one large, sharp pair of scissors for cutting your Aida fabric, and one small, sharp pair of scissors for cutting your embroidery floss.

There are different types of embroidery scissors. Some are shaped like traditional scissors, some are more like clippers. You can also use cosmetic cuticle scissors as embroidery scissors if you have a spare pair lying around!

NEEDLE

To cross-stitch, you need at least one needle (though I highly recommend having a few backup needles, as they can be very sneaky!) Needles come in many shapes and sizes. I prefer a size 5 embroidery, or crewel (pronounced like cruel), needle which has a sharp end (careful!) but allows for a little more freedom with the Aida fabric. You could also use a cross-stitch-friendly tapestry needle, which has a blunt end and won't be as pokey.

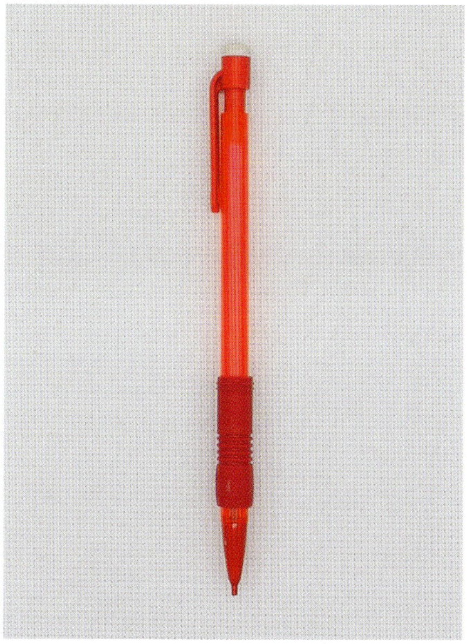

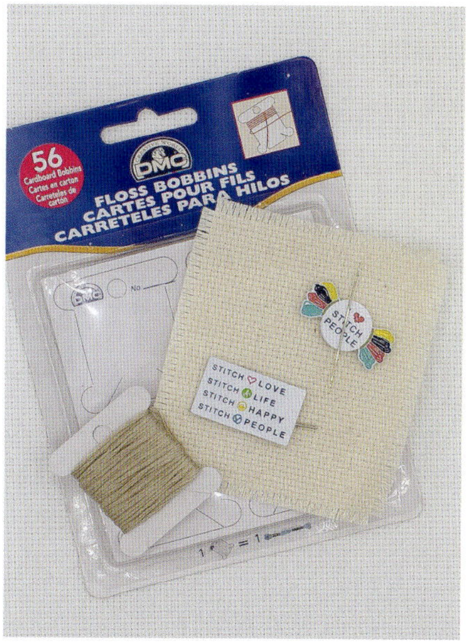

PENCIL

It's useful to have a pencil on hand for cross-stitching. You can use it to mark your pattern, write notes in the book, take notes, and even make light marks on the back side of your fabric! If you have a sewing-friendly heat- or water-soluble pencil or pen, feel free to use that. Personally, I always use a mechanical graphite pencil for convenience and have never had a problem on my fabric. The key is to write lightly!

Never use permanent marker or pen ink on your fabric (unless it's part of the design!).

FELT OR DECORATIVE CARDSTOCK

To finish your piece, you'll need a piece of felt or decorative cardstock paper that's at least as big as the size hoop you're using as the project frame (in our case, 8 inches or 20 cm).

I prefer to back my finished projects with felt, and tend to use neutral colors. White may be see-through so be careful! I suggest a natural finish kind of felt, or gray tone.

HELPFUL, OPTIONAL EXTRAS

The materials described are the essentials you'll need to get stitching. But there are a lot of other tools and products available to make cross-stitching more fun, organized, and easy. For example, cardboard bobbins can be used to wrap and store your floss, either in a plastic organizer or on rings.

You may also find a needle minder helpful. A needle minder is a decorative magnet that clings to your fabric, on which you can rest your needle when it's not in use! From hoop or frame guards, to daylight lamps, magnifying glasses, and magnetic needle cases, there are many fun accessories hobbyists far and wide enjoy collecting and exploring.

preparing to stitch

BEFORE YOU'RE ABLE TO CROSS-STITCH ANY PATTERN, THERE ARE A FEW STEPS OF PREP WORK YOU'LL WANT TO TACKLE. DON'T WORRY—IT'S NOT MUCH!

READY THE FABRIC

Some avid stitchers like to pre-wash their fabric, especially if it is a color other than white. Some also like to pre-iron their fabric to remove any folds that may have been retained in the packaging. These steps are up to you and how tidy you like to be when you work!

CUT THE FABRIC TO SIZE

Use fabric scissors to cut your Aida fabric to an appropriate size for your pattern.

How much fabric should you cut? It depends on the size of your pattern. Remember, size 14 Aida fabric means 14 stitches can fit in an inch (2.5 cm). For example, if you count a finished pattern (or note any provided dimensions), and find it will be 98 squares wide by 70 squares in height, you can find the dimensions by dividing those numbers by the Aida fabric, size 14. So now you know that pattern would be 7" x 5" (18 cm x 12.5 cm).

It's safe to include a 2-inch (5 cm) perimeter of additional fabric around the pattern size. So for this example, I'd recommend cutting a piece of fabric 11" x 9" (28 cm x 23 cm).

Fold your fabric lengthwise, and then again widthwise.

DEFINE THE CENTER POINT

On any given cross-stitch project, it's helpful to mark the center point of your Aida fabric to be able to align your work, matching the center point of a pattern. The easiest way to do this is to fold your fabric length-wise, and then again widthwise. Lightly mark the center point with a pencil on what will be the back of your fabric.

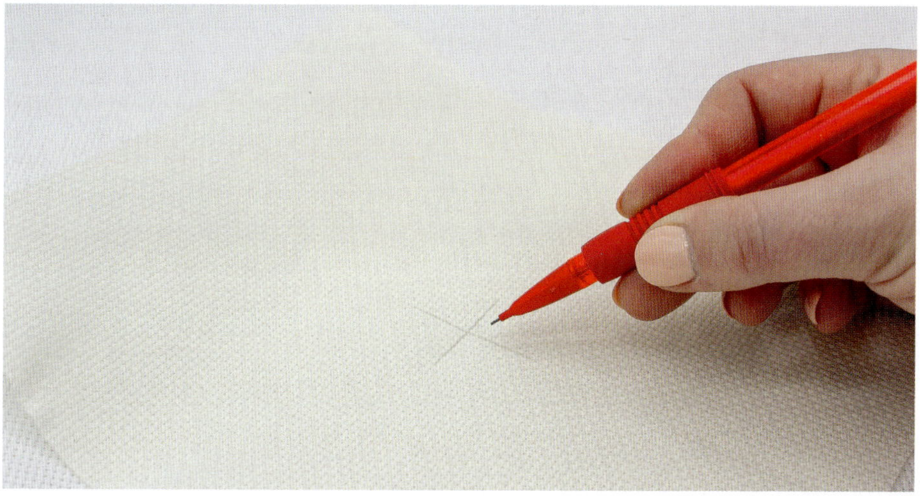

Lightly mark the center point with a pencil.

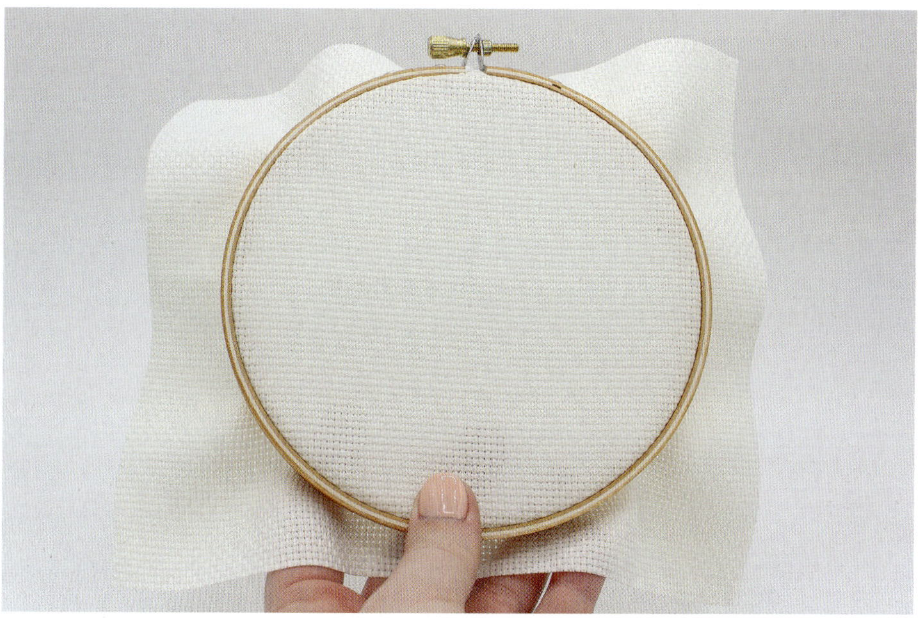

Secure the fabric.

tip

I often secure my fabric in an embroidery hoop the opposite way, so the back side is raised, flush with the edges of the outer hoop. This way, if I have anything on my fingers (dust or dirt from petting my dogs, makeup residue from touching my face, etc.) and it innocently transfers onto the fabric, then it is more likely to do so on the back side of the fabric, and reduces the likelihood of being visible from the front.

When it comes time to finish my work, utilizing the embroidery hoop as a frame, I simply remove my work, flip the fabric around, and re-center it in the embroidery hoop.

How can you tell which side of the fabric is the front or back? It typically doesn't matter, as Aida fabric is, for all intents and purposes, identical on either side.

SECURE THE FABRIC

Now is the time to secure the Aida fabric in your chosen hoop or frame. If you're using a Q-Snap or frame of some kind, follow any given instructions associated with them to properly secure your fabric. For a traditional embroidery hoop, secure the Aida fabric between the inner and outer hoop, pulling the fabric taught and securing the outer hoop with the pin at the top.

Traditionally, it's common to orient the fabric such that the front side of the fabric is raised, flush with the edges of the outer hoop, and the back side of the fabric (where your center point is defined) is lowered within the inner hoop.

THREAD THE NEEDLE

When you begin to stitch, you'll first cut a length of floss. How much? I recommend holding the end of the floss in your fingers and cutting a length roughly around where your bicep is on that same arm.

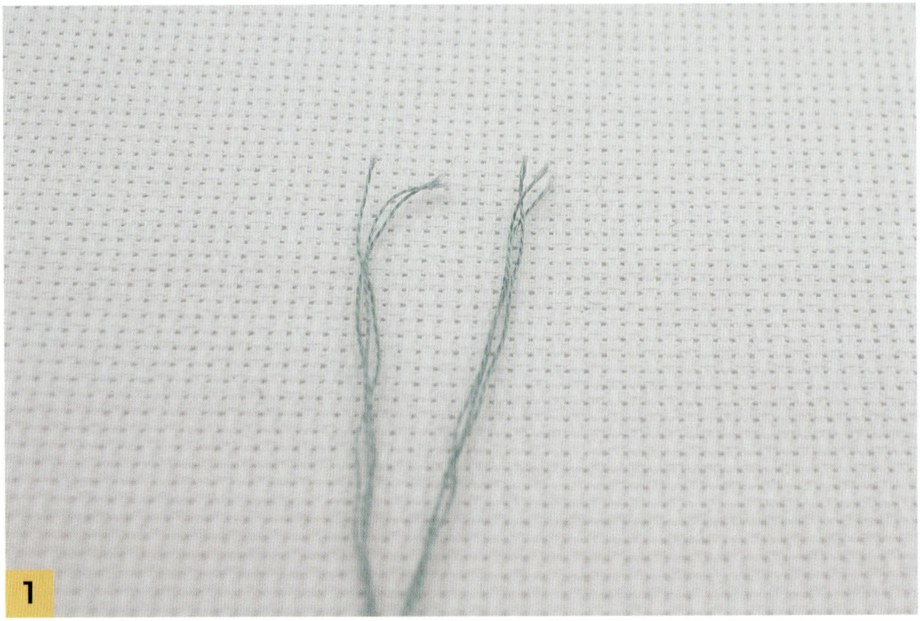

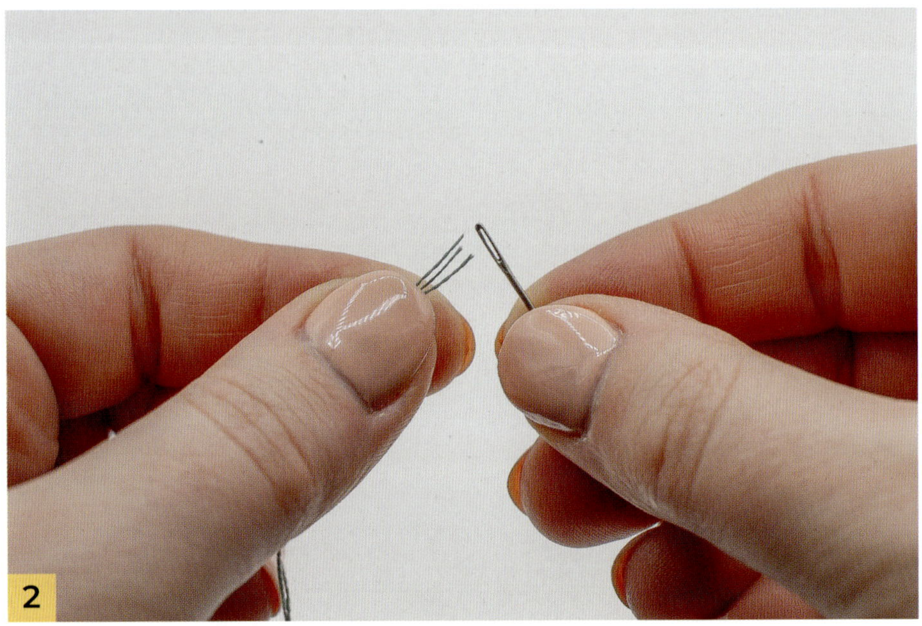

1 Recall that embroidery floss is made up of 6 threads, or strands, but you should only use 3 strands for cross-stitching on size 14 Adia fabric (and only 1 to 2 threads for smaller details!)

2 Now that you've got an arm's length of 3 threads of embroidery floss, thread your needle! Ensure all strands of floss are pulled equally through the eye of the needle. Do not tie any ends into a knot! We'll be "casting on" to secure our floss and this does not require a knot.

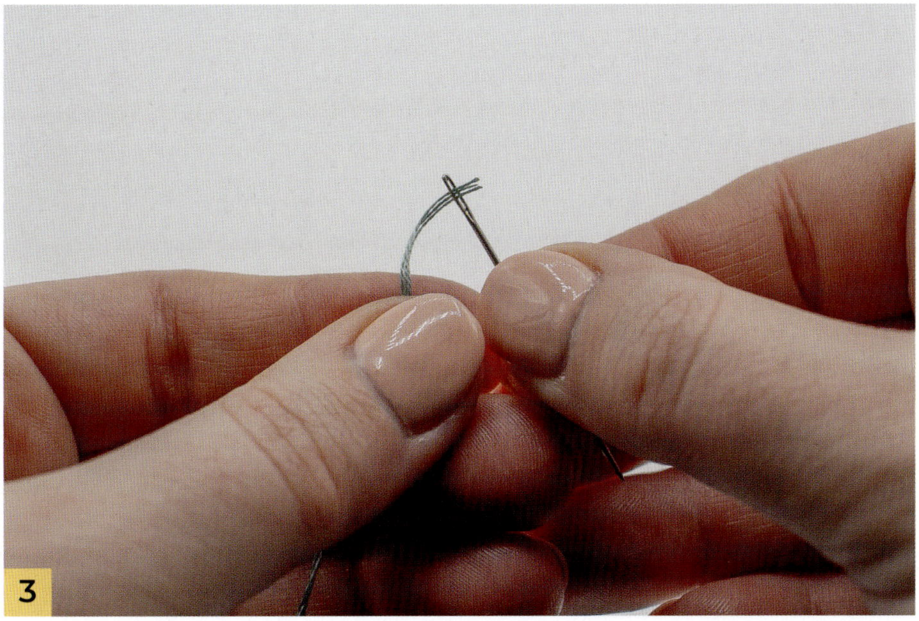

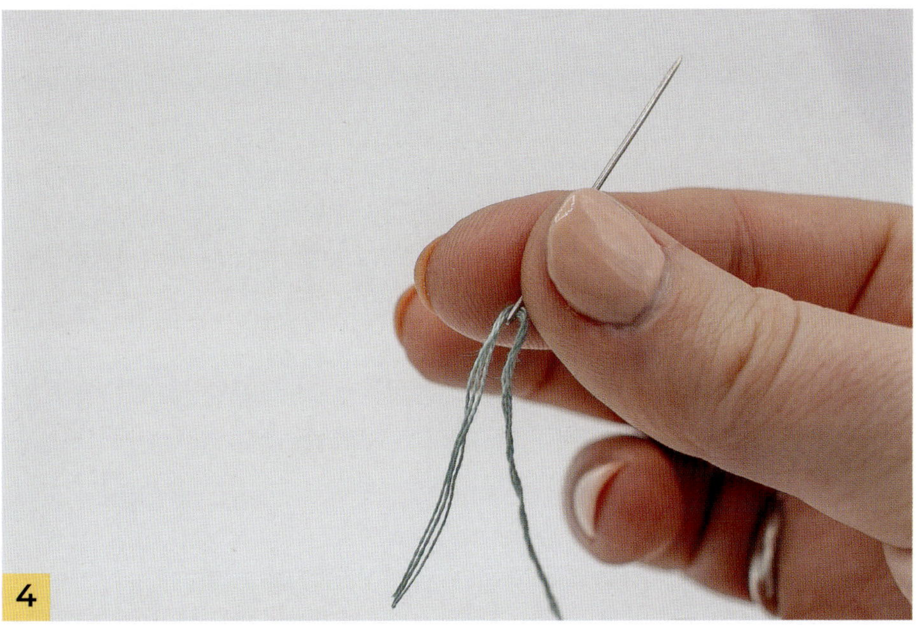

tip

When using DMC floss, pull the loose end from the *number* side of the skein to prevent bunching.

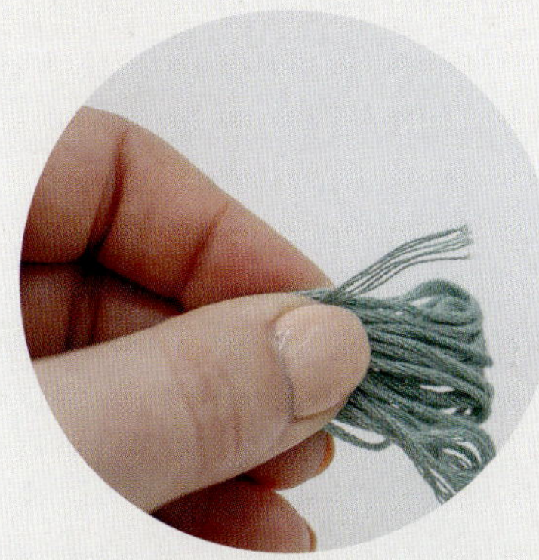

3 The cleanest, sleekest way to cross-stitch and secure your floss is to forego the use of knots. You'll utilize the loops on the back of your work, created during the process of cross-stitching, to secure your ends.

4 Leave a 1-inch (2.5 cm) length of floss out the end of your needle, and keep it secured by holding your needle right at the base of the eye where you'll keep the floss in place as well.

how to cross-stitch

IF YOU'RE A NEW STITCHER, THESE NEXT FEW PAGES WILL INTRODUCE YOU TO CROSS-STITCHING AND THE TYPES OF ADDITIONAL STITCHES MOST COMMONLY USED WITH CROSS-STITCHING PROJECTS.

If you have learned to cross-stitch but it's been a while...I know that feeling! And this section will be a great refresher for you.

For those of you who already have a confident handle on cross-stitching (and completing French knots) you can feel confident skipping this section.

TIPS FOR SUCCESS

Before we get stitching, I'd like to mention a few tips for success that will help to quickly elevate your work to pro status. (Fair warning: this likely won't be the only time you read these from me!)

1 Be consistent layering your cross-stitch diagonals. Any cross-stitch is made simply of two crossing diagonal stitches (like / and \) to create an X shape. As you stitch each individual X try to keep all the bottom diagonals of the cross-stitches going the same direction (like this \\\\) and keep the top diagonals of the cross-stitches going the same direction (like this ////).

2 Keep the tension consistent while stitching. Cross-stitching is a "just right" kind of thing, like Goldilocks and the three bears! You want your stitches to be snug and taught—not loose—but you also don't want to pull too tightly as you stitch. Try not to distort the holes of the Aida fabric.

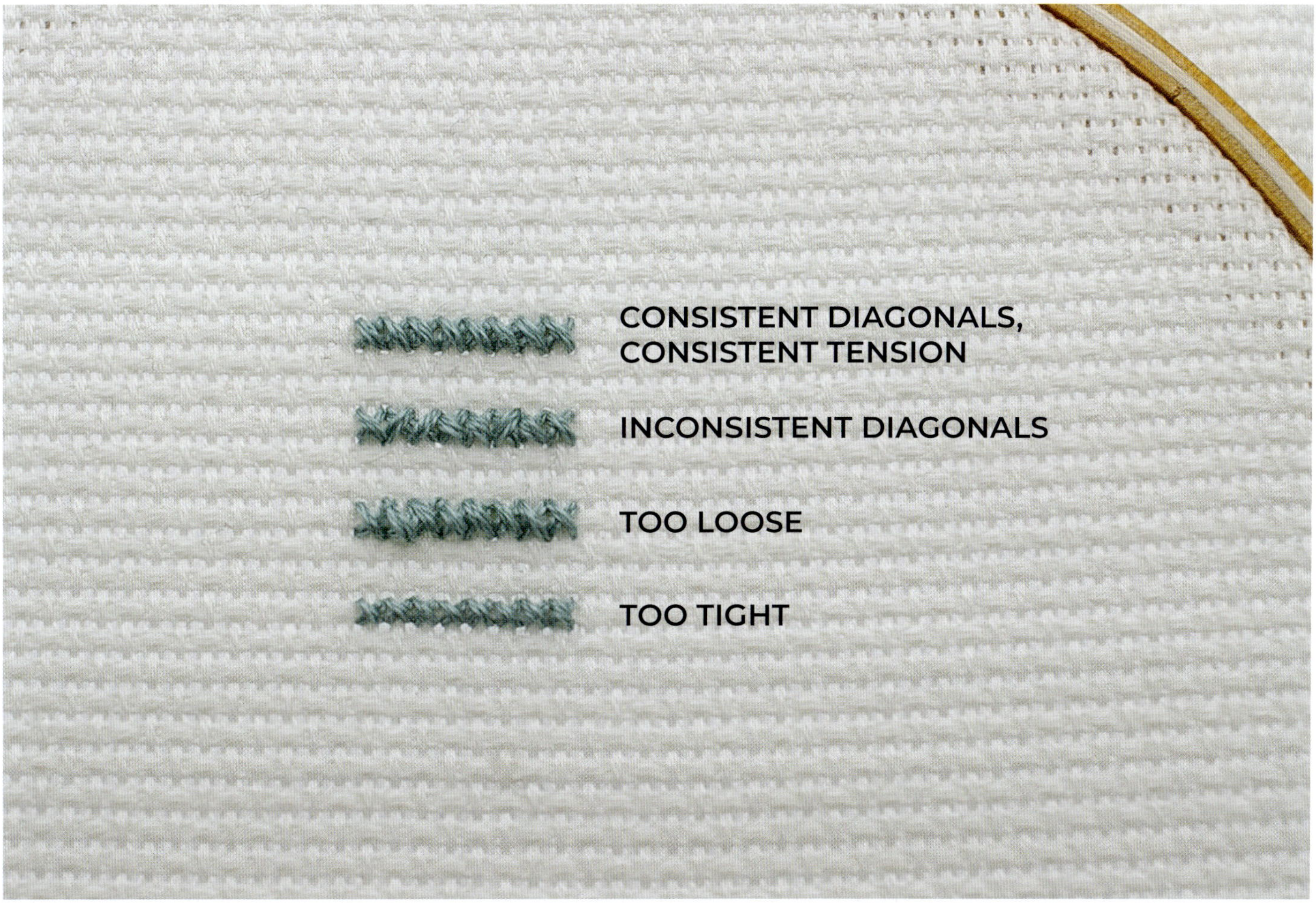

3 "Next-to, not into!" Many cross-stitches will share holes in the Aida fabric. While stitching, try to aim your needle such that the point doesn't catch existing stitches in the holes of the fabric, and that the new stitch will sit snugly next to existing threads. This prevents bunching and knotting.

4 Keep your focus on the front side of your work. Because cross-stitching consists of many "ins-and-outs" or "ups-and-downs," depending on how you think of it, it can be tempting to flip your work from front to back with each stitch you make. I highly recommend you do not do this. Resist the urge! While slow going at first, cross-stitching will be much easier and faster over time if you train your hand-eye coordination and keep your focus on the front side of your work.

This image shows the differences in stitching consistency. The top row is, as Goldilocks would say, "just right!" The tension of the stitching is consistent, and the cross-stitch diagonals are uniform. The second row shows inconsistent diagonals with consistent tension. The third row shows how stitches that are too loose can look a little higgledy-piggledy. The fourth row is an example of cross-stitching that is too tight. See how the holes of the Aida fabric directly around the stitches look a little large?

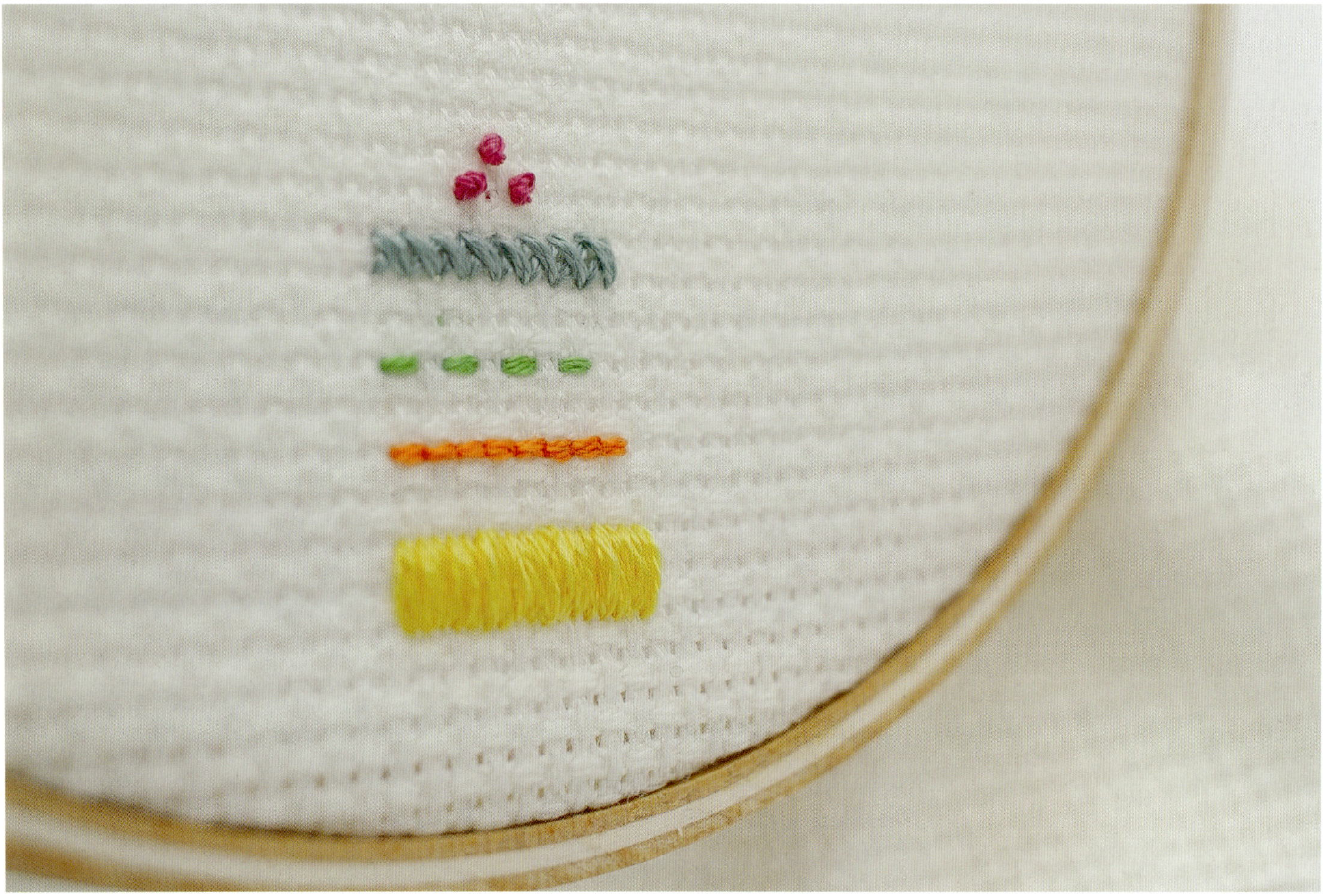

CREATE A CROSS-STITCH

As mentioned in the tips for success (you read them, right???) a cross-stitch consists of creating two overlapping diagonals. Each X created, and with the use of varying colors, combines to create an overall picture of some kind.

Ultimately, there is no right or wrong way to cross two diagonals in a square boundary to make a cross-stitch. The primary thing to remember is to keep the construction of your X stitches the same.

You may complete each X of a cross-stitch individually (like this: XXX) or complete rows, columns, or sections of "under" diagonals (like this: ////), and then double back to complete the same rows, columns, or sections of "over" diagonals (like this: \\\\). You may also combine the two methods depending on the pattern and your needs. I often do!

Visualize your cross-stitch. It will be an X shape within a square boundary, where each outer point of the X utilizes a hole in the Aida fabric.

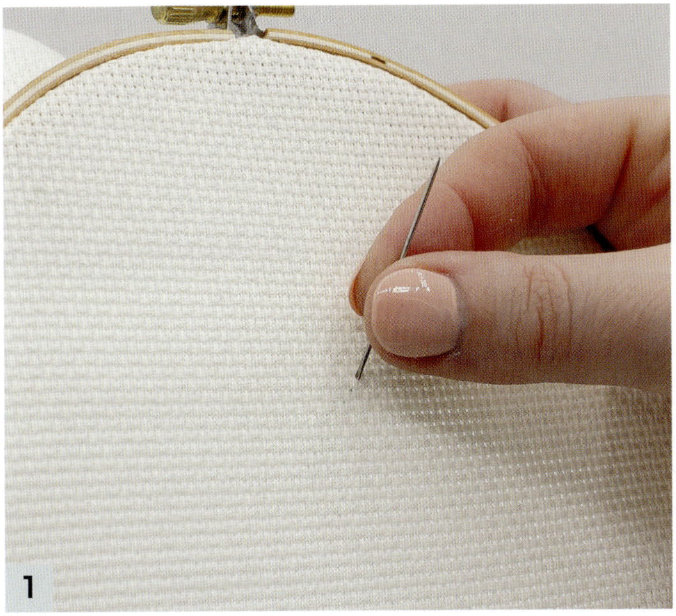

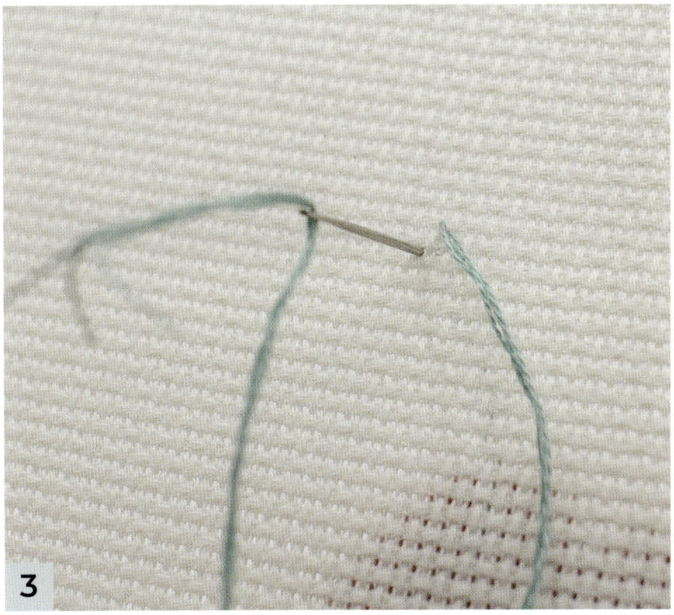

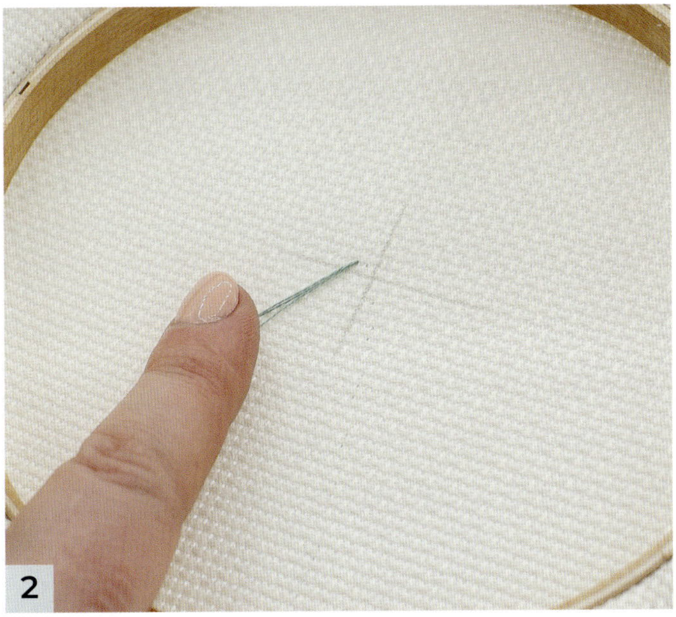

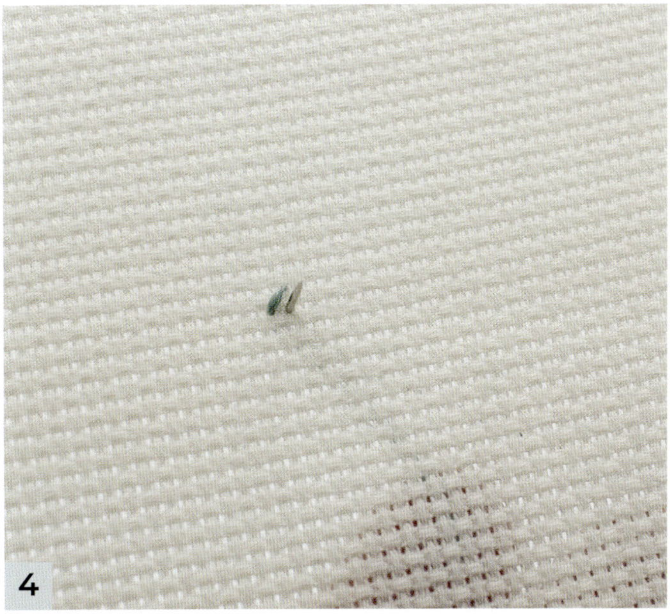

1 To create a cross-stitch, bring your needle up through a hole in the Aida fabric at a good starting point for your pattern. Your needle will come through from the back of your fabric to the front.

2 Keep a finger of your nondominant hand on the tail of the floss to secure it so it doesn't pull through.

3 Then, push your needle back through the fabric, from front to back, creating a straight stitch at a 45° angle.

4 Bring your needle back up through the fabric in an adjacent hole—one of the unutilized corners necessary to create an X shape.

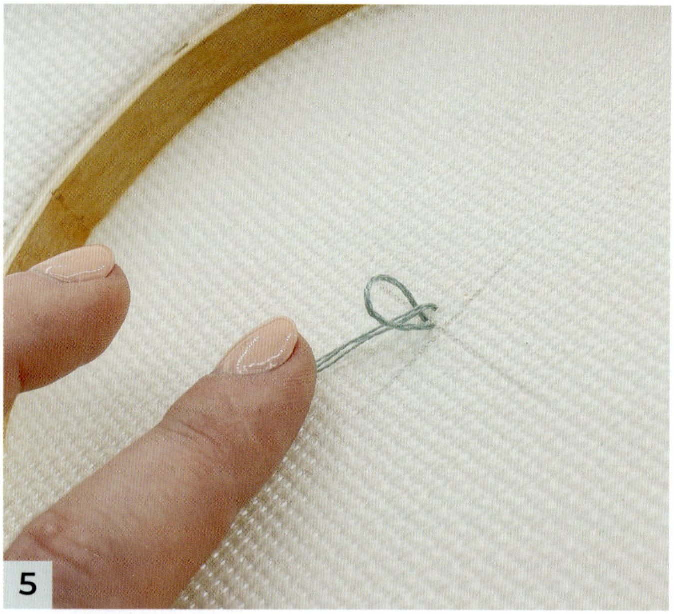

5

5 Pull slowly and utilize the loop that is forming on the back side to secure the loose tail of your floss. See? Secured with no knots!

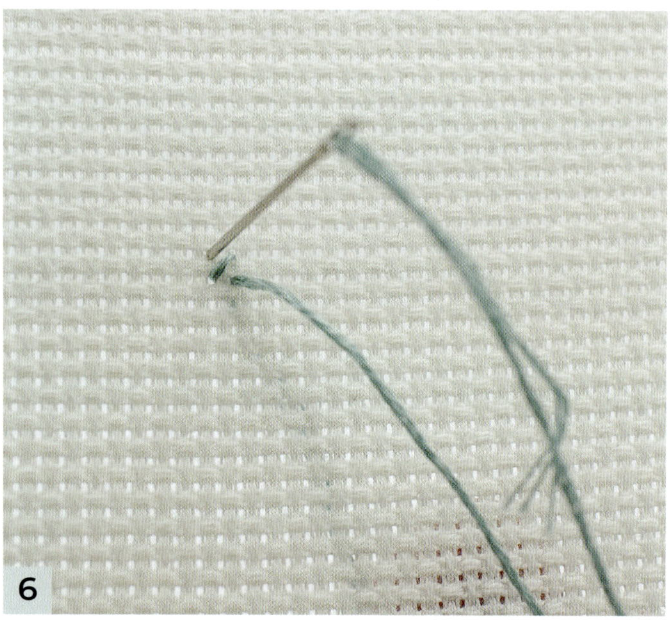

6

6 Push your needle through the final "corner" of the imaginary square in the Aida fabric where your X-shaped stitch will lie.

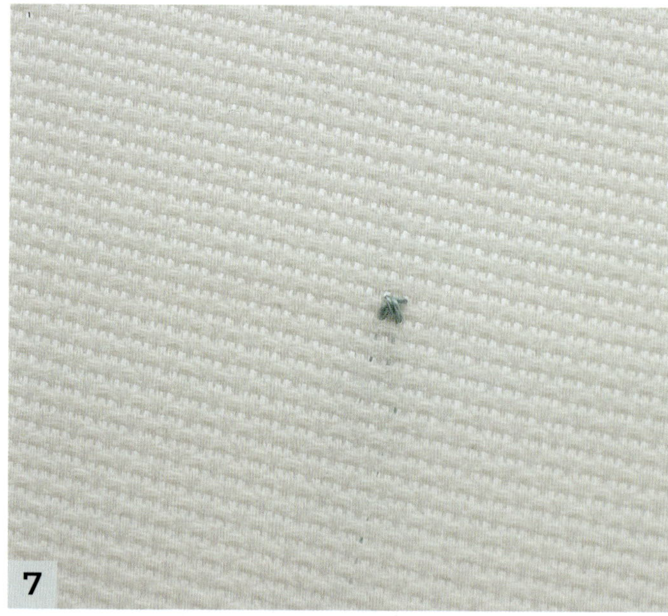

7

7 As you pull the floss taut, you'll have created your first cross-stitch!

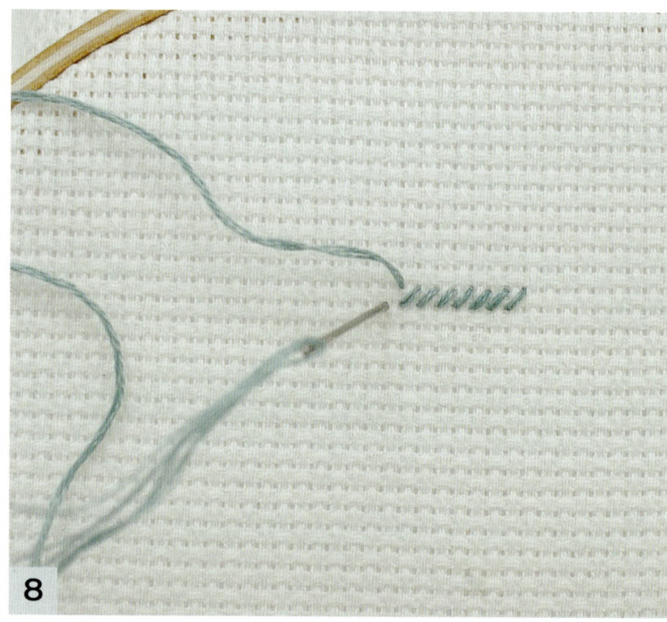

8

8 Remember, you can create multiple cross-stitches in rows or columns of diagonals as shown.

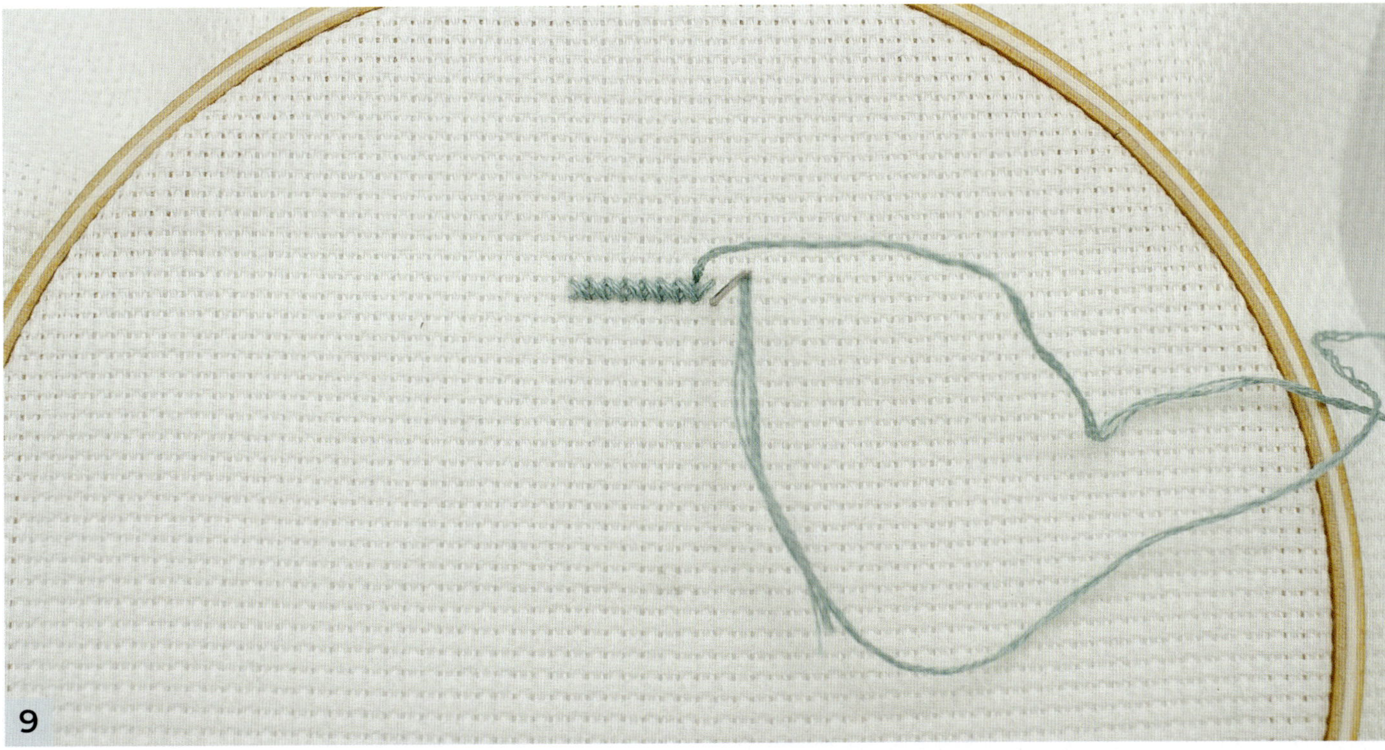

9 Or you can complete each individual X shape as you go, as shown above.

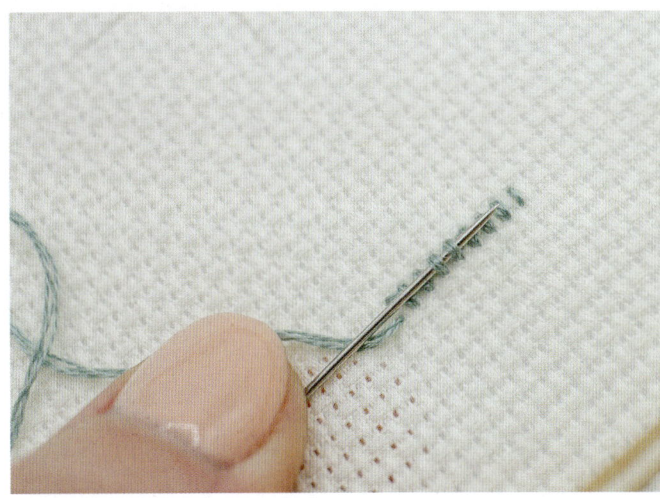

BURY THE THREAD

When you're done with a specific floss color or section of your pattern, you'll want to secure the floss so your stitching doesn't unravel. Simply tuck the needle under a few loops of stitching on the back side of your portrait and pull the needle and remaining thread through. Clip away excess floss with scissors.

This is a good practice for any stitch—cross-stitch or otherwise—to secure the ends of floss.

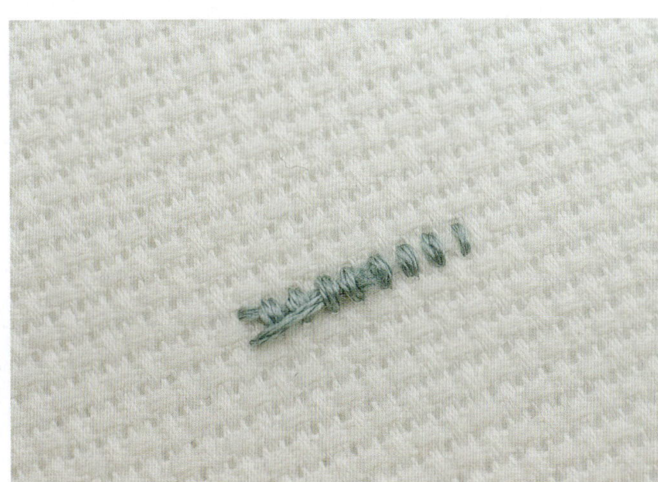

other stitching techniques

THIS IS THE KEY TO CUSTOMIZATION! THERE ARE A NUMBER OF OTHER STITCHES THAT WILL BE USEFUL TO YOU WHILE DESIGNING AND STITCHING YOUR CROSS-STITCHED PATTERNS. TAKE A MINUTE TO LOOK THROUGH THESE AND READ THE DESCRIPTIONS ABOUT HOW YOU MIGHT UTILIZE THEM.

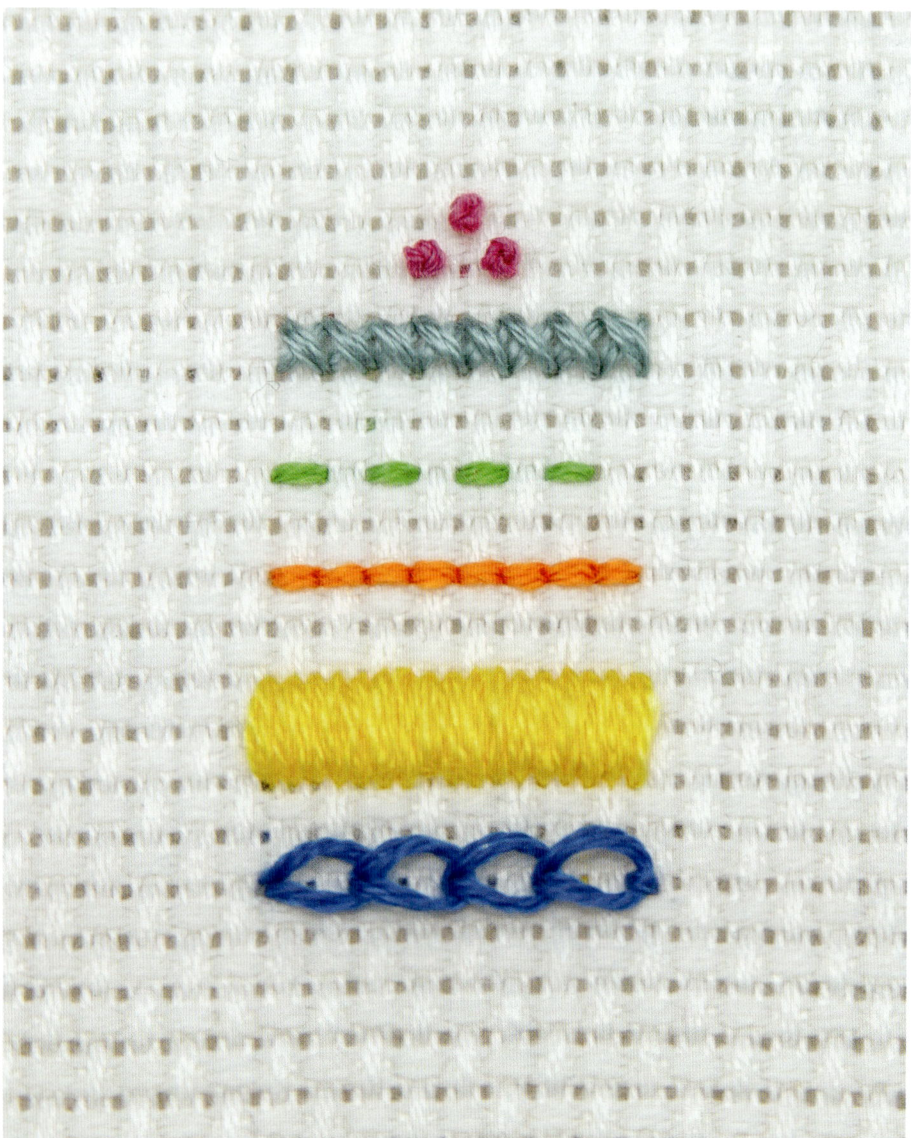

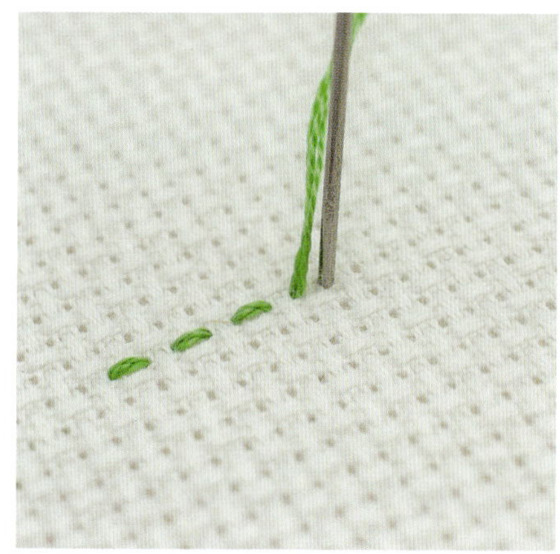

RUNNING STITCH

What: The running stitch is a simple, consecutive up/down style stitch with a dashed look.

Uses: The running stitch is useful for creating simple borders and underlining text.

How: Bring your needle up and down through your fabric in even increments.

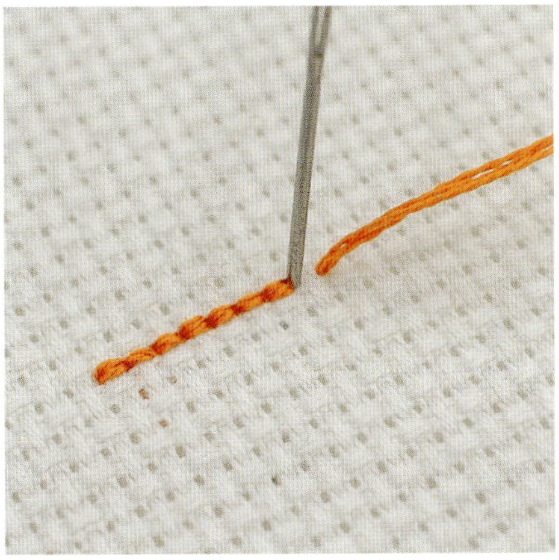

BACKSTITCH

What: Backstitching creates a straight line in a "two steps forward, one step back" kind of sequence.

Uses: The backstitch is useful for outlining characters (should you choose to), adding character details, creating simple borders, and underlining text.

How: Bring your needle up through the fabric and create a straight stitch. Bring your needle up again in a distance that matches the size of the first stitch. Then, bring your needle back toward the first stitch. Repeat this process in a sequence where you bring your needle up a stitch's length away and double back to complete the stitch.

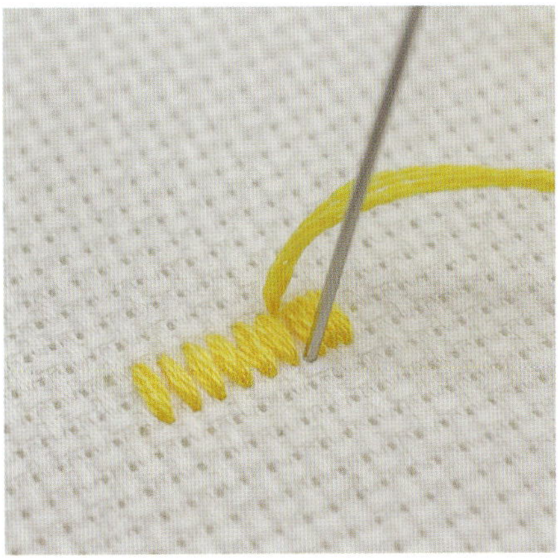

SATIN STITCH

What: The satin stitch is a traditional embroidery stitch, great for filling in large areas of space with one color, made from tightly positioned, parallel straight stitches.

Uses: Satin stitches can be useful for creating effects in character hairstyles, pet fur, or clothing details.

How: Create a section of parallel straight stitches that fill the specific shape you need to fill. In the context of cross-stitching, I find it useful to utilize the holes of the Aida fabric, first, and then double back, filling in stitches in between the holes, stabbing my needle outside the holes of the Aida fabric.

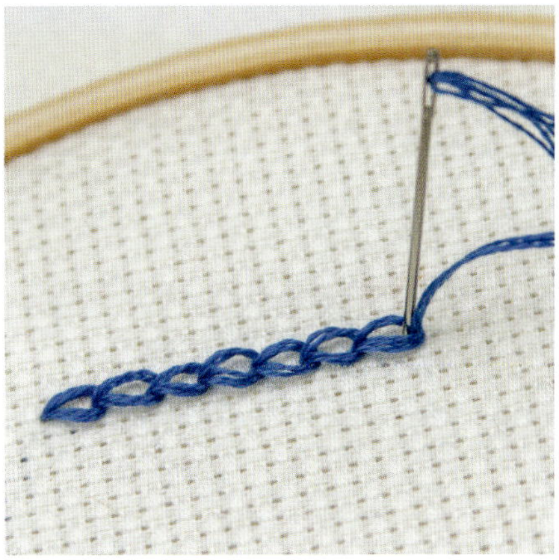

DAISY CHAIN STITCH

What: The daisy chain stitch is made from creating a sequence of interlocking loops that can act as a simple, beautiful border or filler stitch.

Uses: Daisy chains can create border elements or more detailed linear clothing elements like a flower crown or decorative belt. This stitch can also create a knitted effect for clothing details when completed in tight, parallel rows.

How: Bring your needle up at the starting point, and return your needle to the same point. Pulling slowly, a loop will form. Bring your needle up a length away from the starting point, catching the loop and securing it outward. Repeat the process as many times as needed to create the appropriate length chain you need. To create a more linear or more loopy look to the chain, adjust how tightly you pull each stitch.

FRENCH KNOT

What: The French knot is a classic, compact, round knot with a spherical feel.

Uses: French knots are useful for eyes for babies and pets, details for clothing like buttons, polka dots, and floral patterns, or adding a curly look to hairstyles or pet fur.

How: French knots take some practice, but can be fairly simple once you get the hang of them. It's easiest to complete a French knot if the floss is secure to your fabric. So before you begin, loop your floss around existing stitches on the back side of your fabric.

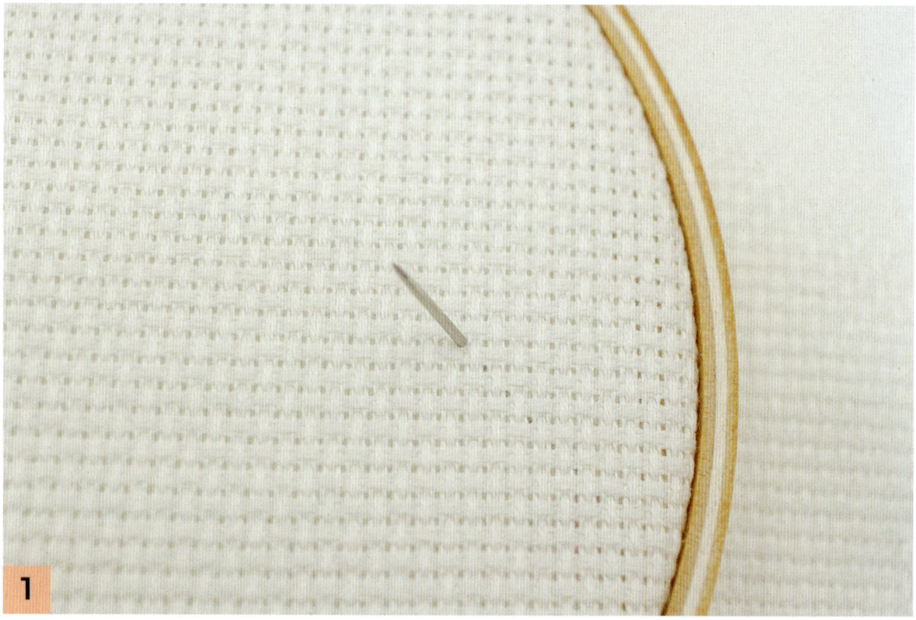

1

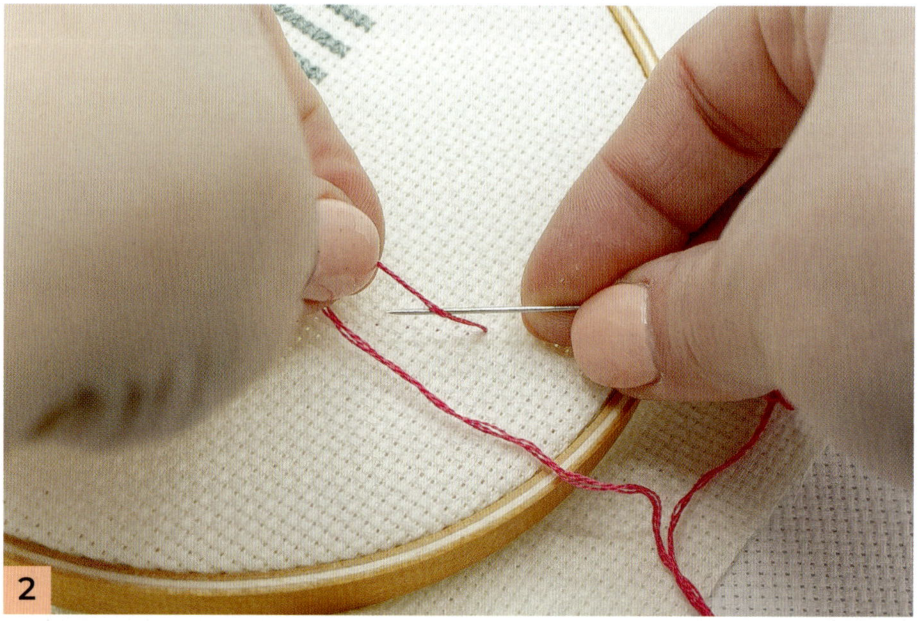

2

1 Bring your needle and floss through the fabric to the front in the place you want the French knot to go.

2 Take hold of the floss with your non-needle fingers, and bring the needle to the origin point on the Aida fabric.

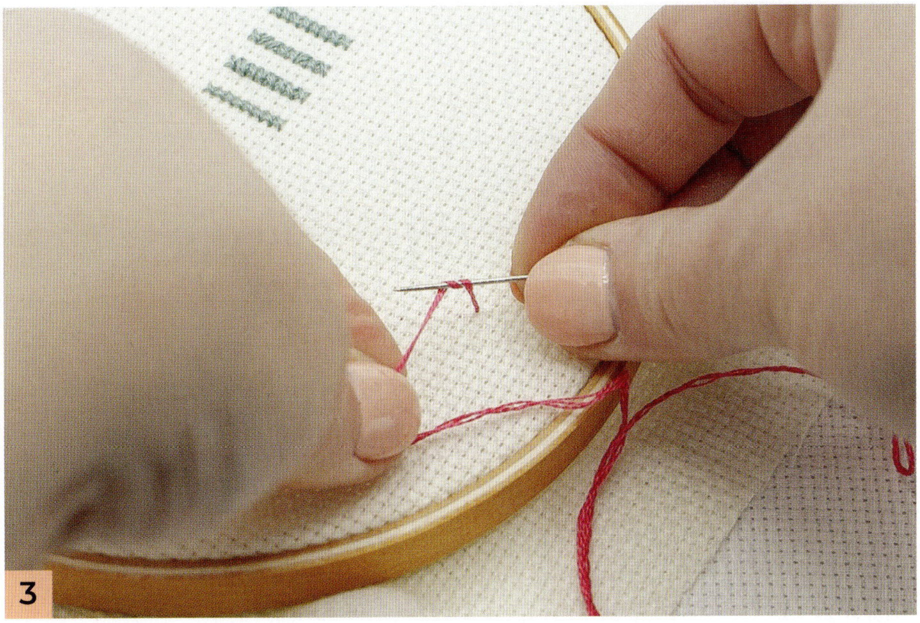

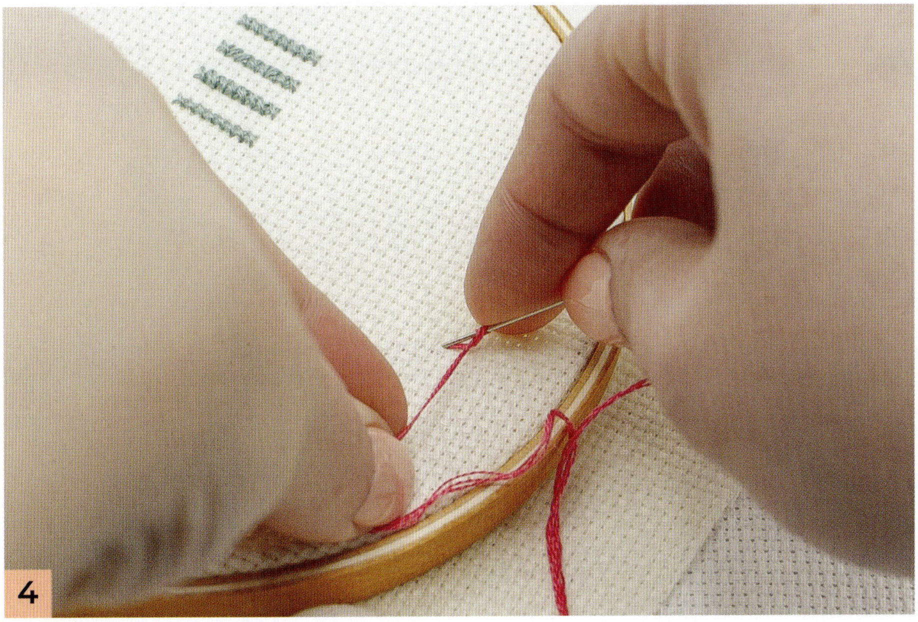

3 Twist the floss around the needle two times with your non-needle fingers. Don't let go of the floss!

4 Push the needle back through the fabric very close to where you brought it up, but not in the same hole.

tip

You can control the size of a French knot with the following three factors:

Threads: The number of threads you use will affect the size. A single thread will create a tiny French knot whereas 6 threads will create a very chunky French knot.

Twists: The number of times you twist the floss around your needle can impact the size of your French knot. Fewer twists will make a smaller knot, more twists will make a larger knot.

Tension: How tight or loose you keep your floss will affect the size of your French knot. A tight tension will create a smaller knot. Allowing a little slack will create a larger, more relaxed-looking French knot.

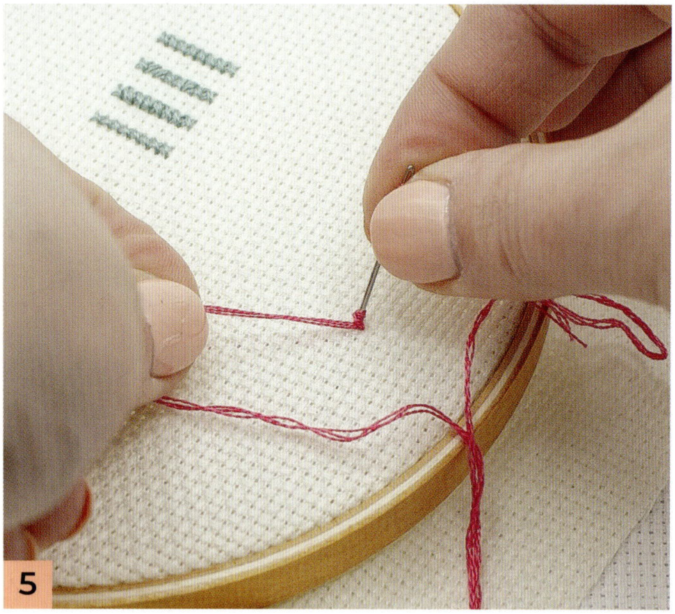

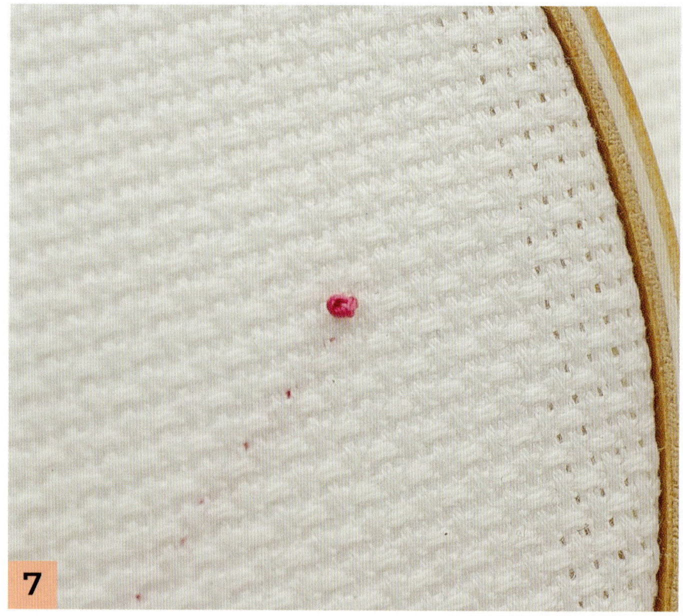

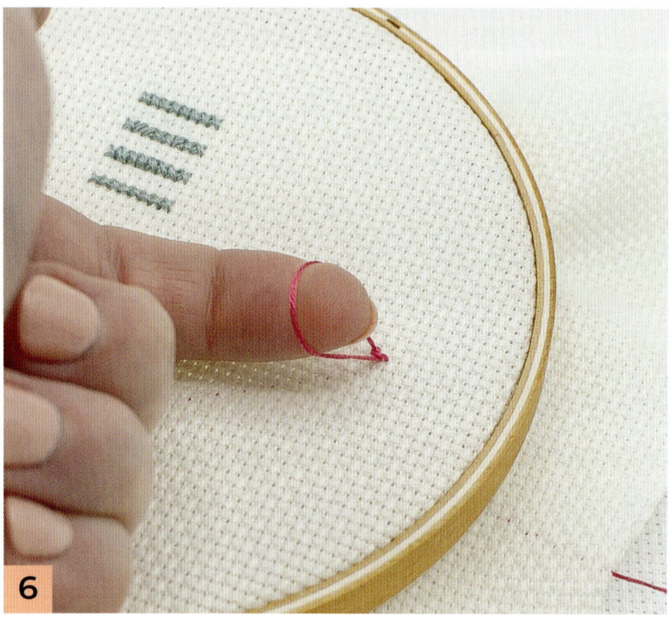

5 Keep the floss taught, and keep your non-needle fingers on the excess floss.

6 Pull your needle slowly. A loop will form around your non-needle finger.

7 Gently slide the loop off and keep pulling the floss tight and a knot will form.

DIAGONAL HALF STITCHES

Many of the patterns in this book utilize half stitches, which are exactly what they sound like—stitches, that take up half as much space as a cross-stitch. They can be completed in a number of ways, depending on your needs. Here are the two most popular ways to complete a diagonal half stitch.

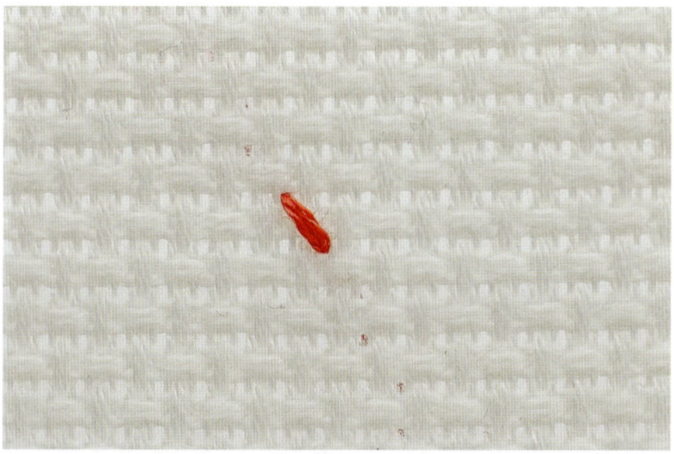

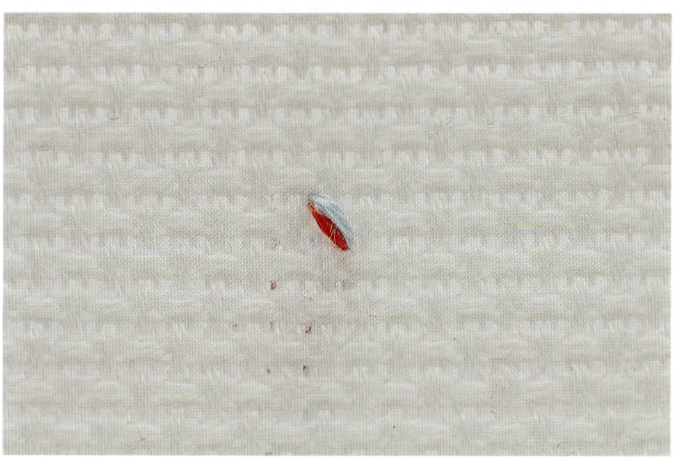

DIAGONALS ONLY

You may wish to complete a half stitch by stitching the diagonal portion only. If two colors share the square, stitch their diagonals side by side, utilizing the same holes in the Aida fabric.

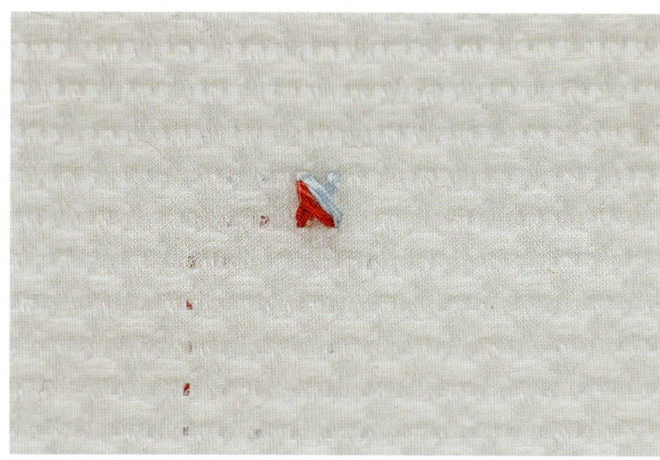

QUARTER STITCH

If you need a fuller look in the square of the Aida fabric, complete a quarter stitch, from a hole in the Aida fabric into the center of the square. Then complete a diagonal to fill the area. If two colors share the square, complete this with each color, and the diagonals will sit side by side and utilize the same holes in the Aida fabric.

VERTICAL AND HORIZONTAL HALF STITCHES

Another type of half stitch that Stitch People patterns utilize is a half-length or half-width stitch. These can be completed in a number of ways, depending on your needs. Here are the two most popular ways to complete a rectangle half stitch, which may be oriented either vertically or horizontally.

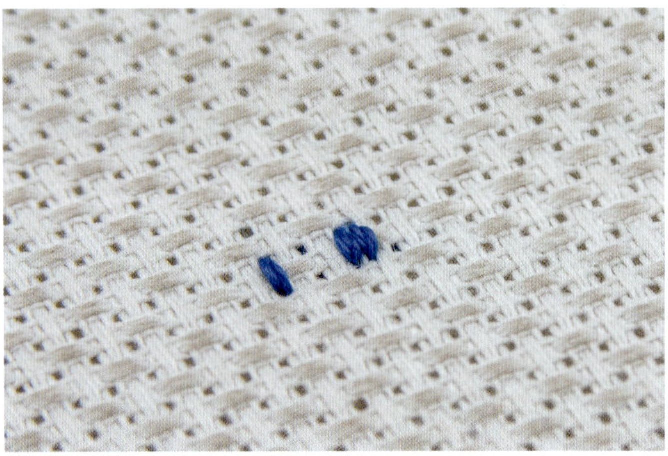

STRAIGHT STITCHES

Depending on the context of the stitch, and your personal preference, you can either complete a rectangle half stitch using a single straight stitch or two straight stitches side by side like a tiny satin stitch.

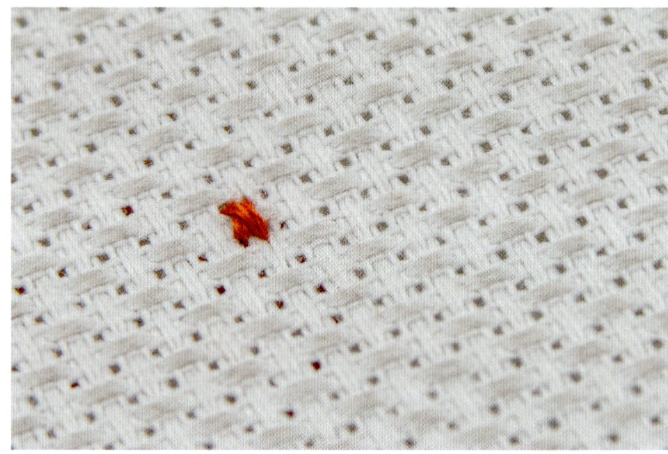

CROSS-STITCHES

Stitch each half of the rectangle half stitch with cross-stitches, but do not utilize four holes in the Aida fabric. Instead, use two holes of the Aida fabric, and finish the stitches between the holes of the Aida fabric on the other side of the stitch.

2:1 STITCHES

Another common stitch utilized in Stitch People patterns is one I'm not sure is an "official" stitch. I call them 2:1 stitches, where the diagonal is 2 squares long on one side and 1 square wide on another. Here's how I recommend stitching them:

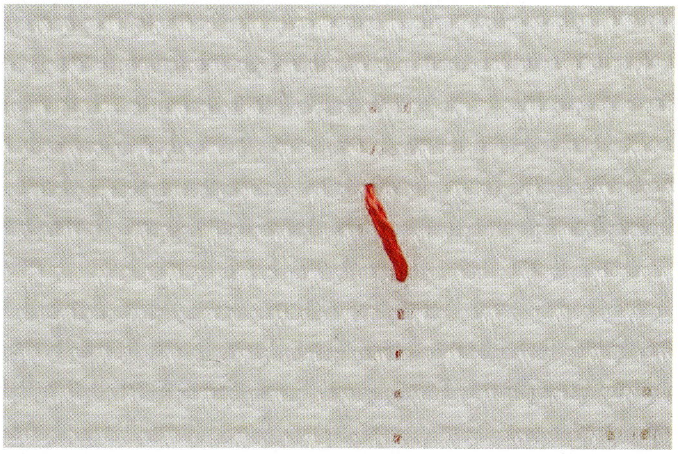

Stitch your first diagonal with the 2:1 ratio.

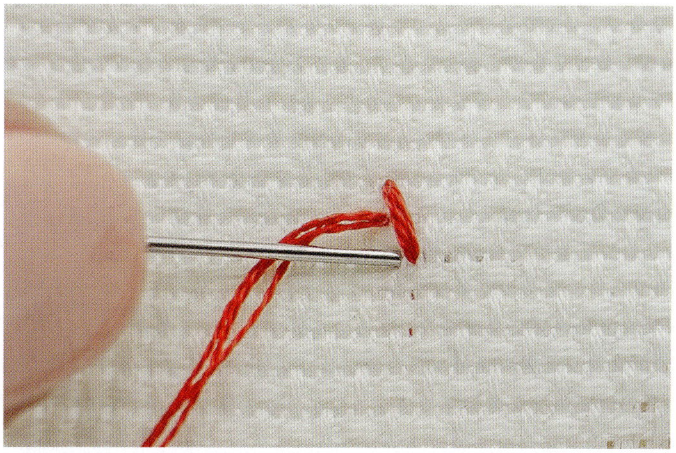

Then create a small filler stitch, where one end of the diagonal utilizes a hole of the Aida fabric, and you poke the needle and thread outside the holes of the Aida fabric at the other end of the diagonal.

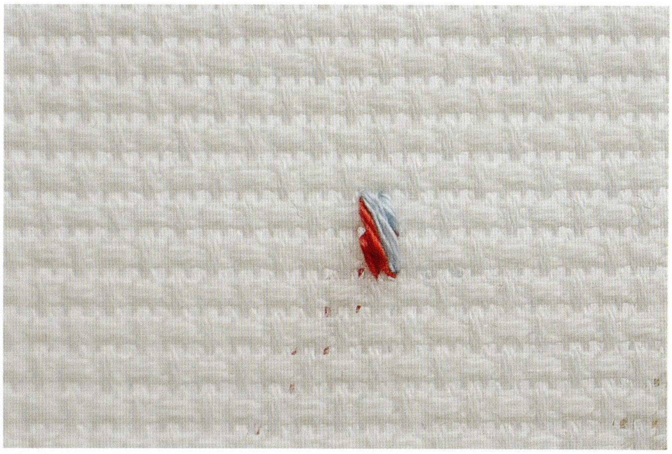

Where two colors share the diagonal, complete them each in a similar fashion. The diagonals will sit side by side and utilize the same holes of the Aida fabric.

customize your cross-stitch

MAKE IT YOUR OWN! THE PATTERNS IN THIS BOOK CONTAIN DIFFERENT GROUPS OF PEOPLE IN MANY ITERATIONS, BUT YOU'LL LIKELY WANT TO MAKE ADJUSTMENTS TO MAKE THESE PATTERNS TRULY YOUR OWN.

COLOR

The simplest adjustment you can make to customize a pattern is to change the colors. From the clothing colors to the skin tones and the hair colors, so much about a person can be customized by simply personalizing the floss colors you use.

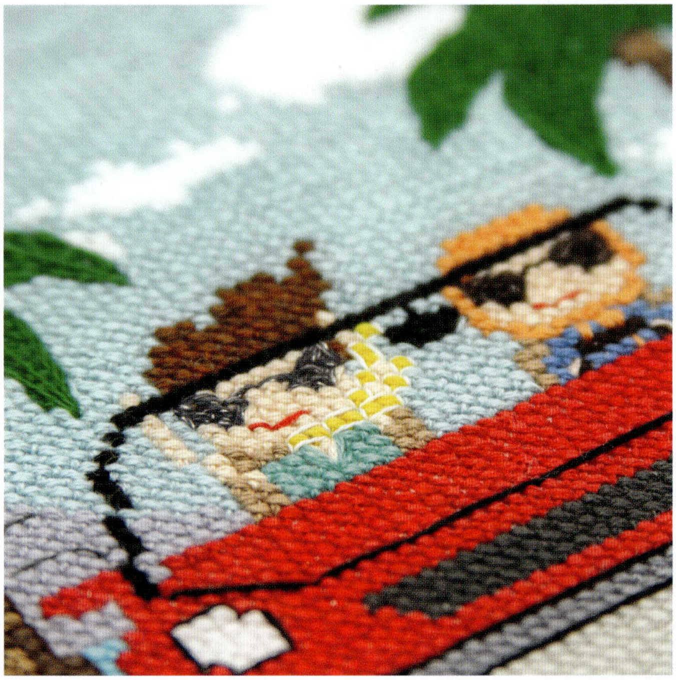

Clothing colors can be easily matched with your own eye, depending on the article of clothing, but skin tones and hair colors can be a little more difficult! While skin tones and hair colors can vary extensively, below are some go-to recommendations for natural-looking colors. If you'd like it, a more extensive color recommendations guide can be found in our book *Do-It-Yourself Stitch People*.

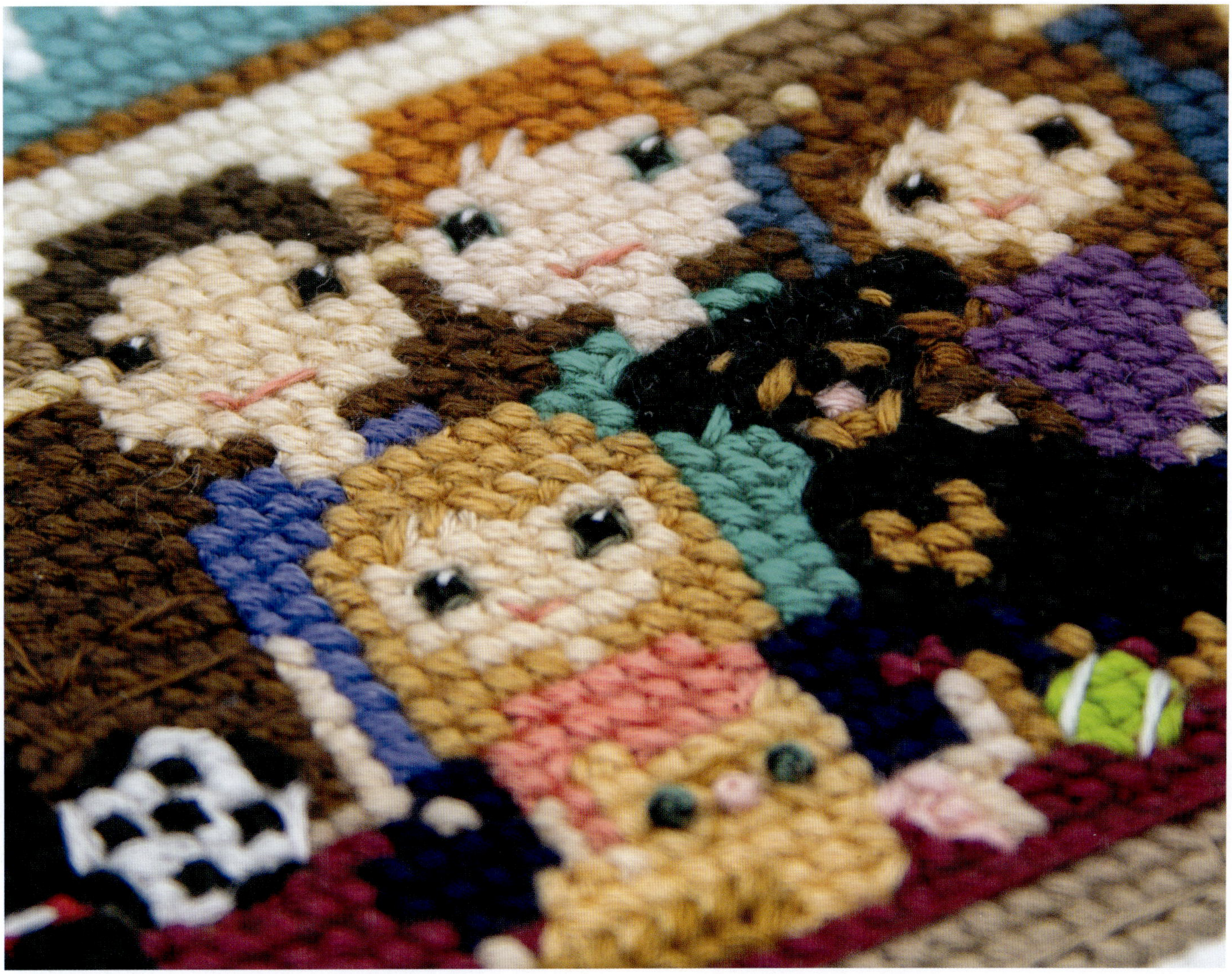

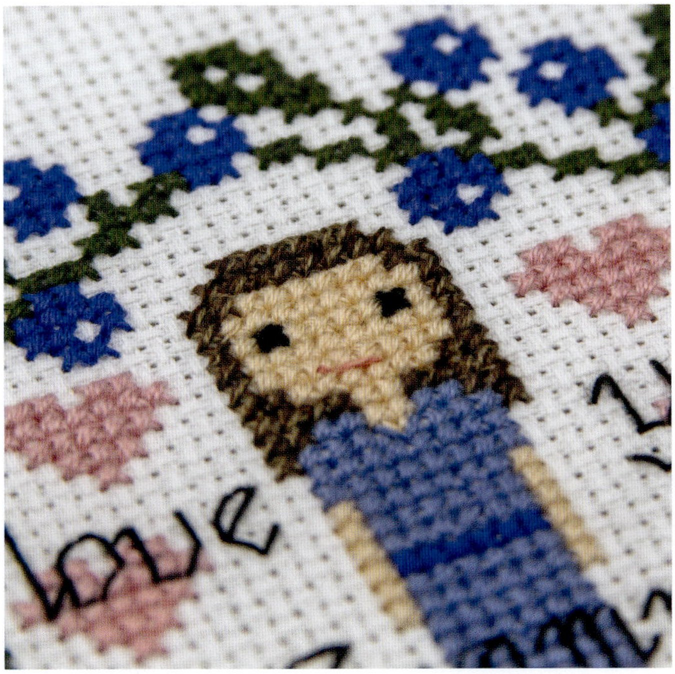
love

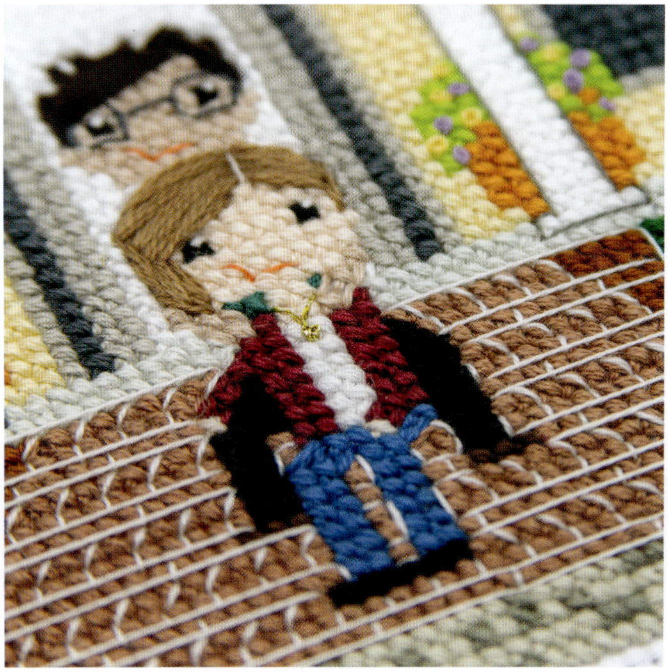

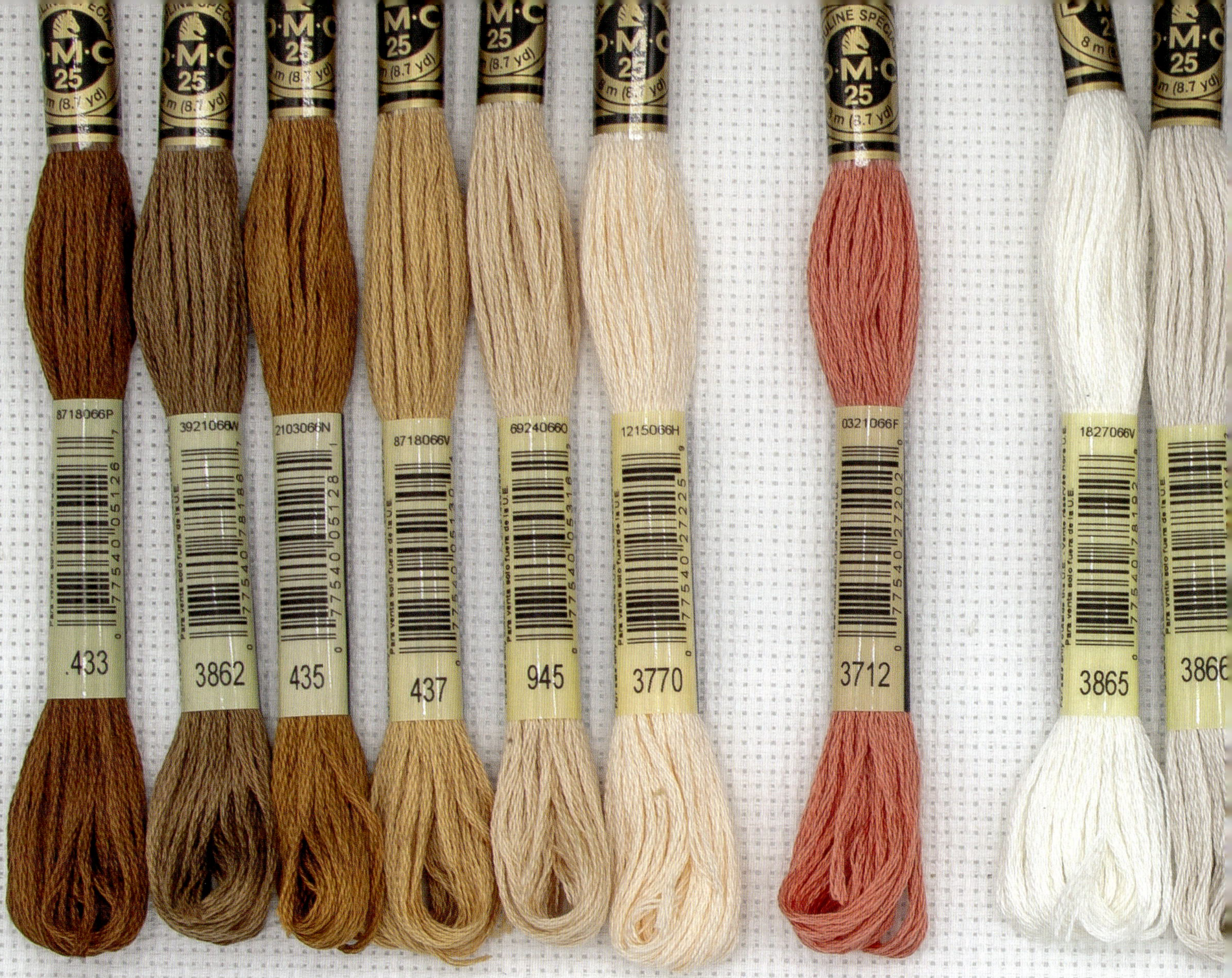

SKIN TONES

DMC 433: Medium Brown
DMC 3862: Dark Mocha Beige
DMC 435: Very Light Brown
DMC 437: Light Tan
DMC 945: Tawny
DMC 3770: Very Light Tawny

LIPS

DMC 3712
(Medium Salmon)
is my favorite natural-looking lip color. Light, but not too much so. Peachy, but not orange. If needed, basically any lipstick color can be matched with a DMC floss color; do your best to find a match!

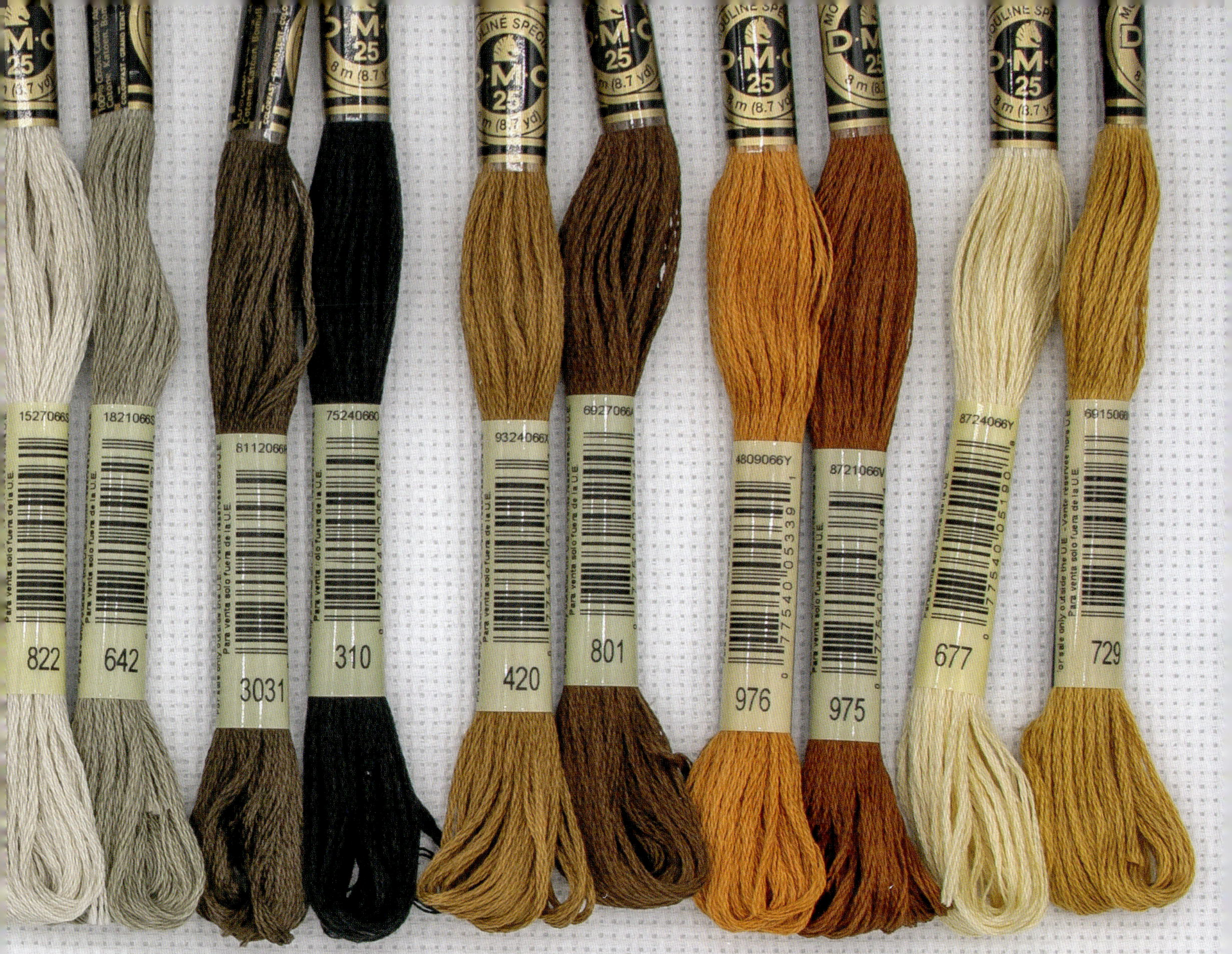

EYES

DMC 310
(Black)

HAIR COLORS

Light red: DMC 976 (Medium Golden Brown)
Dark red: DMC 975 (Dark Golden Brown)
Light blonde: DMC 677 (Very Light Old Gold)
Dark blonde: DMC 729 (Medium Old Gold)
Light brown: DMC 420 (Dark Hazelnut Brown)
Dark brown: DMC 801 (Dark Coffee Brown)
Light/warm black: DMC 3031 (Very Dark Mocha Brown)
Dark/true black: DMC 310 (Black)
Light gray: DMC 822 (Very Light Beige Gray)
Dark gray: DMC 642 (Dark Beige Gray)
Light white: DMC 3865 (Winter White)
Dark white: DMC 3866 (Ultra Very Light Mocha)

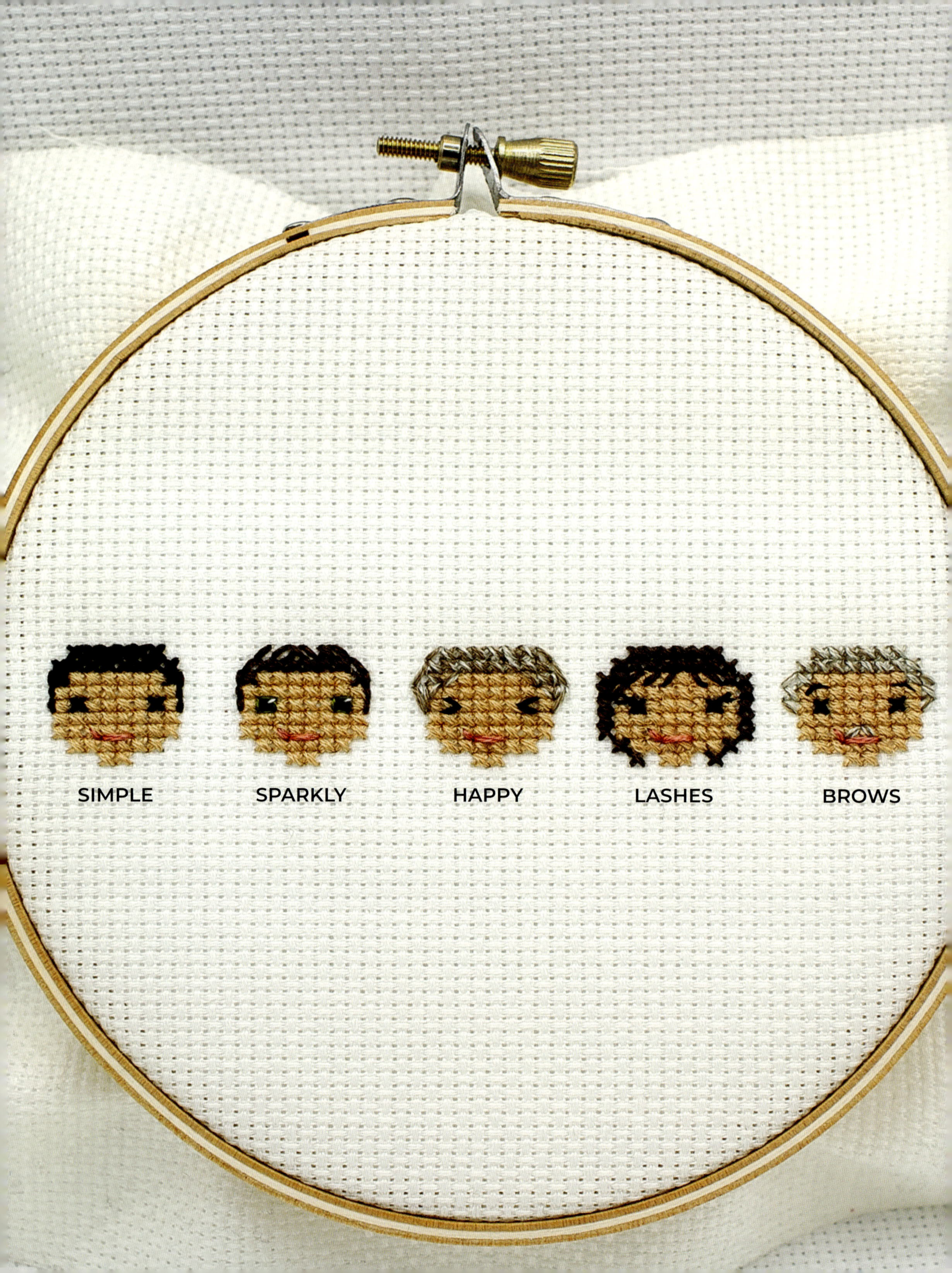
SIMPLE
SPARKLY
HAPPY
LASHES
BROWS

EYES

In group photos, you'll notice that eyes usually appear darker rather than their true color, due to depth, distance, lashes, and irises. I recommend using DMC 310 to stitch eyes or a very dark version of gray, blue, green, or brown. You can also outline a cross stitch of DMC 310 with a single thread of a light blue, green, or gold. Resist the urge to cross-stitch the eyes in a lighter color, as it can look a bit alien-like!

Simple

Complete each eye with a single cross-stitch, using 3 to 4 threads of DMC 310 or a very dark brown, green, or blue.

Sparkly

Complete each eye with a single cross-stitch of 3 black threads (DMC 310). Outline each eye with straight stitches, using 1 thread of blue, green, gray, or brown. Then complete a quarter-sized diagonal straight stitch in the top-right corner of each eye using 1 thread of DMC Blanc.

Happy

Cross-stitch the eye's "square" in the pattern using the same color as the skin tone. Then complete two squinty diagonal straight stitches with 2 threads of DMC 310. The diagonals should extend from the outermost corners of each eye and meet at a point between the holes of the Aida fabric, on the inside of the eye toward where the bridge of the nose would be.

Lashes

Cross-stitch each eye with 3 to 4 threads of DMC 310. Then, using 2 threads of DMC 310, straight stitch a horizontal and diagonal quarter stitch outward from the eye's outside corner.

Brows

Cross-stitch each eye using 3 to 4 threads of DMC 310. Straight stitch a full-length horizontal stitch and a diagonal quarter stitch above each eye using 1 thread of brown, black, or gray floss.

SIZE

Another (relatively) simple way to adjust a pattern to make it your own is to change the height or width of the characters in the pattern. Height is easiest—which is why Stitch People style patterns typically stick to a stylized, uniform width as explained in the introduction. But if you're feeling confident, you can make width adjustments as well.

HEIGHT ADJUSTMENTS

When adjusting the height of characters, simply add or remove a single row starting with one row in the legs. If it's not quite enough of an adjustment, add or remove an additional row across the torso and arms.

If you remove height, fill in the additional space according to what the rest of the pattern background is.
If you're adding height, you'll have to replace some of the existing pattern with the colors of the legs, and/or torso and arms.

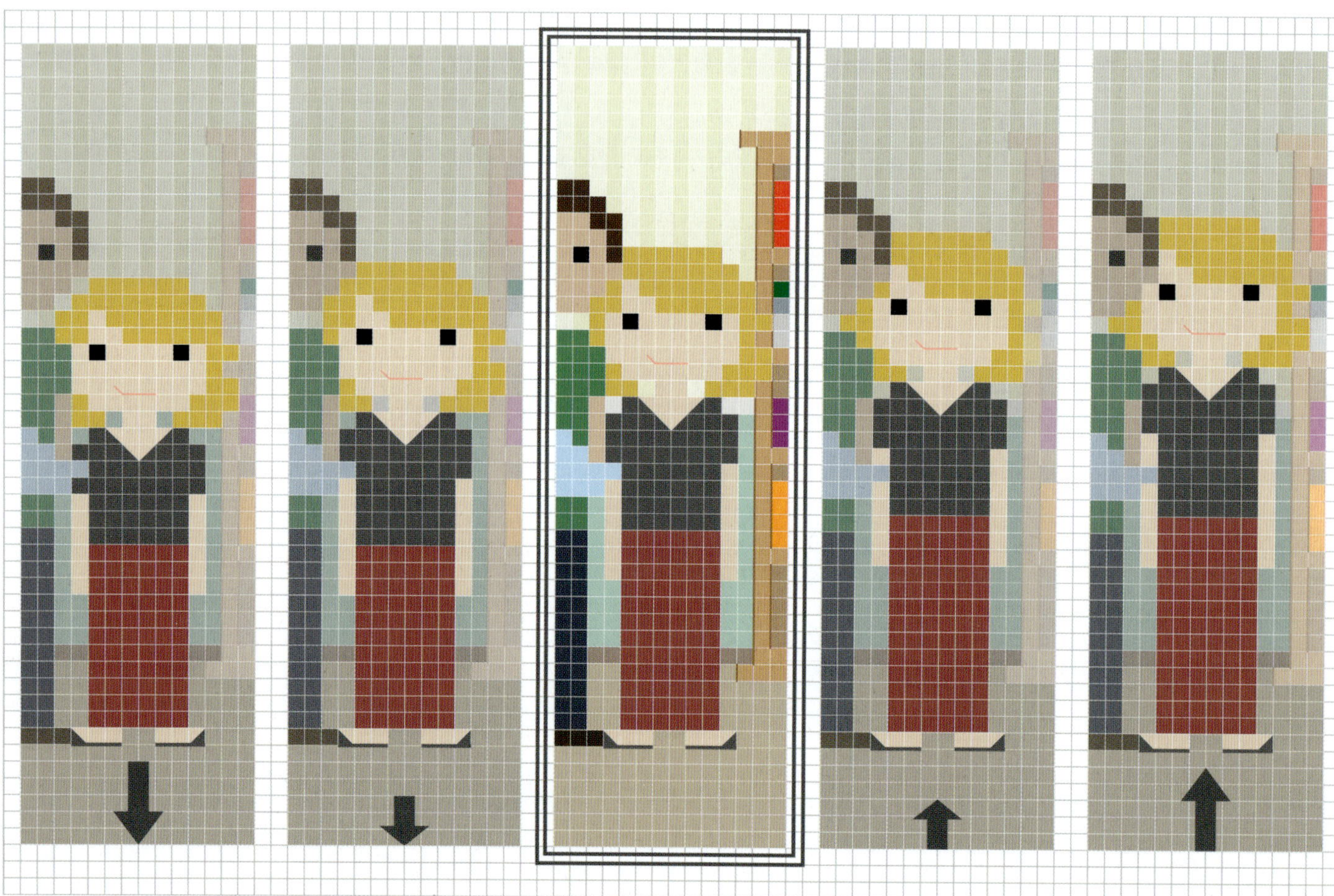

Row removed from legs, row removed from torso and arms

Row removed from legs

Original pattern

Row added to legs

Row added to legs, row added to torso and arms

note

While the background is dimmed out to emphasize the changes in height, note the subtle changes needed to be made to the background to accommodate height changes.

WIDTH ADJUSTMENTS

Width adjustments are a little trickier to manage merely due to the design constraints of the little characters. Refer to the example shown to understand the theory behind them. In short, you'll be adding a full column of width on either side of the Stitch People character, making each leg one square wider, as well as adding a square of width on either side of the torso and up into the shoulders.

You'll stitch the wider body pattern instead of whatever else the pattern currently has in the background. Don't double stitch, cross-stitching the background and then cross-stitching the person on top, or your work will look inconsistent and chunky.

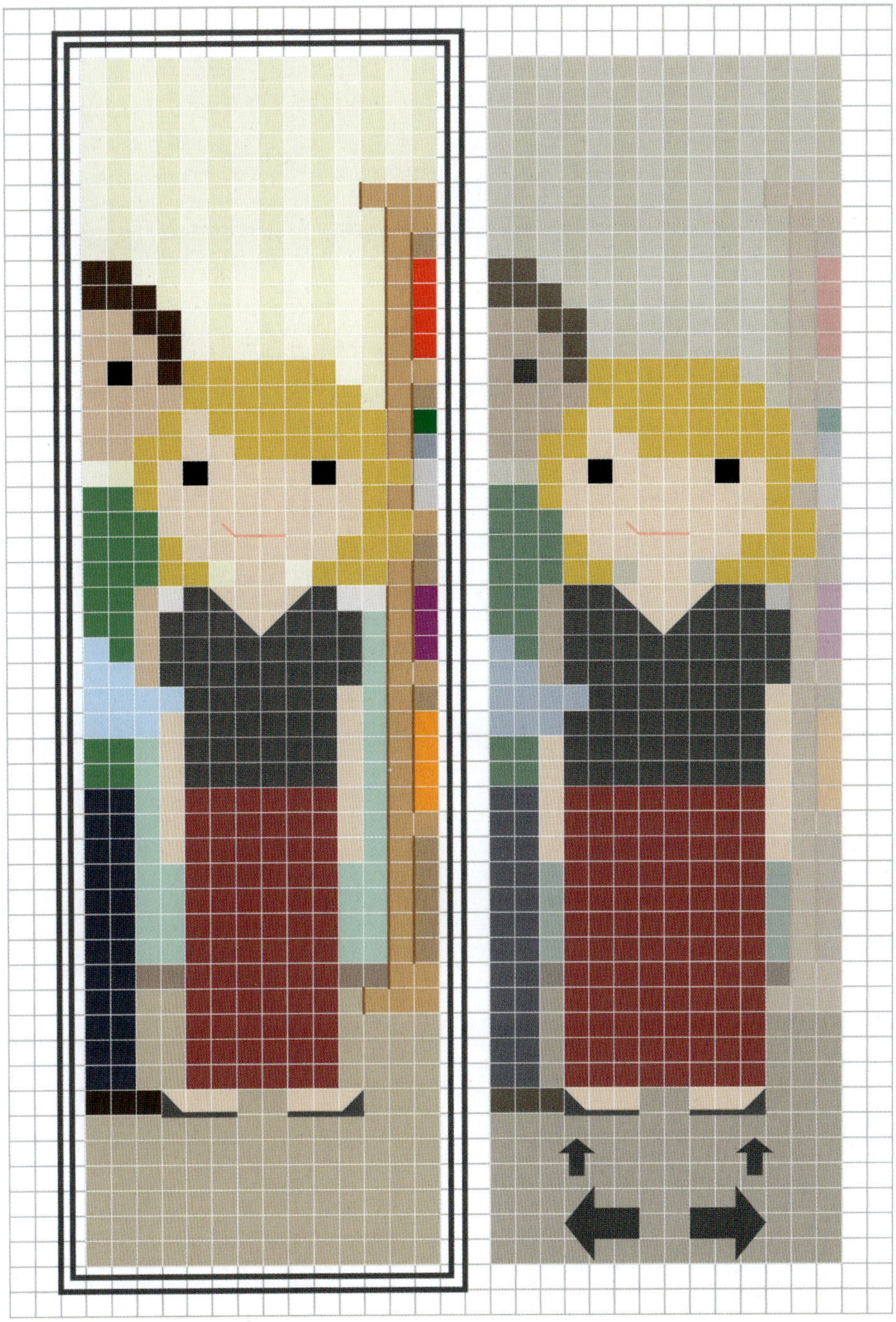

Original pattern

A column has been added on either side of the character, from the shoulder to the bottom of the leg. The center remains 2 squares wide to accommodate the neck and keep the head centered. The feet do not move.

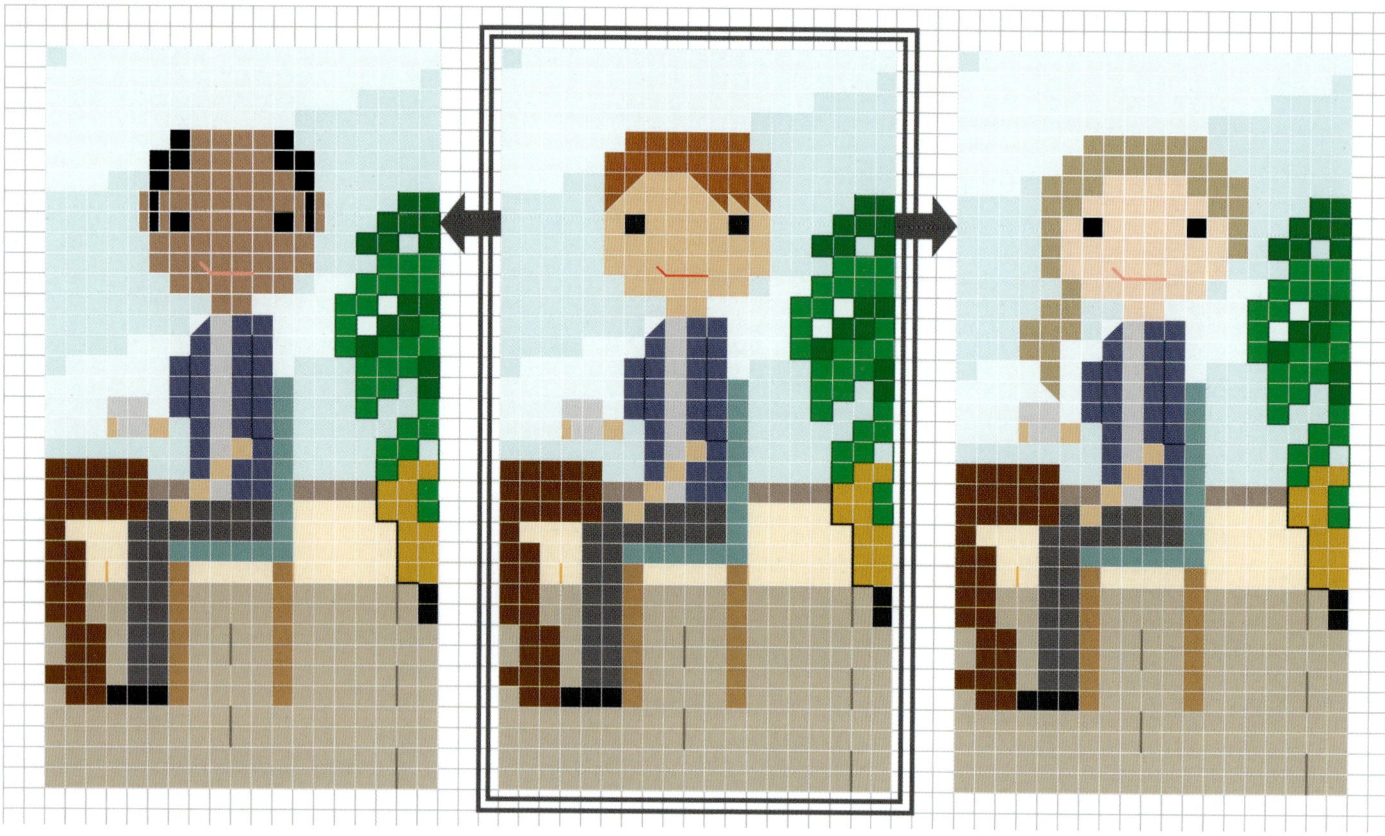

HAIRSTYLES

The last surefire way to customize a portrait character is to change the hairstyle completely. This is also the most complicated customization, as it requires changing the pattern in a relatively significant way. But it may just be worth it!

While there are hundreds, if not thousands, of hairstyles in the world, the patterns on the following pages offer a number of basic options.

To "swap" the hairstyle of a character in a pattern, simply stitch one of the following hairstyle patterns, from the neck up, instead of what's shown in any given pattern. This requires some planning ahead so you can adjust the background of the pattern accordingly—either removing squares of the background design to make room for a larger hairstyle, or filling in like squares of the background design to accommodate a lighter hairstyle.

Of course, adjust the floss colors you use according to the needs of your pattern.

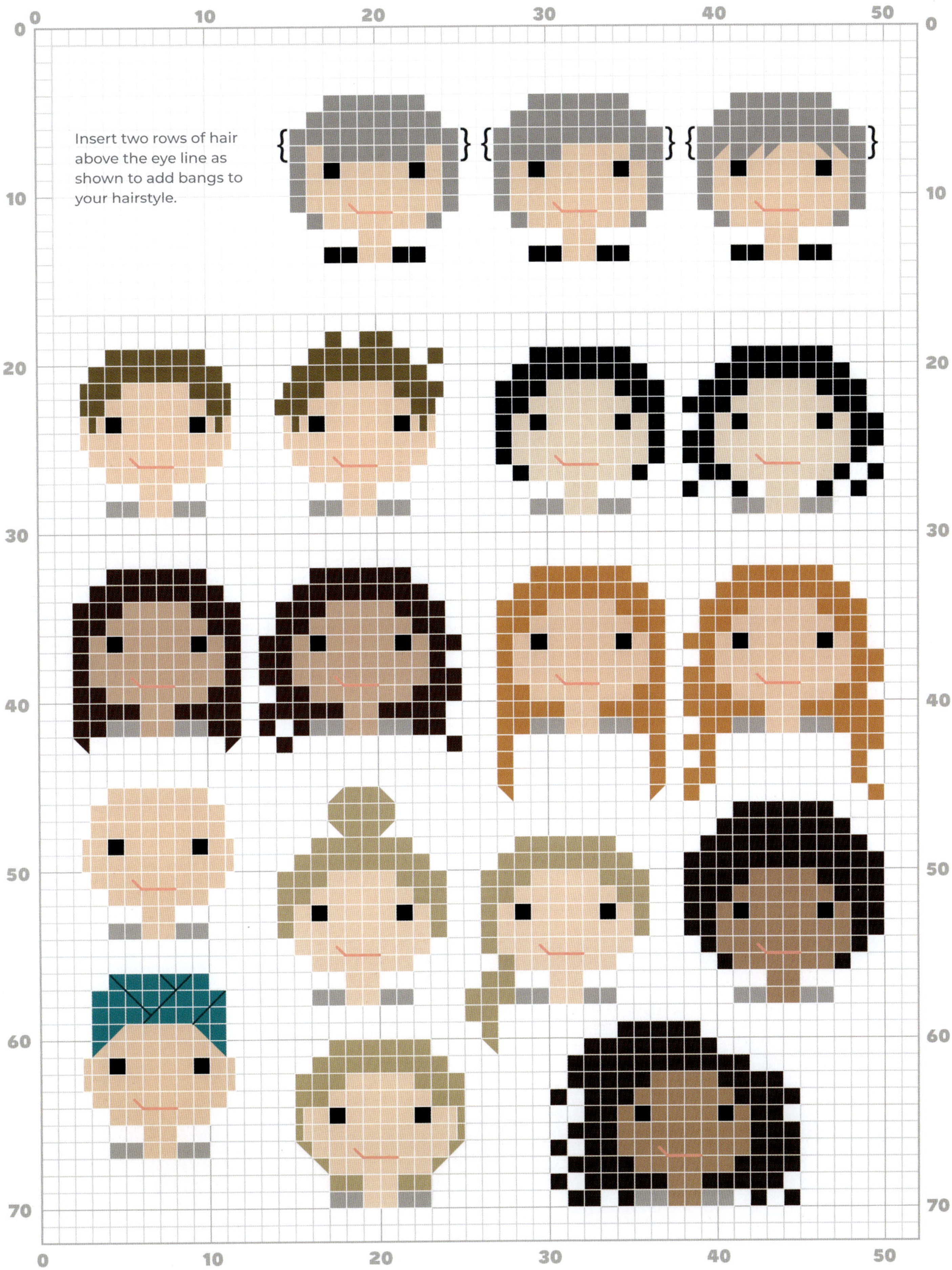
Insert two rows of hair above the eye line as shown to add bangs to your hairstyle.
0
10
20
30
40
50
60
70

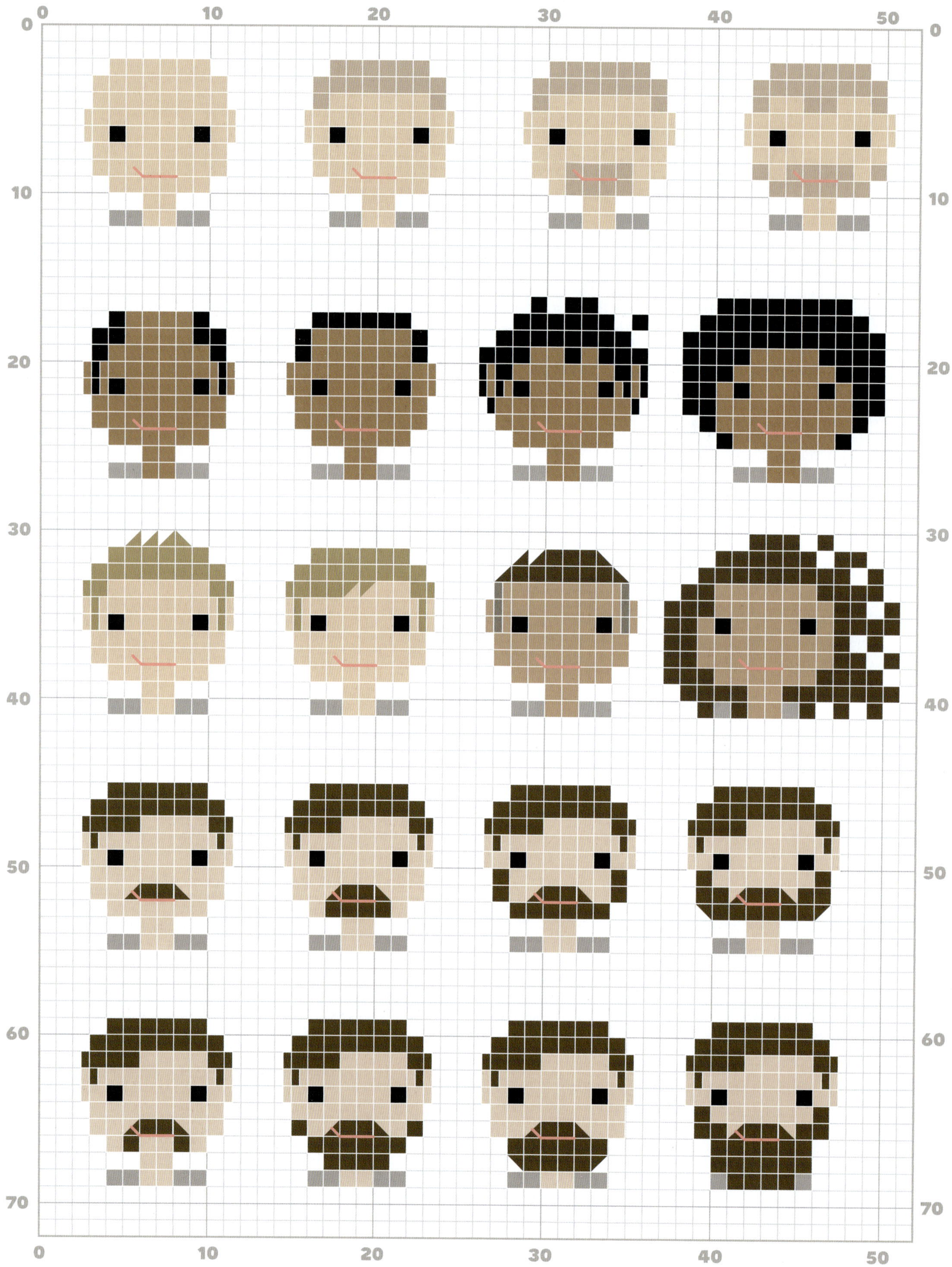
0
10
20
30
40
50
60
70

BORDERS & ALPHABETS

Other ways to infuse your cross-stitched portraits with your unique personality and creative style are to add, remove, and/or adjust the borders or text within and around a pattern. Not every border, phrase, or color scheme will be to your liking and that's totally okay! Take the reins of your creative imagination and feel free to remove a border, adjust the border design, or change the colors. Alternatively, you can change the text within a given pattern or add text where there is none, putting words or a phrase above/below a pattern or to the left or right.

This will take some design work on your part, but you can do it! Copy each letter from the alphabet you like onto the blank graph paper at the back of the book to work out your name or phrase. Count out the width and height, and center it up to the pattern you're using. Make sure you're using enough fabric to stitch it all!

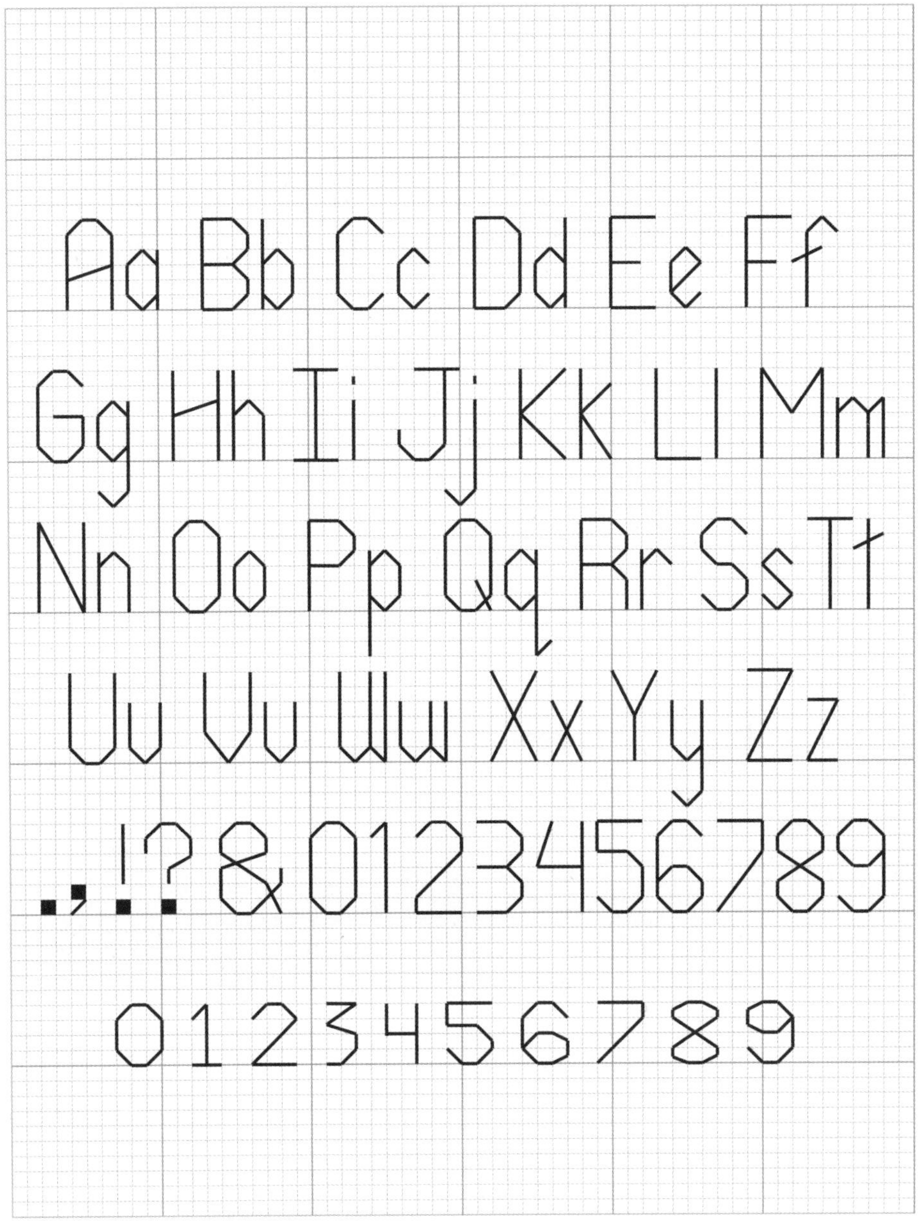

ALPHABET INSTRUCTIONS

The instructions are the same for adding any words or phrases to your patterns.

1. Use the blank graph at the back of the book to sketch things out (see page 109).

2. Choose the alphabet you like to copy each letter from the alphabet onto the blank graph paper to work out your words or phrase (see page 106).

3. Count out the total width and height of your sketched words or phrase, and center it up to the pattern you're using.

4. Make sure you've planned to have enough fabric for the total pattern, including the words!

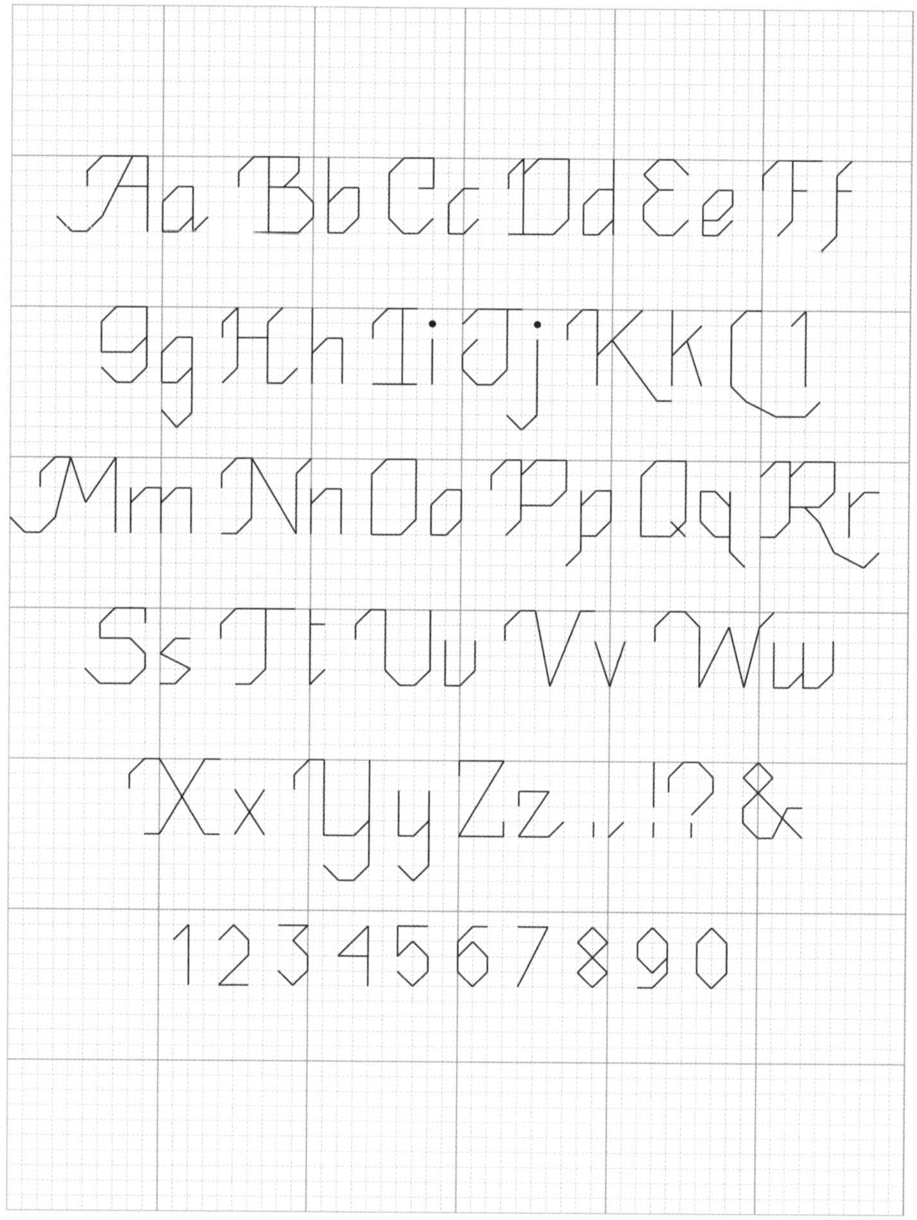

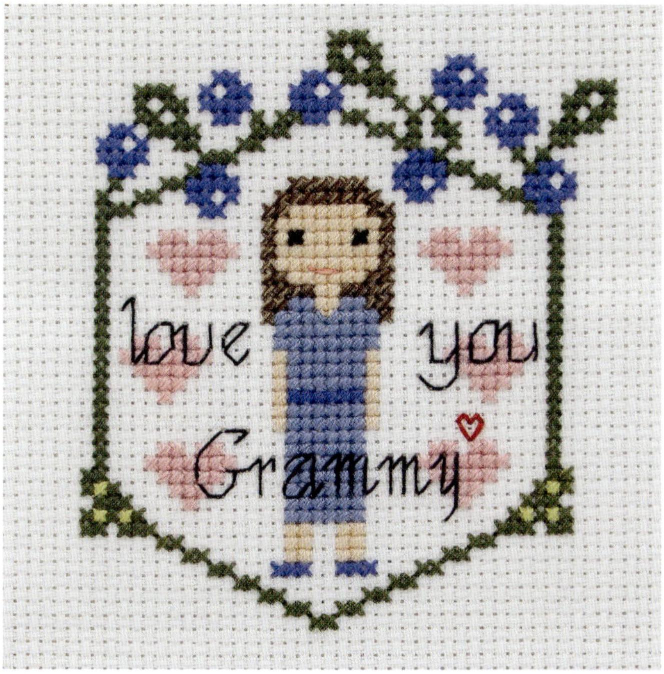

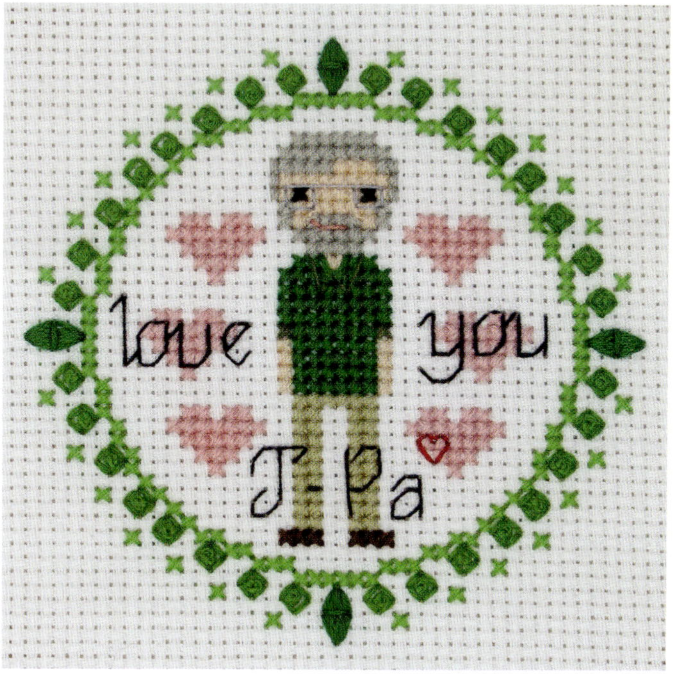

PHRASE IDEAS

If you'd like to add a phrase of some kind to your pattern but don't know where to begin, here are a few examples you can use as a foundation and customize according to the needs of your friends and family.

Family-related:

- Smith Family Vacation 2022
- The Goodwins
- The Mizrahi Family
- Some call it chaos, we call it family
- What matters most is at home
- This is Us
- Family is everything
- Love you any season of the year

Friend- and activity-related:

- Inhale the future, exhale the past
- Coffee is always a good idea
- My Chosen Family
- Friendship refreshes the soul
- Good friends make great adventures
- The Best Crew

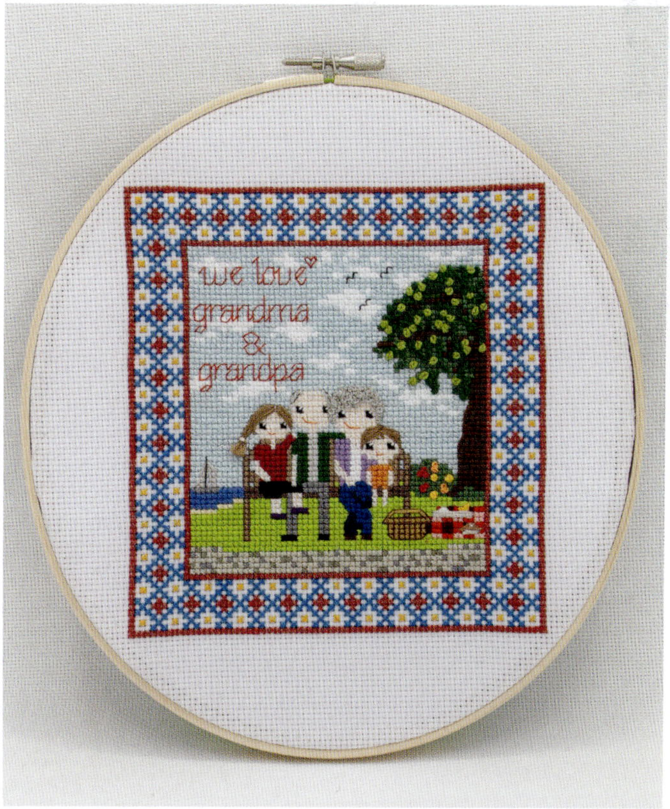

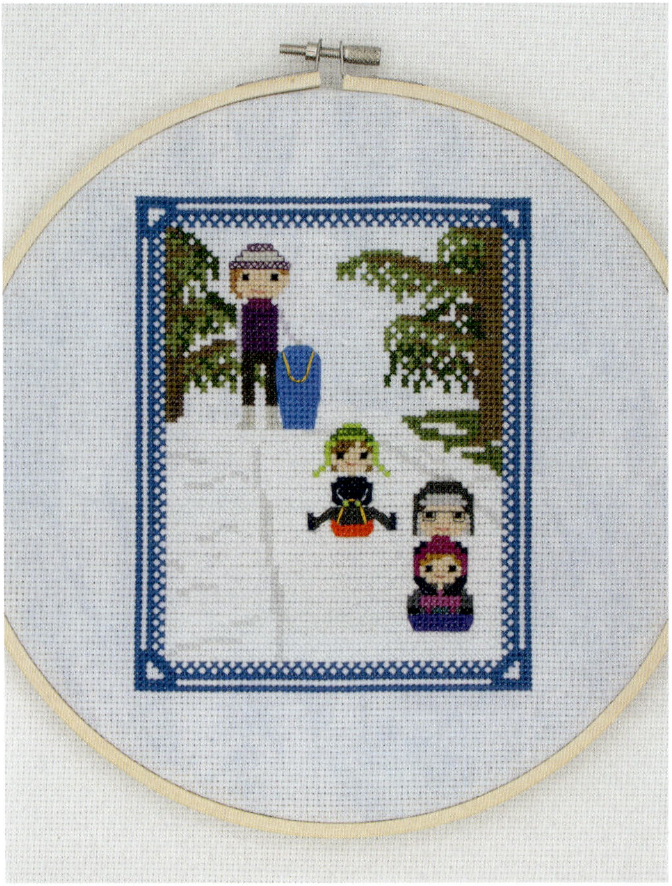

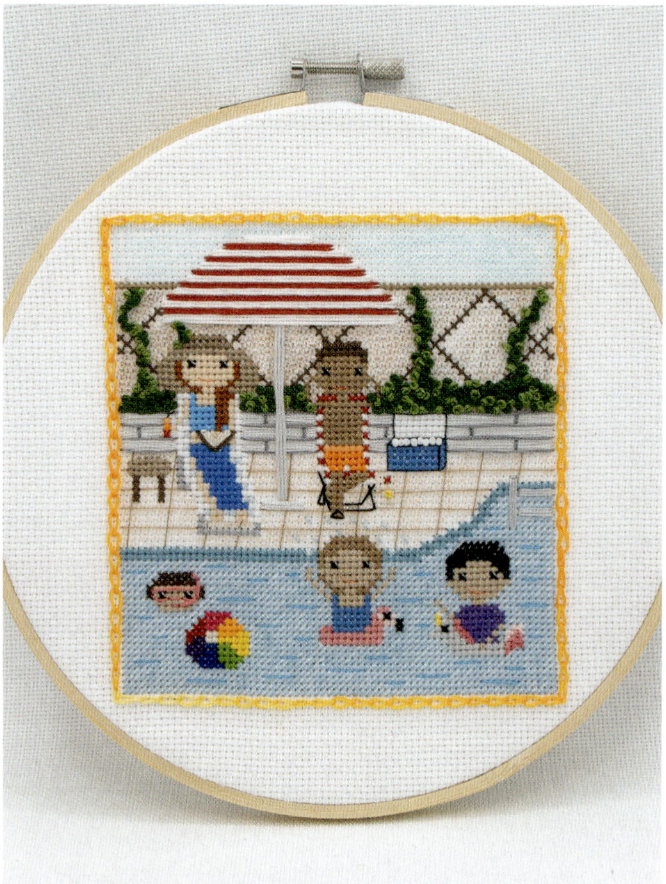

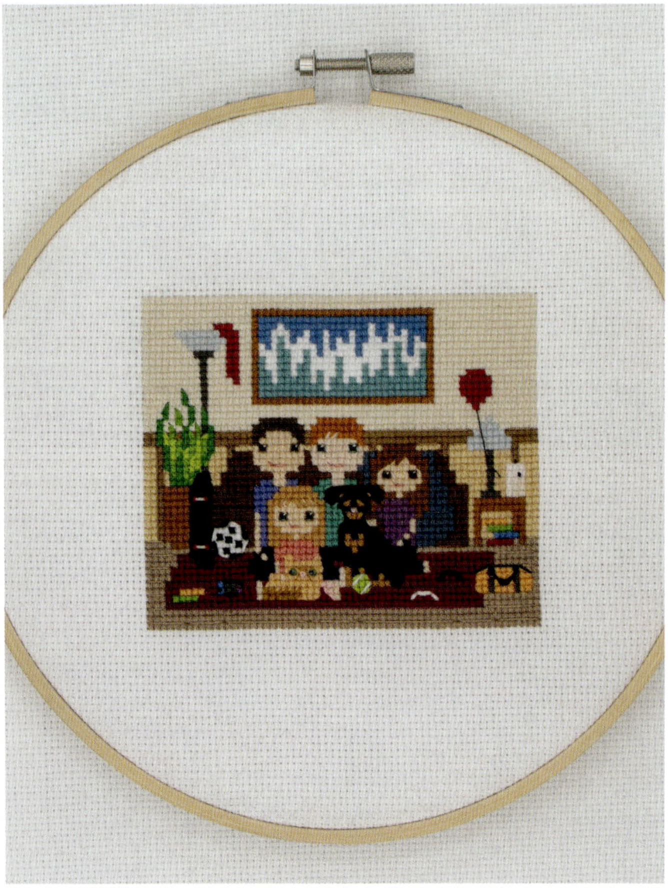

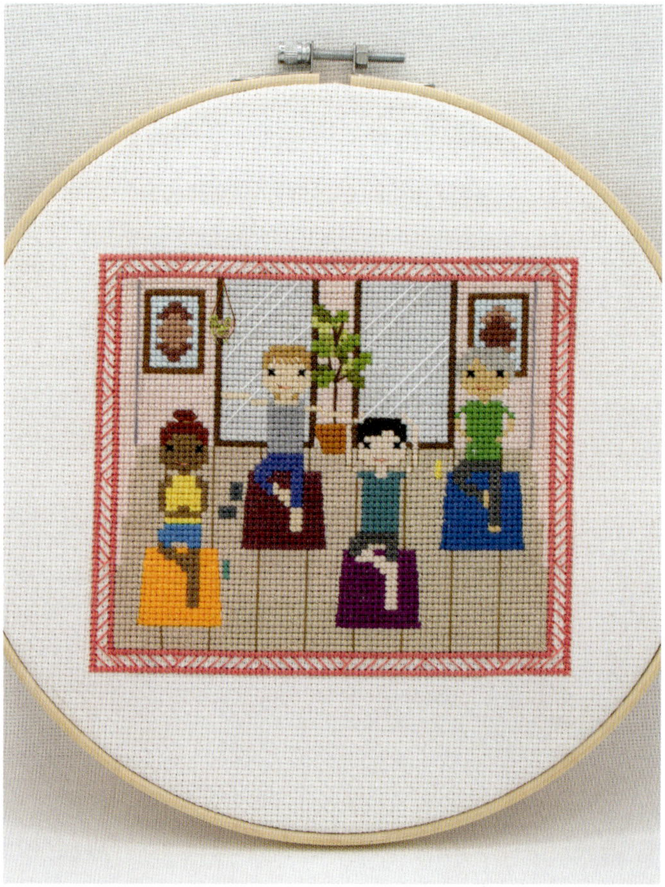

PATTERNS

All of the patterns on the following pages represent various scenes and scenarios for gatherings and outings with your friends and family. Any adult character can represent a male, female, friend, family member, or significant other—that comes down to slight adjustments in the hairstyles, skin tone floss colors, and clothing colors you choose for your portrait's characters.

Remember the suggestions in the "Customize Your Cross-Stitch" section for making each character truly your own, including the size adjustments that can help you make changes to the children in the patterns.

PATTERN SIZING

Something to keep in mind with the patterns is you can adjust their size. If the full pattern is too much for your stitching time constraints or a particular-sized frame, you can use your best judgment to remove squares from the top, bottom, left, and right sides. I recommend removing equal numbers of rows or columns from the left/right and/or the top/bottom.

BORDERS

Each pattern has a border included as part of the design. Consider this your official permission to change or remove any of the borders! You can swap the border with another design in the collection or remove it, entirely. That's up to you!

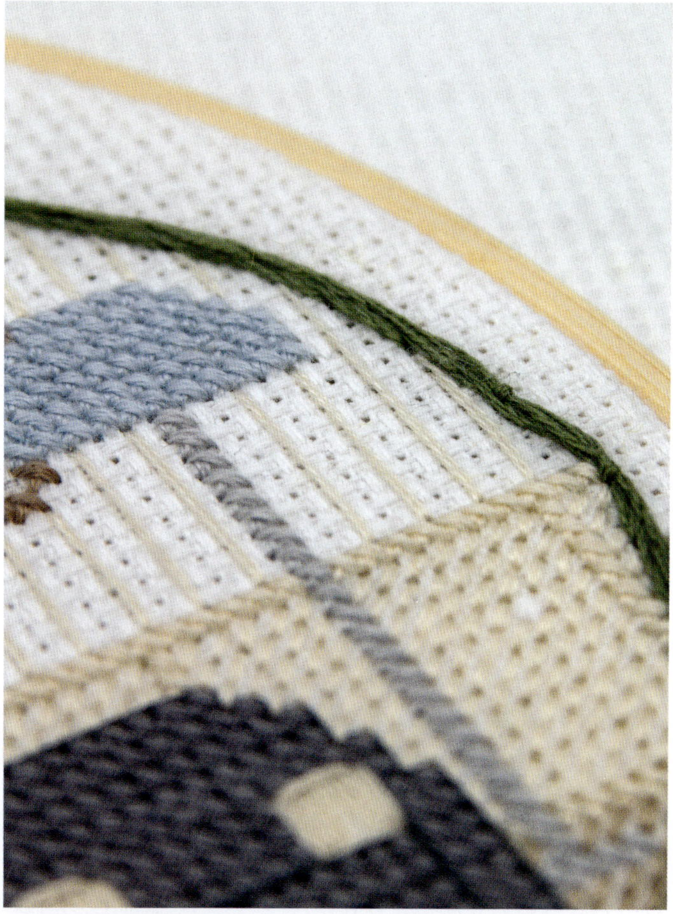

This portrait utilizes various lengths of straight stitches to create different background effects.

family night in

WHAT'S BETTER THAN A NIGHT IN WITH THE FAMILY FOR GAMES OR A MOVIE?

Pattern Dimensions:
65 squares wide
x 51 squares high

Finished Dimensions on Size 14 Aida Fabric:
4.6" x 3.6" (12 cm x 10 cm)

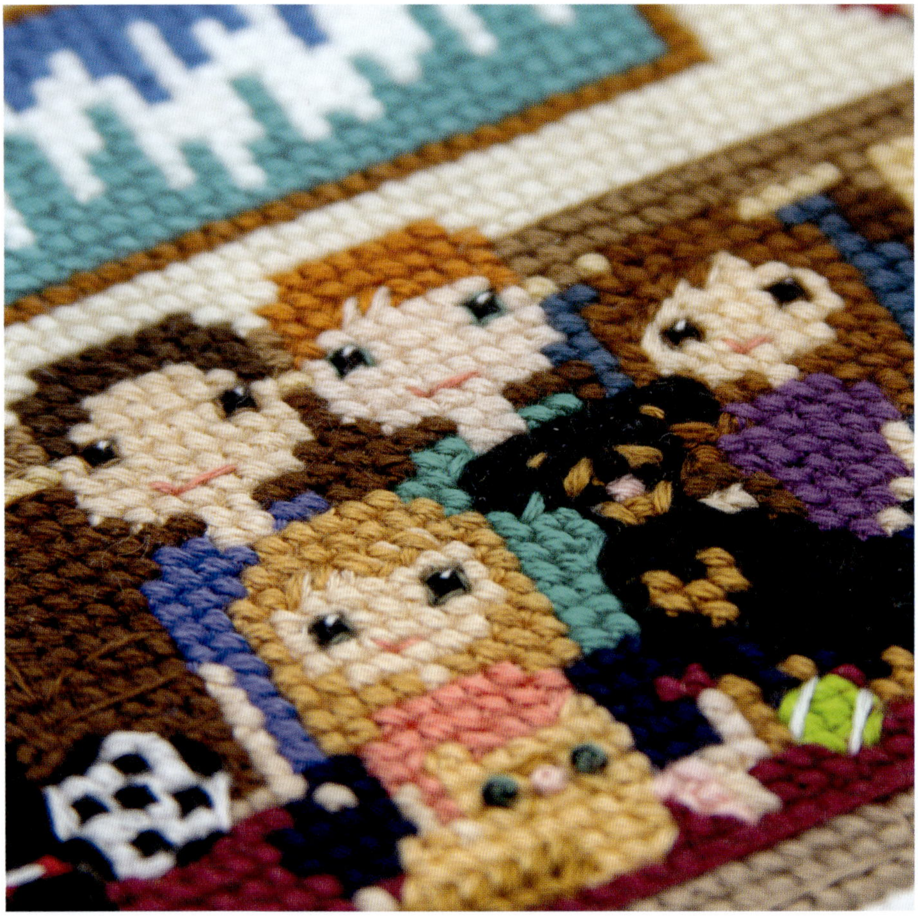

INSTRUCTIONS

1 Cut the fabric 8.5" x 7.5" (22 cm x 20 cm), mark the center point, and secure it in the center of an embroidery hoop. Customize the pattern as needed.

2 Swap hairstyles as needed. Use the provided hairstyle options at the front of the book as a basis for adjusting children's hairstyles (see page 44).

3 Make notes or sketch out any other pattern adjustments you'd like, removing certain elements or adjusting the height or width of any character.

This portrait was lovingly stitched by Teresa Victor!

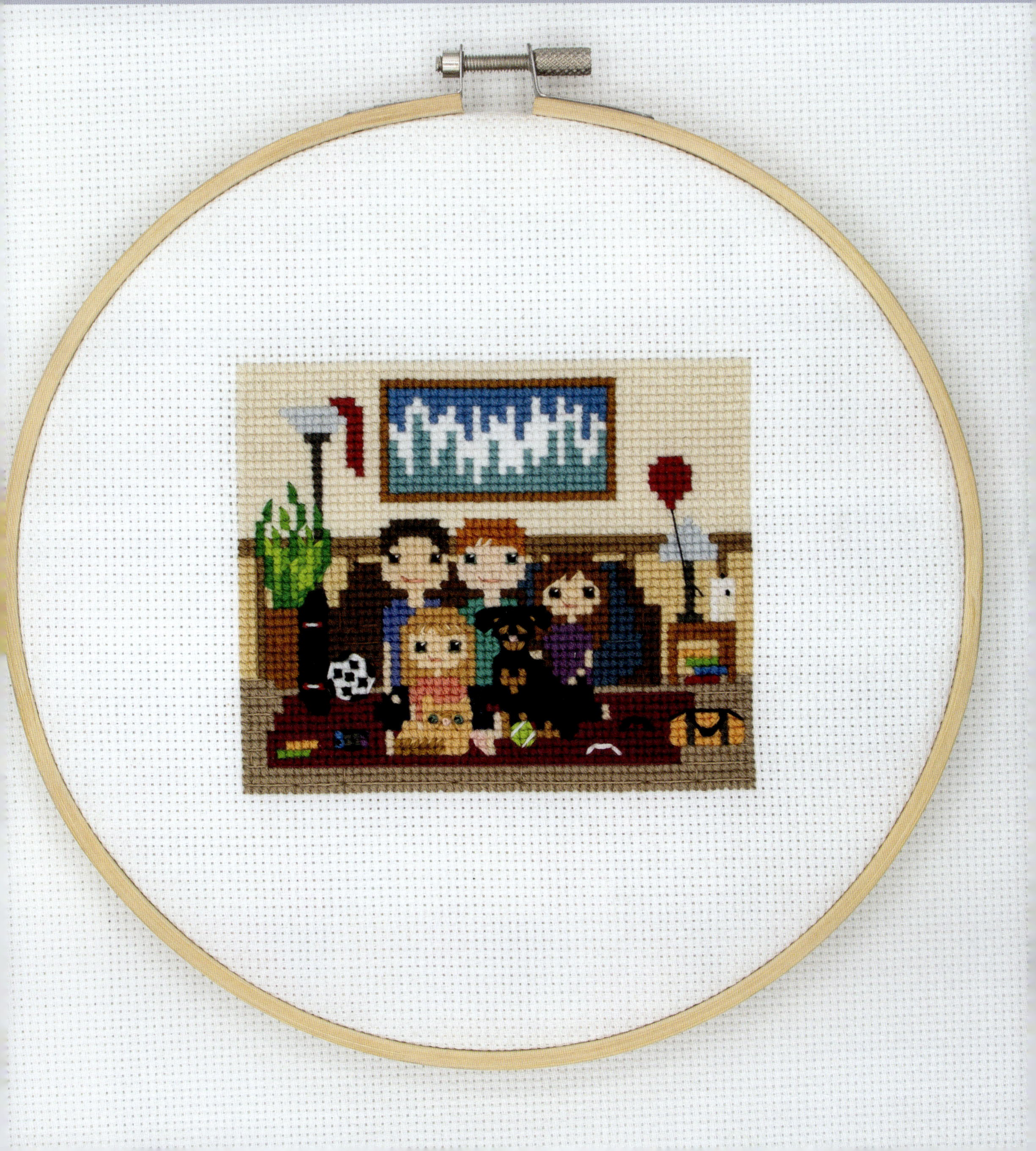

4 Choose the floss color for each character's skin tone and hair color.

5 Choose floss colors for each characters's clothing. Don't forget you can choose more than one color!

6 Select floss colors for the pattern that reflect similar items in your home—floor color, rug color, sofa color, wall color(s), etc.

7 Use 3 strands of floss to cross-stitch each square in the pattern.

8 Use 1 strand of floss to backstitch all linear details, except use 2 threads for the mouths.

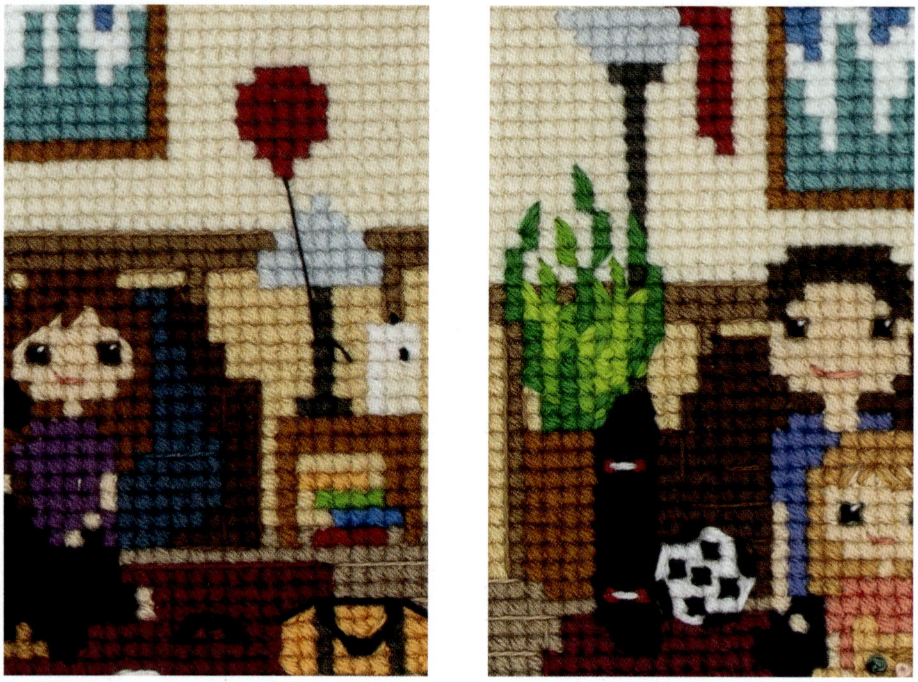

By combining 1 thread of three different colors, you can create the illusion of a patterned fabric. Alternately, you can utilize straight stitches and French knots atop the cross-stitching for stripes or polka dots.

customization tip!

Notice how clean a portrait can look without a border. Whether small or more ornate, sometimes a border simply doesn't match the aesthetic of either the stitcher or the lucky recipient of the portrait! Keep this option in mind if you're short on time or prefer a more minimal aesthetic.

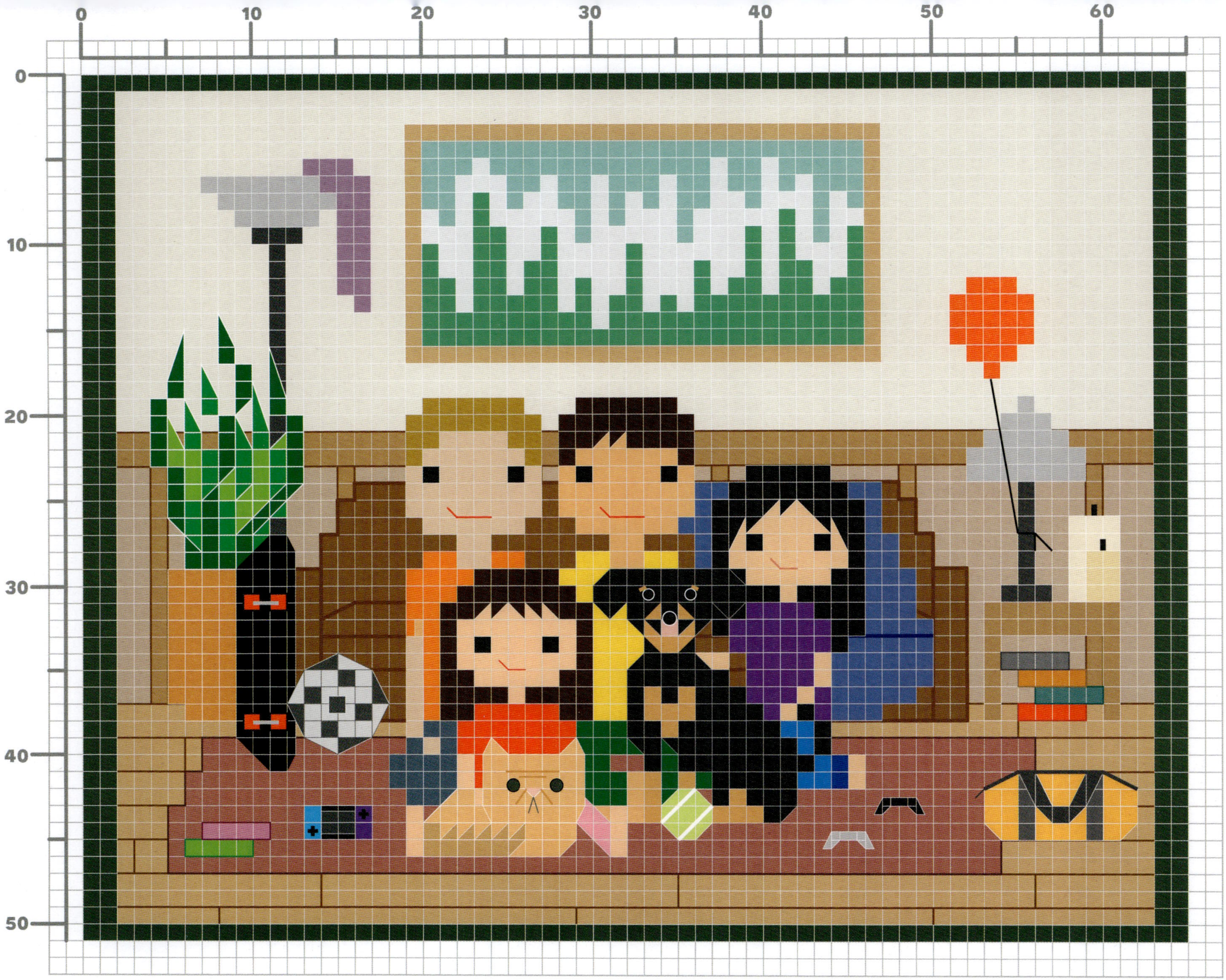
0
10
20
30
40
50
60
0
10
20
30
40
50

baby announcement

STITCH UP A NURSERY SCENE TO ANNOUNCE THE ARRIVAL OF A NEW FAMILY MEMBER!

Pattern Dimensions:
86 squares wide
x 54 squares high

Finished Dimensions on Size 14 Aida Fabric:
6.1" x 3.9"
(15.5 cm x 10 cm)

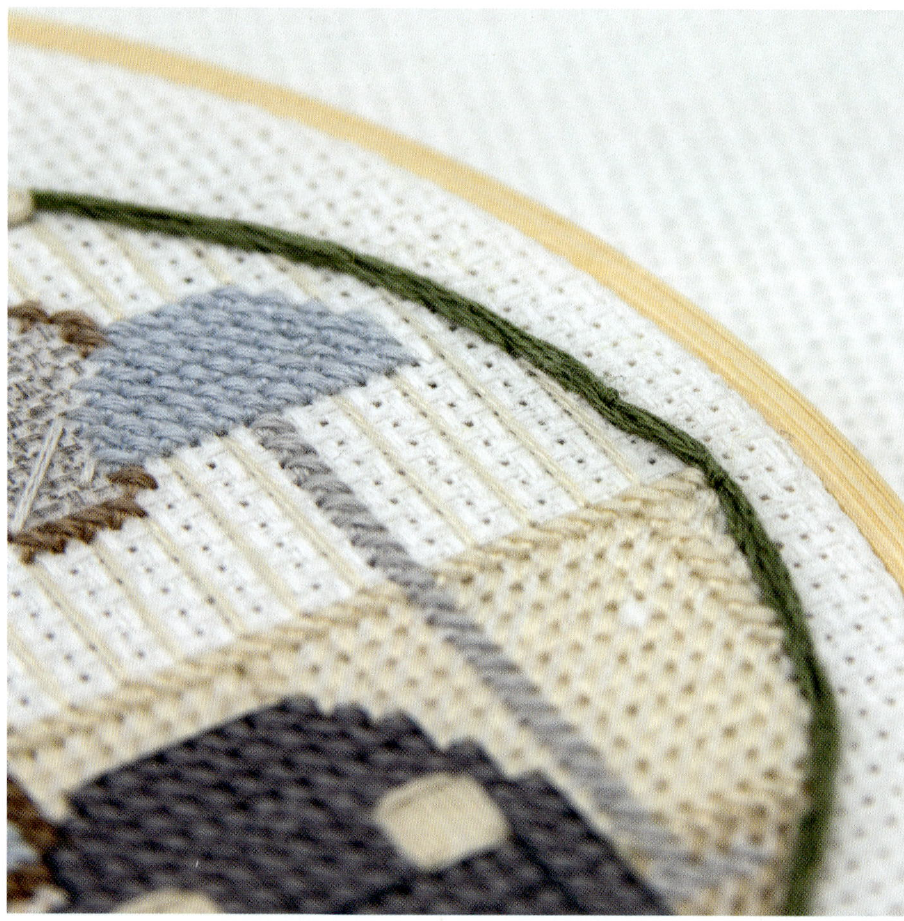

INSTRUCTIONS

1 Cut the fabric 10" x 8" (26 cm x 21 cm), mark the center point, and secure it in the center of an embroidery hoop. Customize the pattern as needed.

2 Swap hairstyles as needed and make any height or width adjustments you'd like (see page 42).

3 Make notes or sketch out any other pattern adjustments you're interested in, removing elements, swapping the border, or adjusting the pattern's dimensions by removing columns or rows.

This portrait was lovingly stitched by Amanda Irvin! Follow her on Instagram @erinandelizabeth.

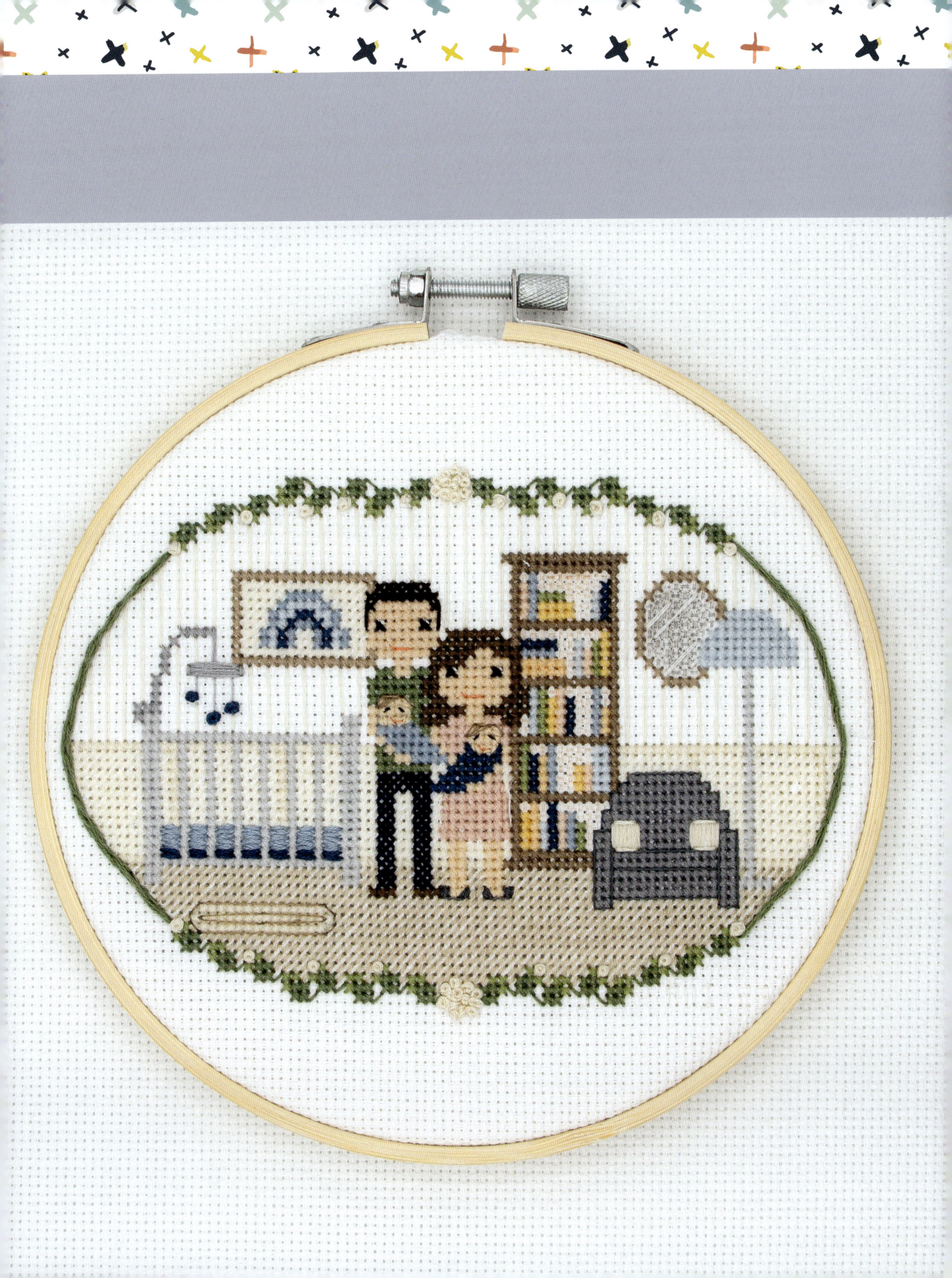

4 Choose the floss color for each character's skin tone and hair color as well as clothing (see page 38).

5 Select floss colors for the pattern that reflect similar items in your home—floor color, furniture colors, etc.

6 Use 3 strands of floss to cross-stitch each square in the pattern.

7 Use 1 strand of floss to backstitch all linear details, except use 2 threads for the mouths.

8 Stitch the elements of the mobile as French knots using 2 threads of floss.

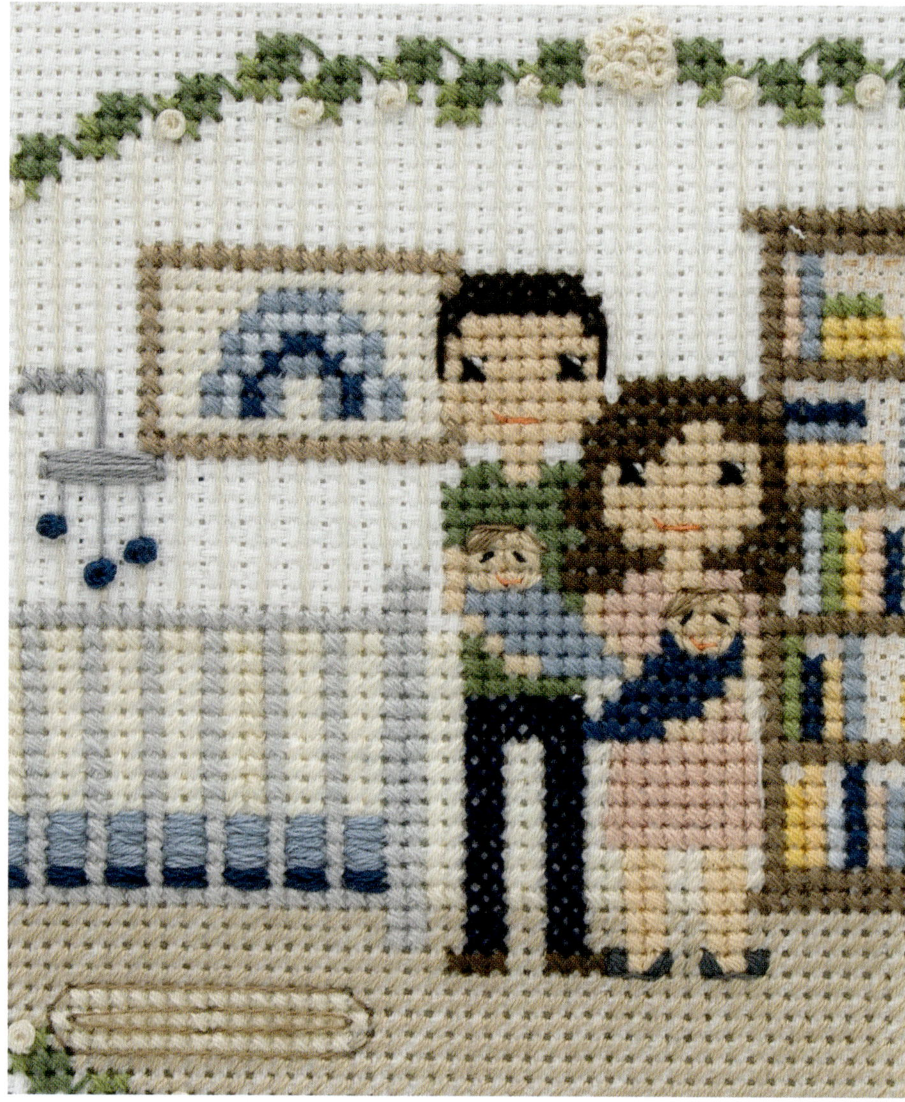

Notice how French knots are utilized in the floral border and mobile, straight stitches create hair for each baby and define the rug on the floor, and satin stitches fill in the blankets of the crib and the shape of the mobile.

customization tip!

This portrait is an excellent example of ways you can customize your portrait. Not only is the color palette totally unique, the background displays some gorgeous time-saving techniques!

The wall was completed by filling in the bottom half with diagonal half stitches, and the vertical stripes on the top half are long, straight stitches against the plain Aida fabric. Similarly, the carpet was stitched using only diagonal half stitches. And did you notice how this stitcher copied the baby pattern in the opposite direction, and stitched it into mom's arms? Twins!

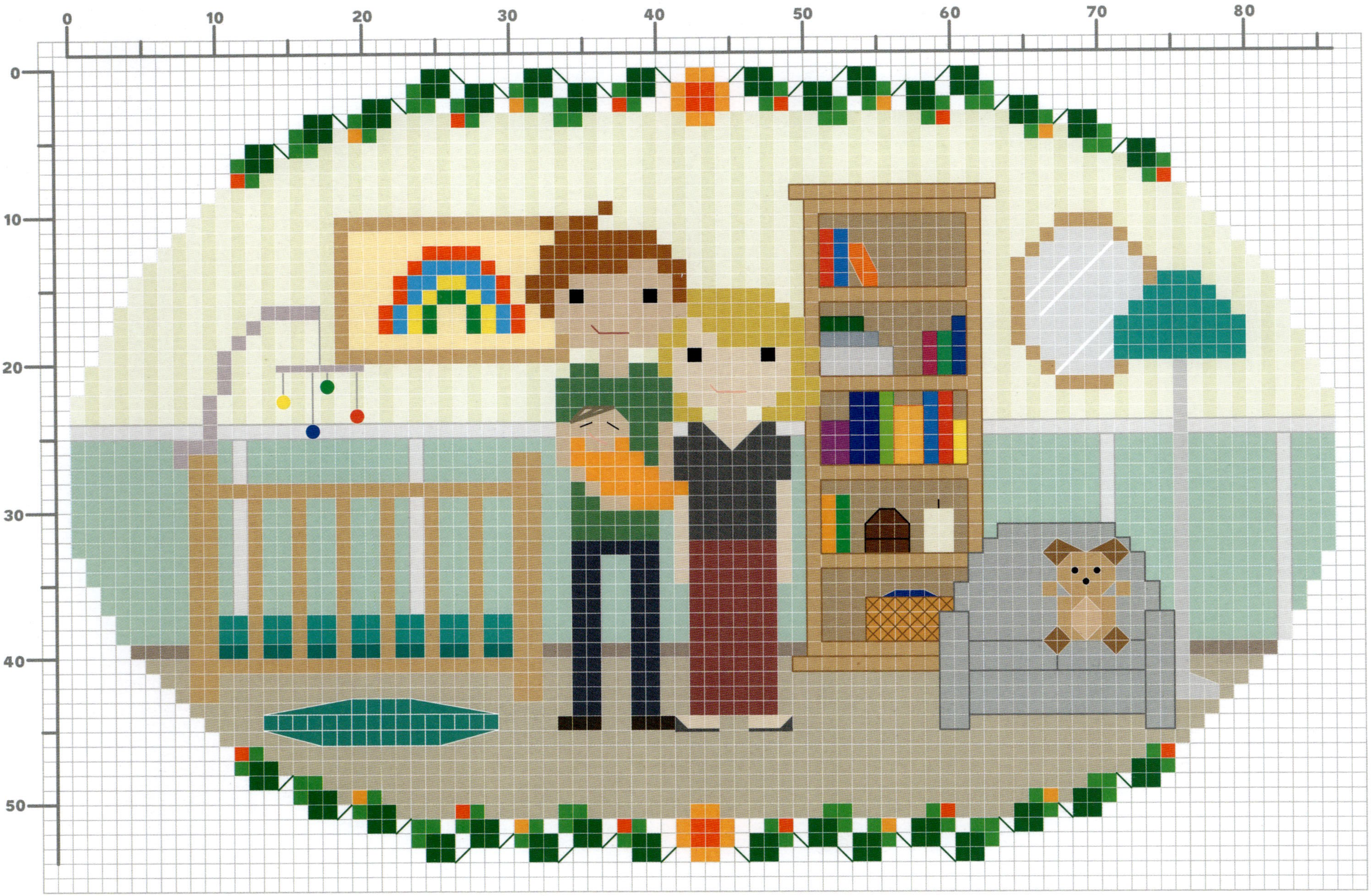
0
10
20
30
40
50
60
70
80
0
10
20
30
40
50

a happy home

A PATTERN FOR A COZY COUPLE OR HAPPY HOUSEMATES.

Pattern Dimensions:
60 squares wide
x 62 squares high

Finished Dimensions on Size 14 Aida Fabric:
4.3" x 4.4"
(11 cm x 11.2 cm)

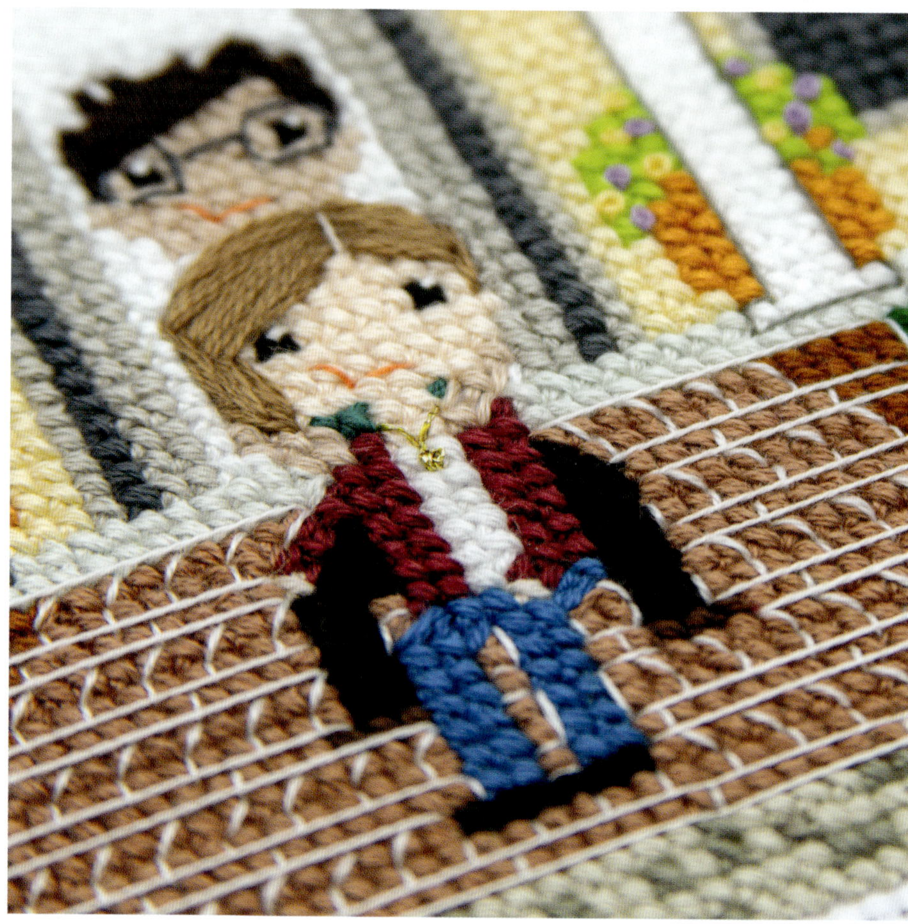

INSTRUCTIONS

1 Cut the fabric 8" x 8" (21 cm x 21 cm), mark the center point, and secure it in the center of an embroidery hoop. Customize the pattern as needed.

2 Plan if you'd like to stitch the pattern as-is or swap the couple with the side-by-side character positioning.

3 Change the hairstyles as needed and make any height or width adjustments (see page 42).

4 Make notes or sketch out any other pattern adjustments you're interested in, like removing or changing the border, or adjusting the pattern's dimensions by removing columns or rows.

This portrait was lovingly stitched by Erika Cota! Follow her on Instagram @arkacota.

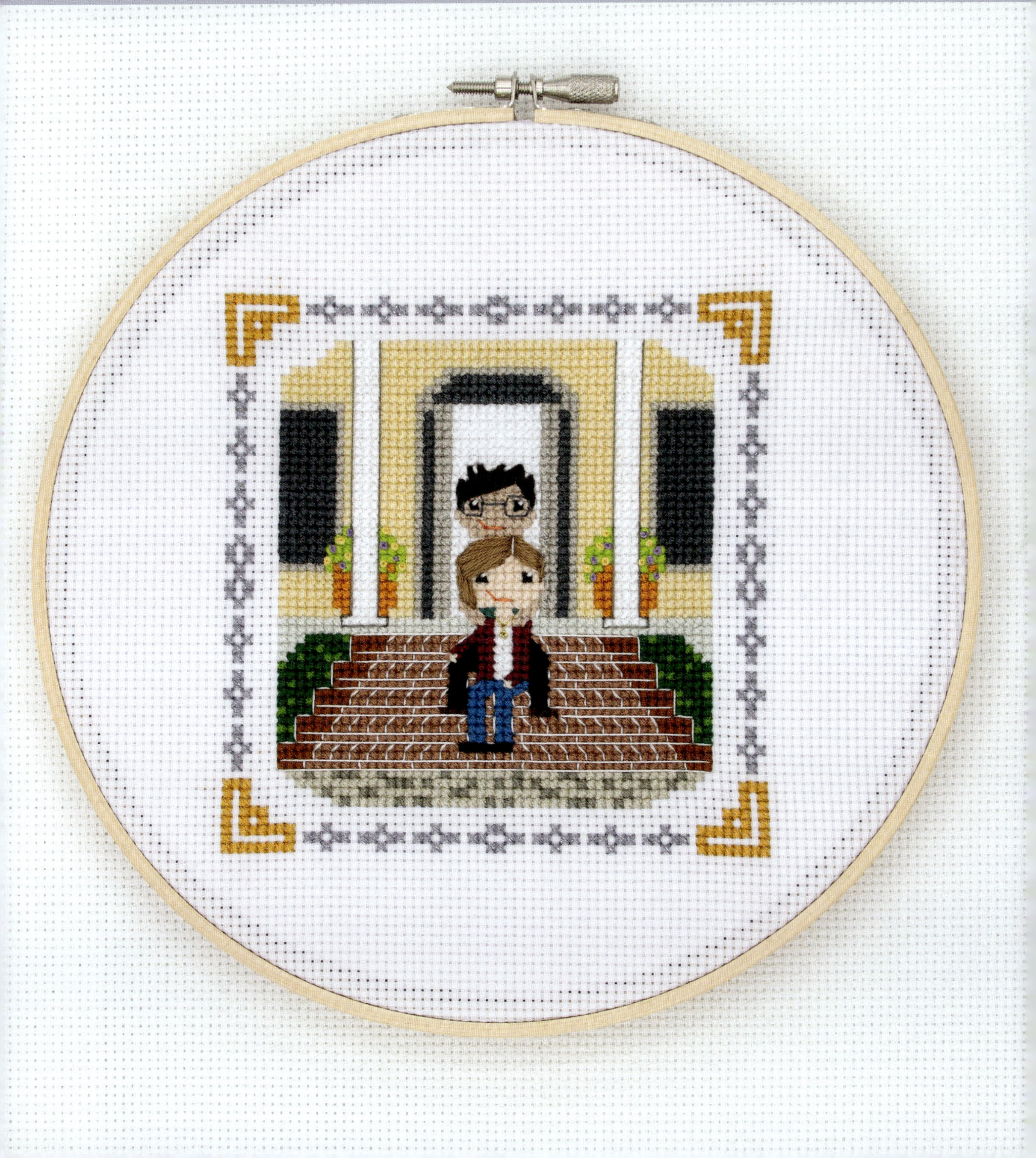

5 Choose your desired floss colors for each character's skin tone and hair color as well as clothing (see page 38).

6 Select floss colors for the pattern that reflect similar items in your home—floor color, furniture colors, etc.

7 Use 3 strands of floss to cross-stitch each square in the pattern.

8 Use 1 strand of floss to backstitch all linear details, except use 2 threads for the mouths.

9 Stitch the circles (flowers in the greenery) with French knots using 2 threads of floss.

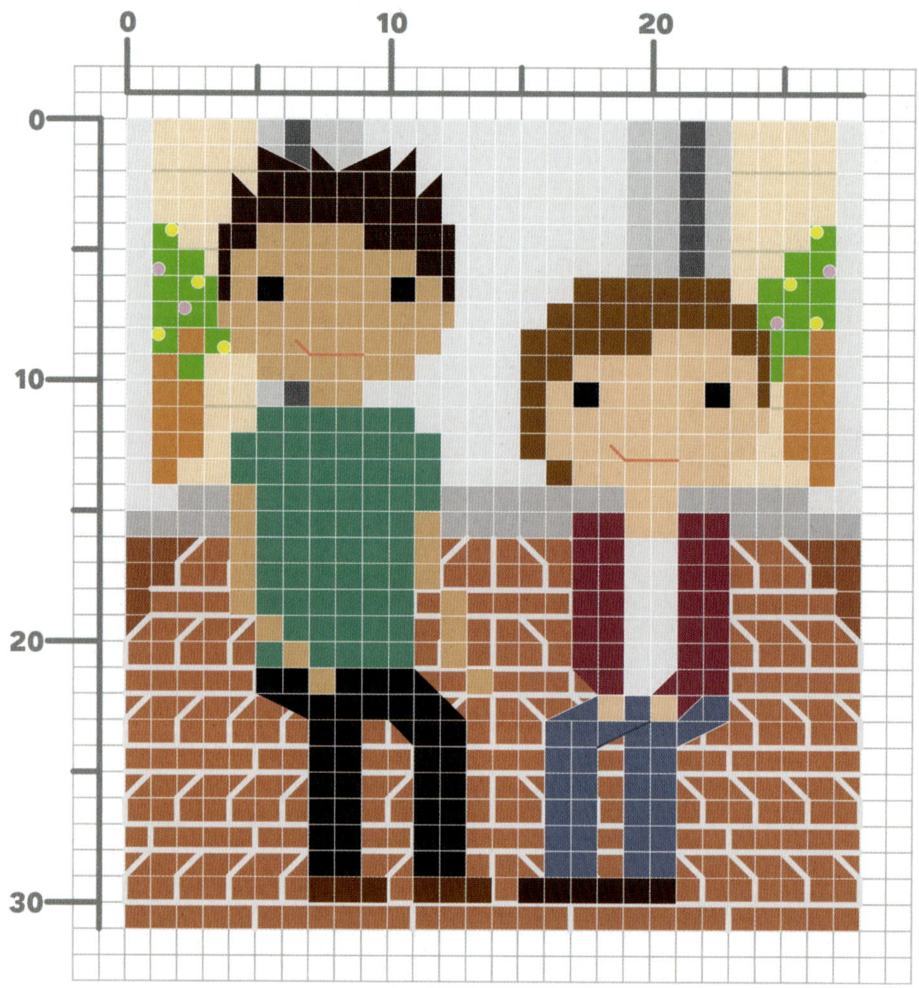

This alternate layout can be used for roommates or a couple that prefers their space!

customization tip!

It's all in the details! Delicate French knots adorn the potted plants, providing a pop of color. An even more subtle French knot sits between 2 single-thread straight stitches to represent a necklace, and both hairstyles are easily stitched with parallel straight stitches, or satin stitches, to create the effect of more realistic-looking hair.

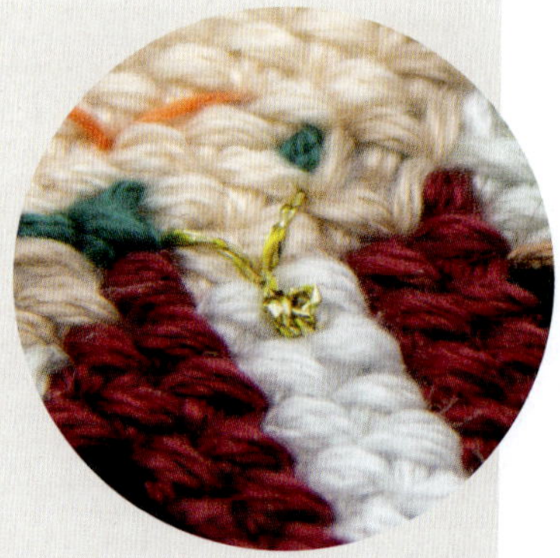

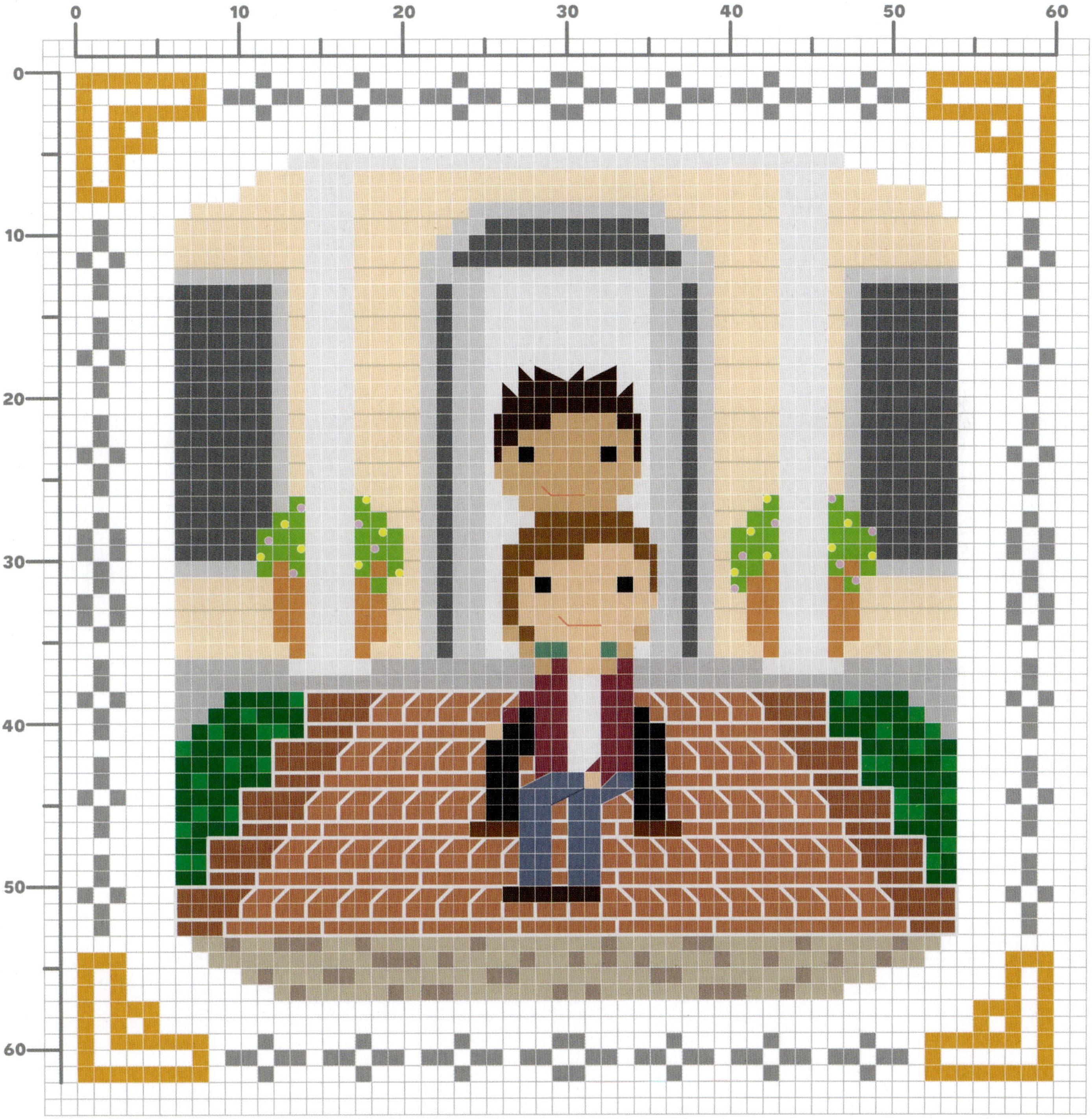
0
10
20
30
40
50
60
0
10
20
30
40
50
60

yoga class

WHAT BETTER WAY TO COMMEMORATE YOUR APPRECIATION FOR YOUR EXERCISE CLASS PALS?

Pattern Dimensions:
80 squares wide
x 70 squares high

Finished Dimensions on Size 14 Aida Fabric:
5.7" x 4.3"
(14.5 cm x 11 cm)

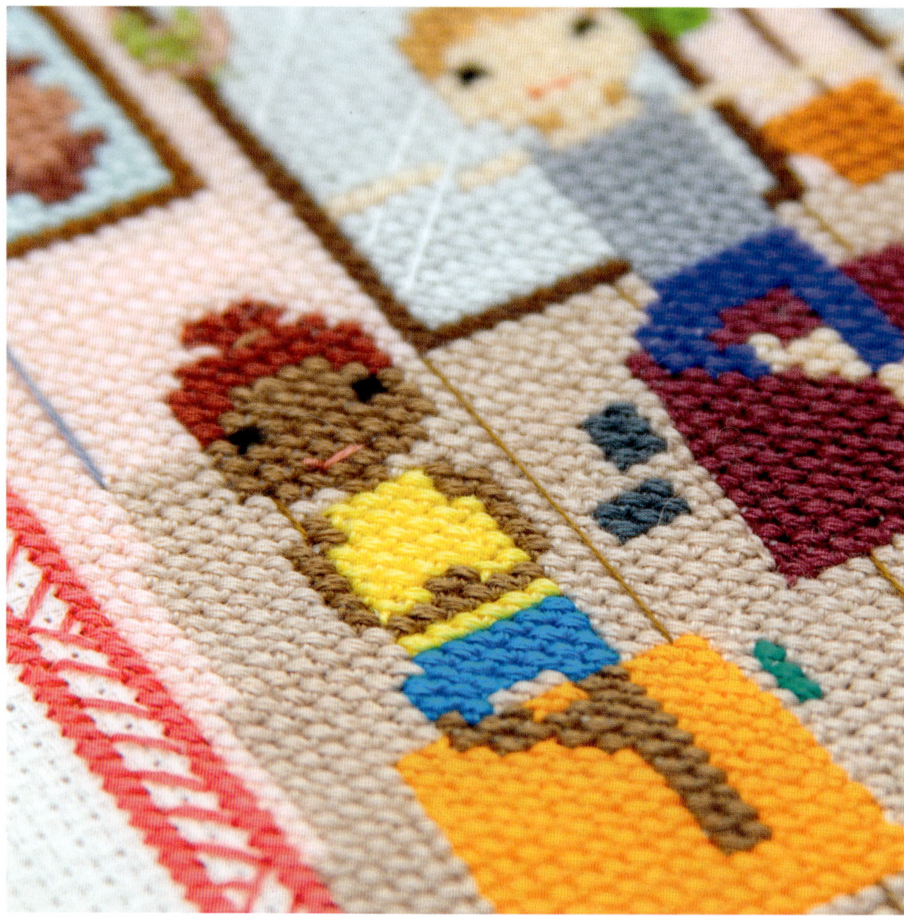

INSTRUCTIONS

1 Cut the fabric 10" x 8" (26 cm x 21 cm), mark the center point, and secure it in the center of an embroidery hoop. Customize the pattern as needed.

2 Change the hairstyles as needed and make any height or width adjustments to the characters in the pattern (see page 42).

3 Choose floss colors for each character's skin tone and hair color (see page 38).

4 Choose floss colors for the clothing and yoga mats. Don't forget you can combine threads of different floss colors and utilize French knots and straight stitches for details.

This portrait was lovingly stitched by Christy Pawloski! Follow her on Instagram @sunlightstitchery.

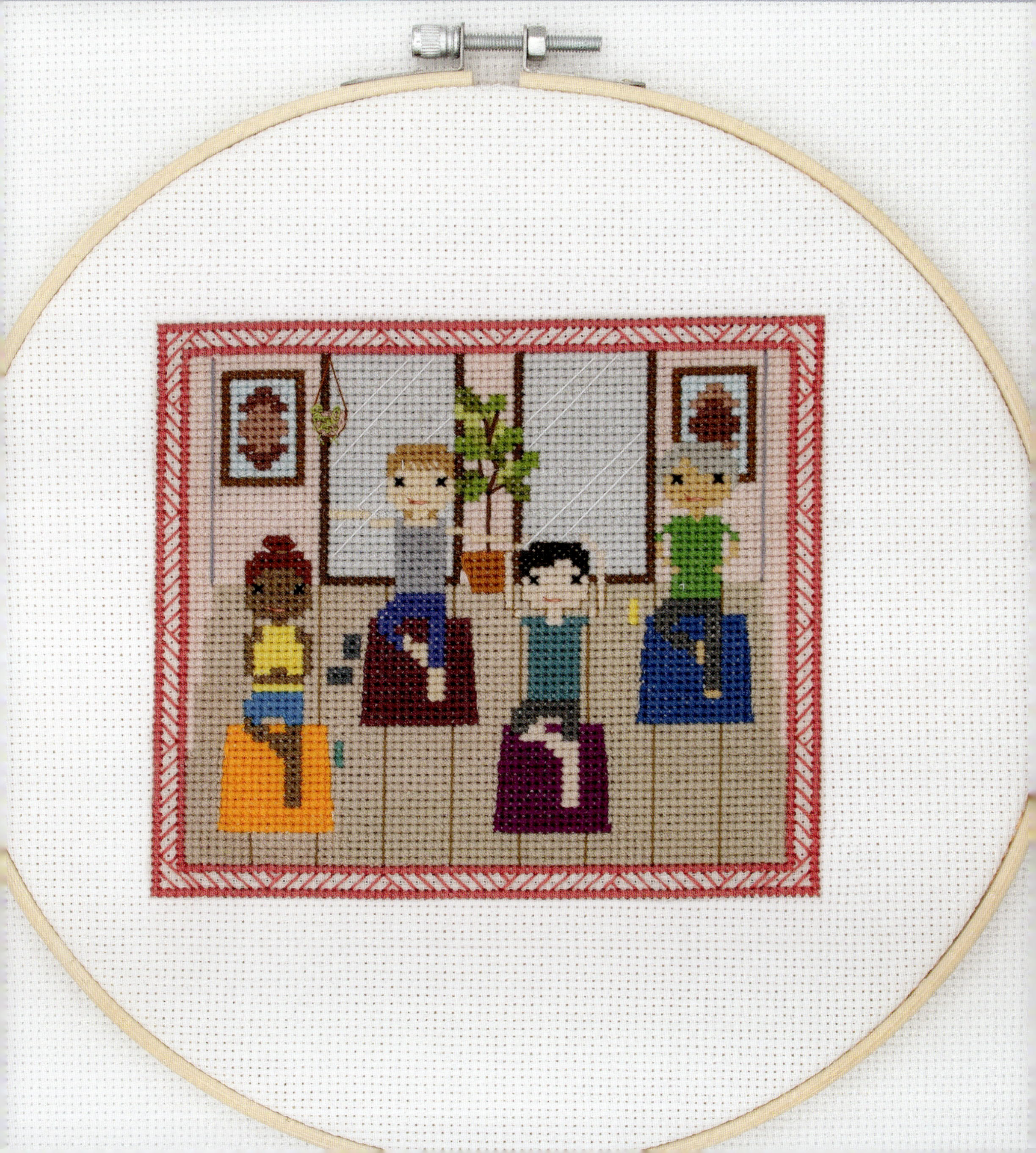

tip

Remember, you can adjust the dimensions of any pattern by removing columns or rows evenly from all sides to reduce the pattern size or simply reduce your stitching time!

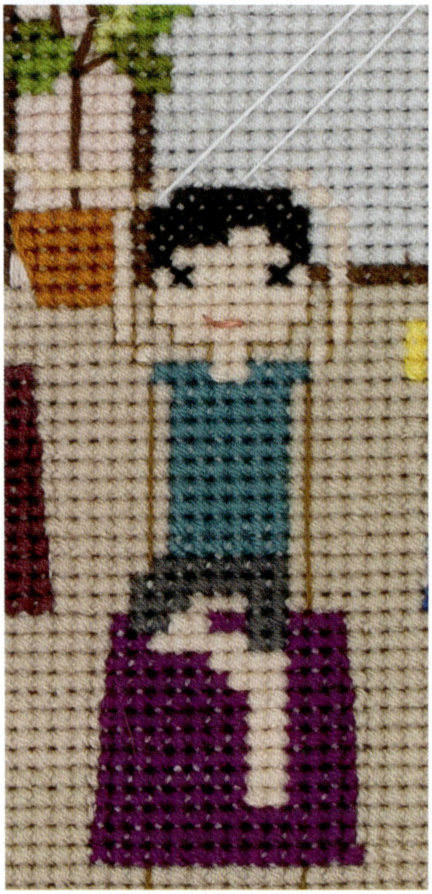

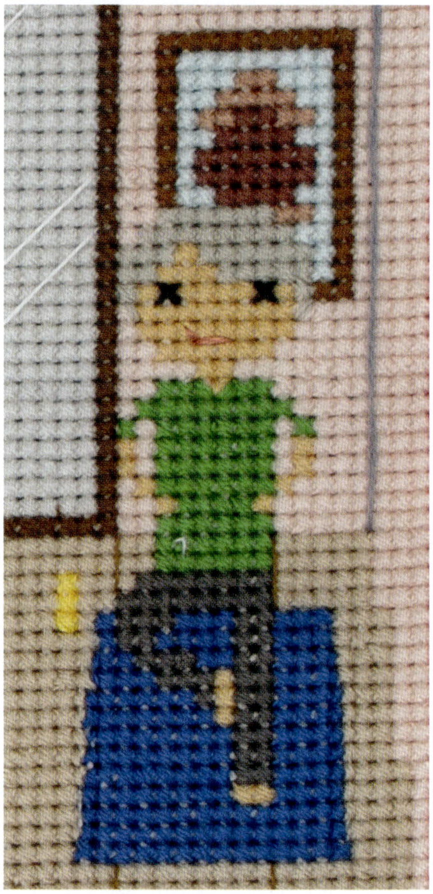

The pattern shows four different yoga positions, but if you prefer everyone match, you can pick your favorite position and swap out the arms, accordingly.

5 Select floss colors for the pattern that reflect the yoga studio you attend: flooring, wall color, etc.

6 Use 3 strands of floss to cross-stitch each square in the pattern.

7 Use 1 strand of floss to backstitch all linear details, except use 2 threads for the mouths.

8 Stitch the circles (hanging plant) with French knots using 2 threads of floss.

customization tip!

Don't forget that anything in any scene can be customized to match something specific or meaningful in real life! Beyond the hairstyles, skin tones, and clothing colors of each character, you can personalize the details of, for example, the yoga mats, water bottles, and color of art on the walls!

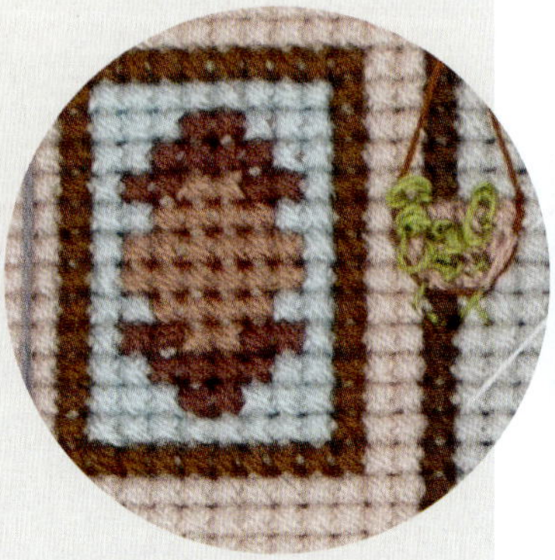

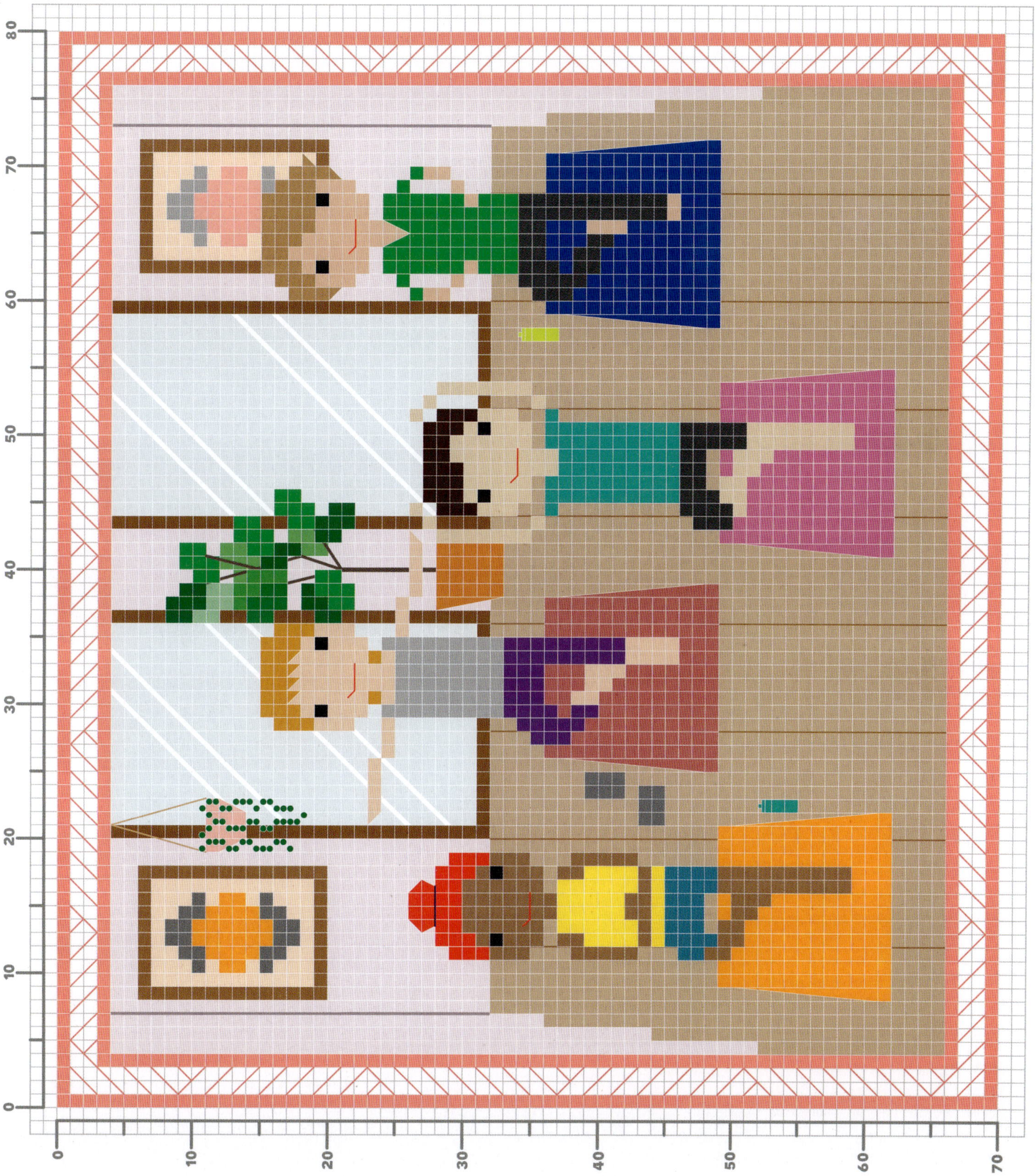

road trip

WHETHER IT'S A GIRLS' TRIP OR A COUPLE'S ADVENTURE, IT'S GOING TO BE A GORGEOUS PORTRAIT!

Pattern Dimensions:
76 squares wide
x 81 squares high

Finished Dimensions on Size 14 Aida Fabric:
5.4" x 5.8"
(14 cm x 15 cm)

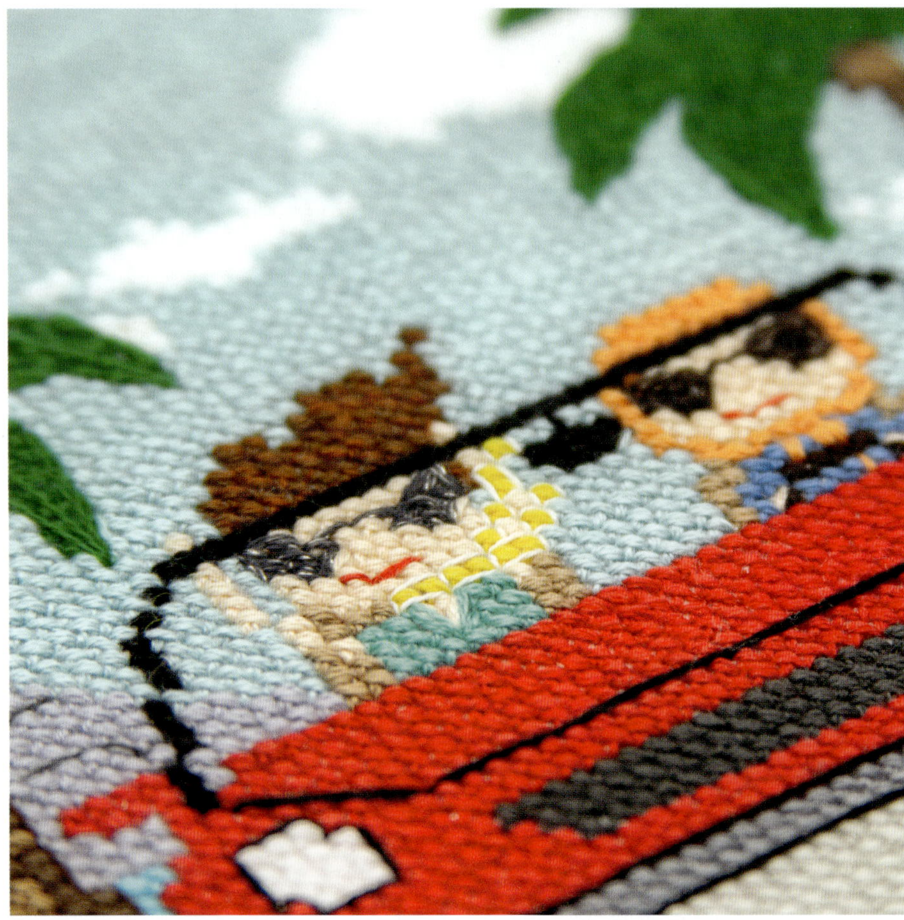

INSTRUCTIONS

1 Cut the fabric 9" x 10" (23 cm x 26 cm), mark the center point, and secure it in the center of an embroidery hoop. Customize the pattern as needed.

2 Change the hairstyles as needed and make any height or width adjustments to the characters in the pattern (see page 42). Reference other patterns for faces if you want to remove the sunglasses.

3 Choose floss colors for each character's skin tone and hair color (see page 38).

4 Choose floss colors for the car, car seats, and scenery.

This portrait was lovingly stitched by Andrea Emslie. Follow her on Instagram @stitchyandrea.

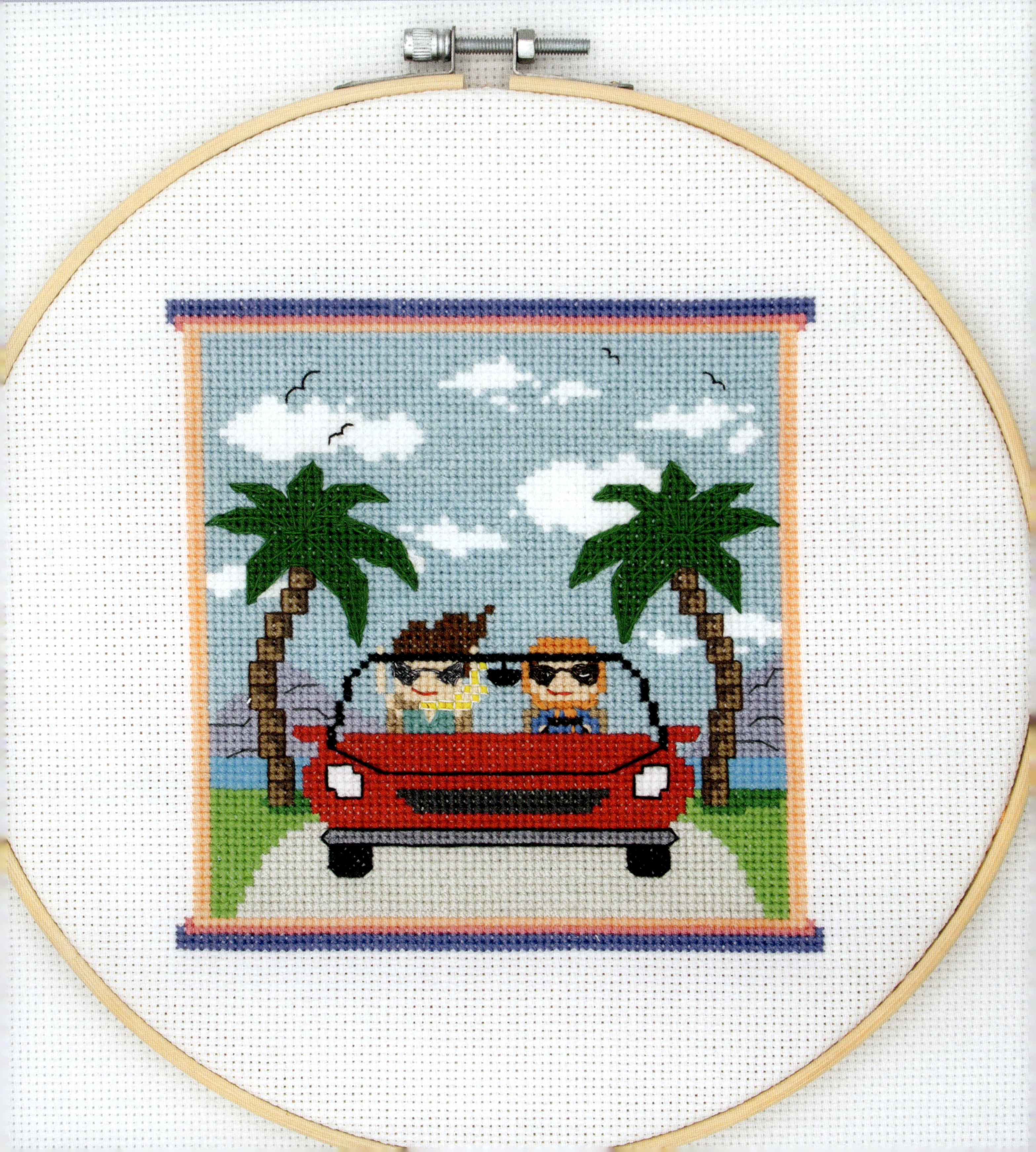

tip

Remember to utilize other stitches like straight stitches, satin stitches, French knots, and more to add details to the elements in your portraits.

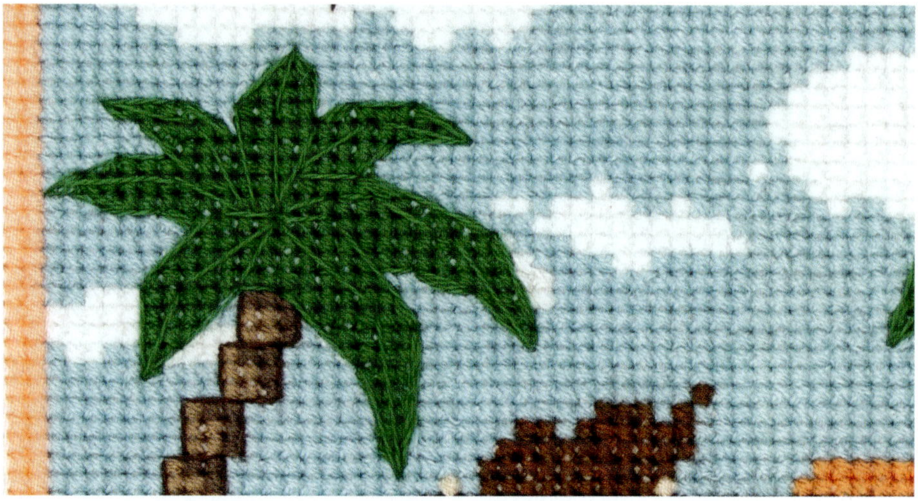

5 Use 3 strands of floss to cross-stitch each square in the pattern.

6 Use 1 strand of floss to backstitch all linear details, except use 2 threads for the mouths.

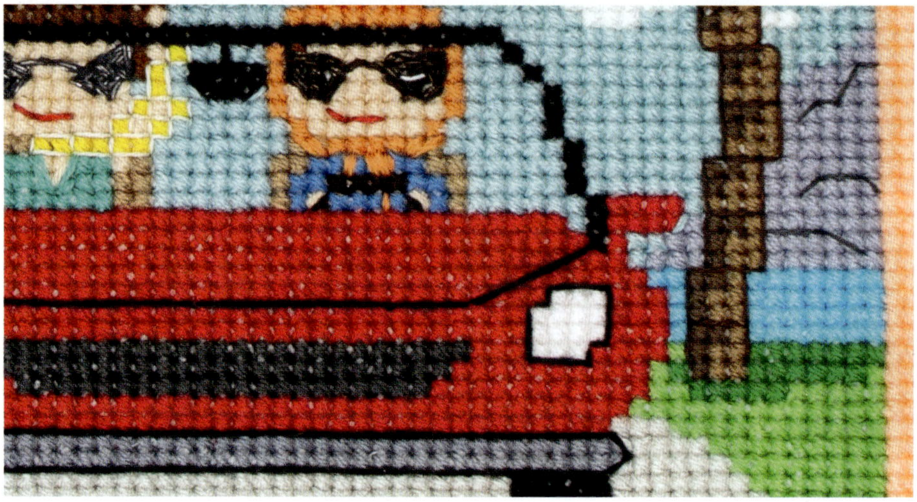

Utilizing one thread of straight stitching atop the finished cross stitching can help give a sense of direction and life to elements of your portrait. The direction of the palm tree's leaves, the edges of the tree, and the hood of the car become clearer as a result!

customization tip!

If you look closely, you might notice the sunglasses of these traveling ladies appear to be shiny. By getting creative with your floss choices, and using options like DMC's metallic-looking Light Effects floss, you can create dynamic effects in your portraits.

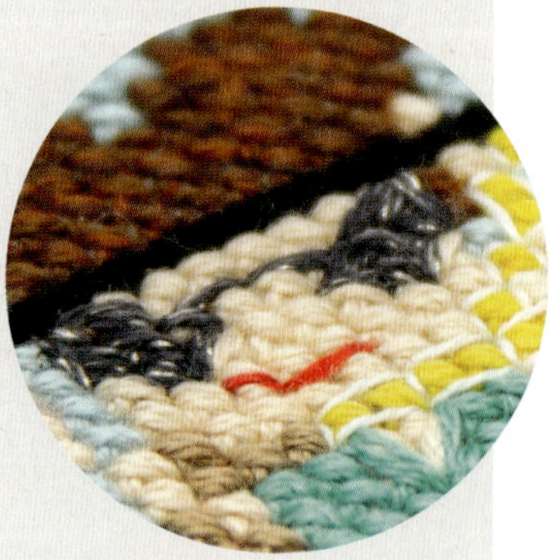

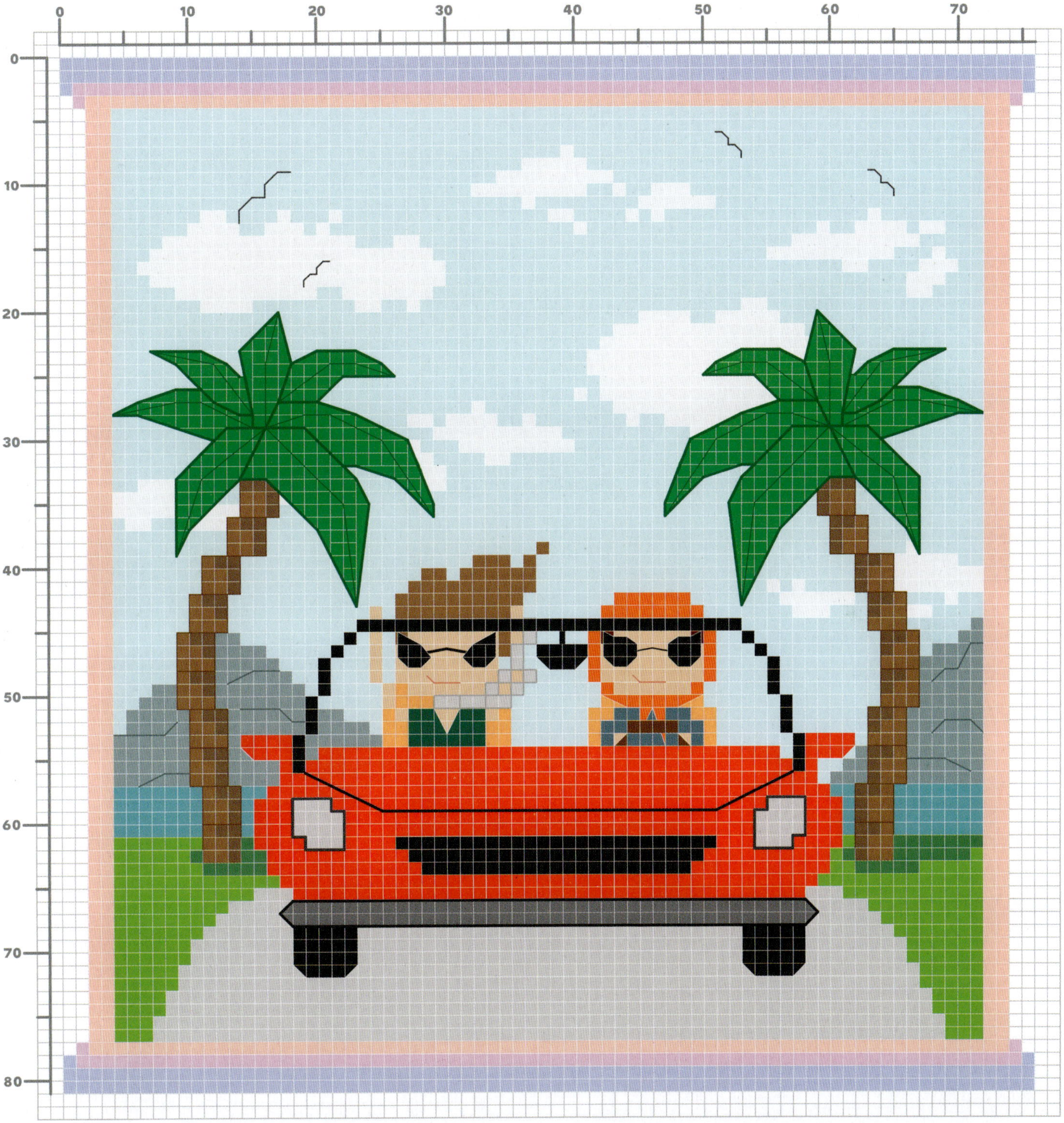
0
10
20
30
40
50
60
70
0
10
20
30
40
50
60
70
80

GRANDPARENT APPRECIATION *scenes*

CROSS-STITCH YOUR LOVE FOR GRANDMA AND GRANDPA!

Pattern Dimensions:
77 squares wide
x 83 squares high

Finished Dimensions on Size 14 Aida Fabric:
5.5" x 5.9"
(14 cm x 15 cm)

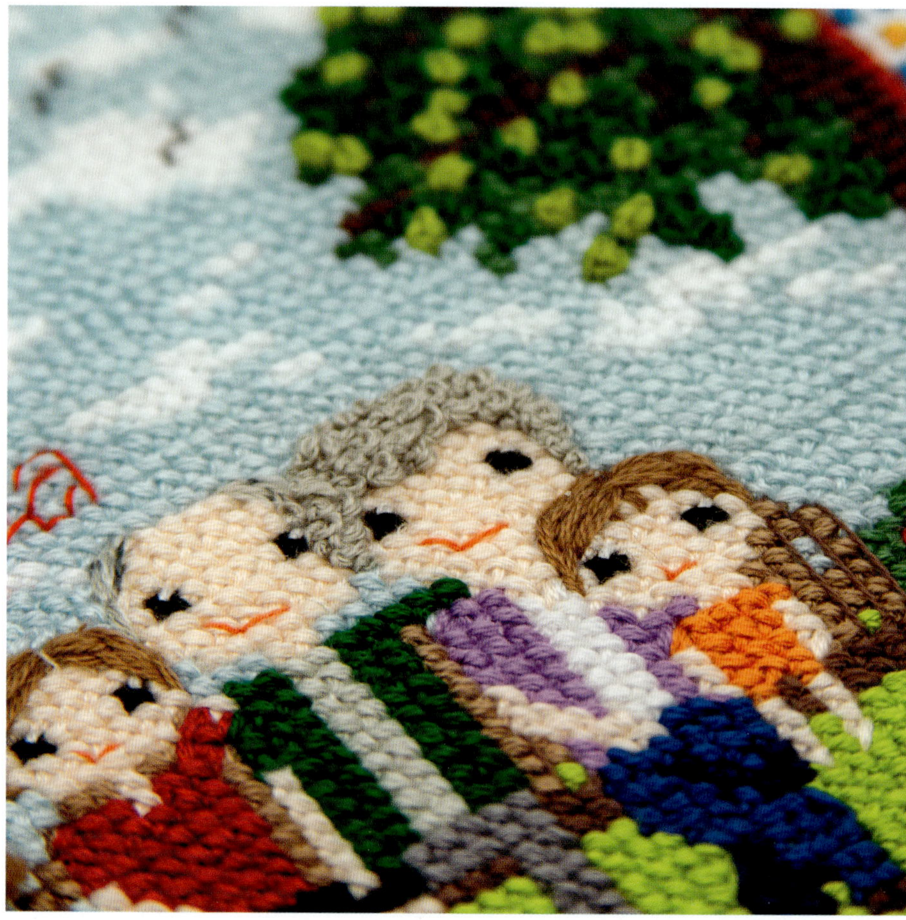

INSTRUCTIONS

1 Cut the fabric 9.5" x 10" (25 cm x 26 cm), mark the center point, and secure it in the center of an embroidery hoop. Customize the pattern as needed.

2 Change the hairstyles if you'd like, and make any height or width adjustments to the characters in the pattern.

3 The text is optional and you may cross-stitch the sky without the text overlay.

4 Choose floss colors for each character's skin tone and hair color.

5 Choose floss colors for each character's clothing and the scenery.

This portrait was lovingly stitched by Erika Cota! Follow her on Instagram @arkacota.

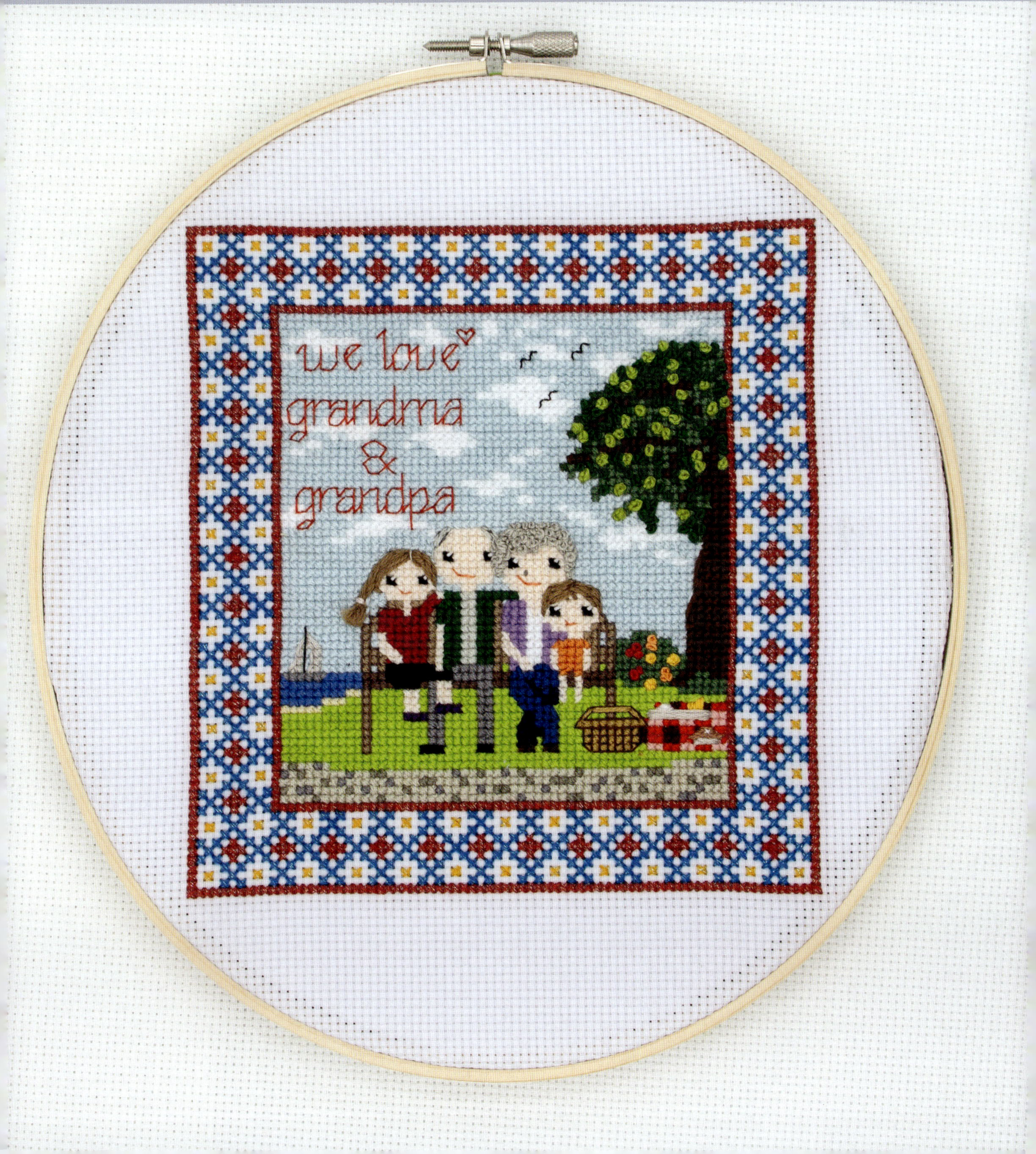
we love
grandma
&
grandpa

note

The children in this pattern can represent a roughly four- to seven-year-old, and a one- to three-year-old respectively. Use the children in the "Family Night In" pattern as alternate patterns or replace with adult forms, using the "A Happy Home" sitting forms as a guide.

6 Use 3 strands of floss to cross-stitch each square in the pattern.

7 Use 1 strand of floss to backstitch all linear details, except use 2 threads for the mouths and text.

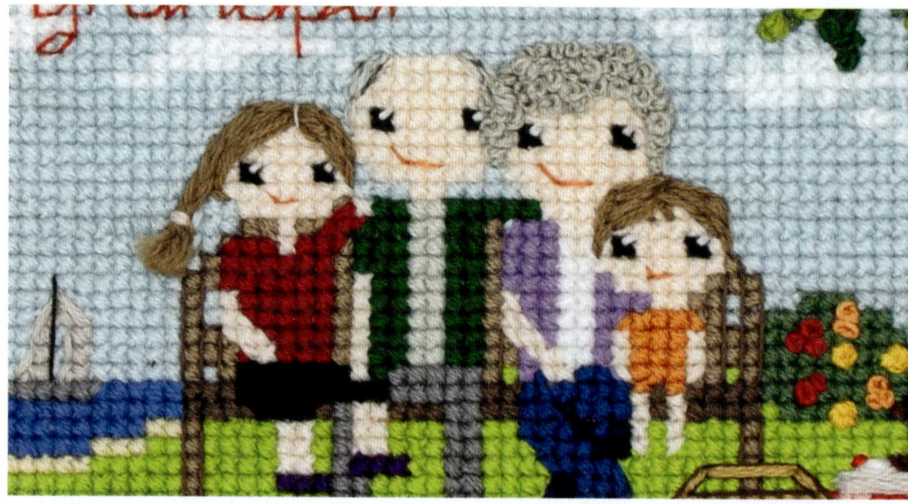

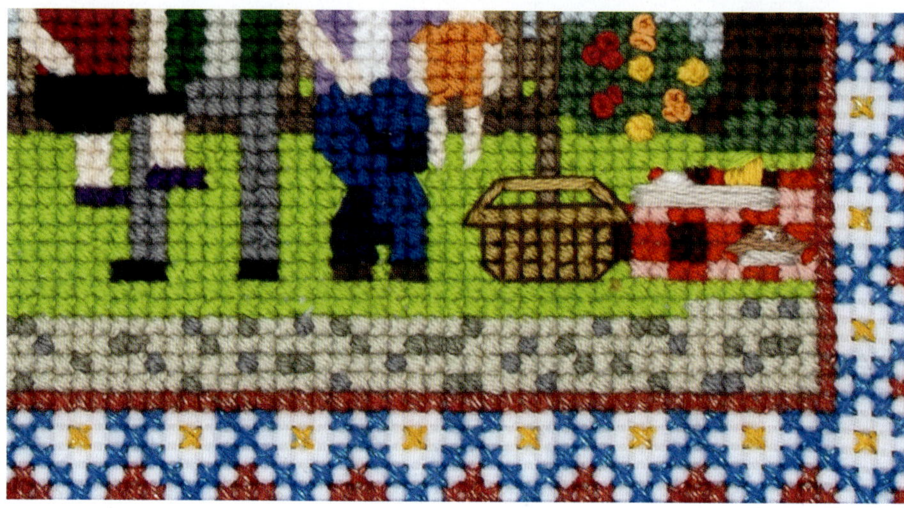

Notice how everyone's eyes look "sparkly" in this portrait. Changing the type of eye you stitch can affect the overall tone of your characters (see page 41).

customization tip!

Not only does this portrait utilize DMC Mouliné Étoile floss in the border, giving it a unique sparkle, but the hairstyles have been stitched to more accurately reflect the people. Parallel straight stitches, or satin stitches, top the heads of Grandpa, Grandson, and Granddaughter (who also sports a braid of embroidery floss). Grandma's hair is a tight collection of French knots to represent her curls.

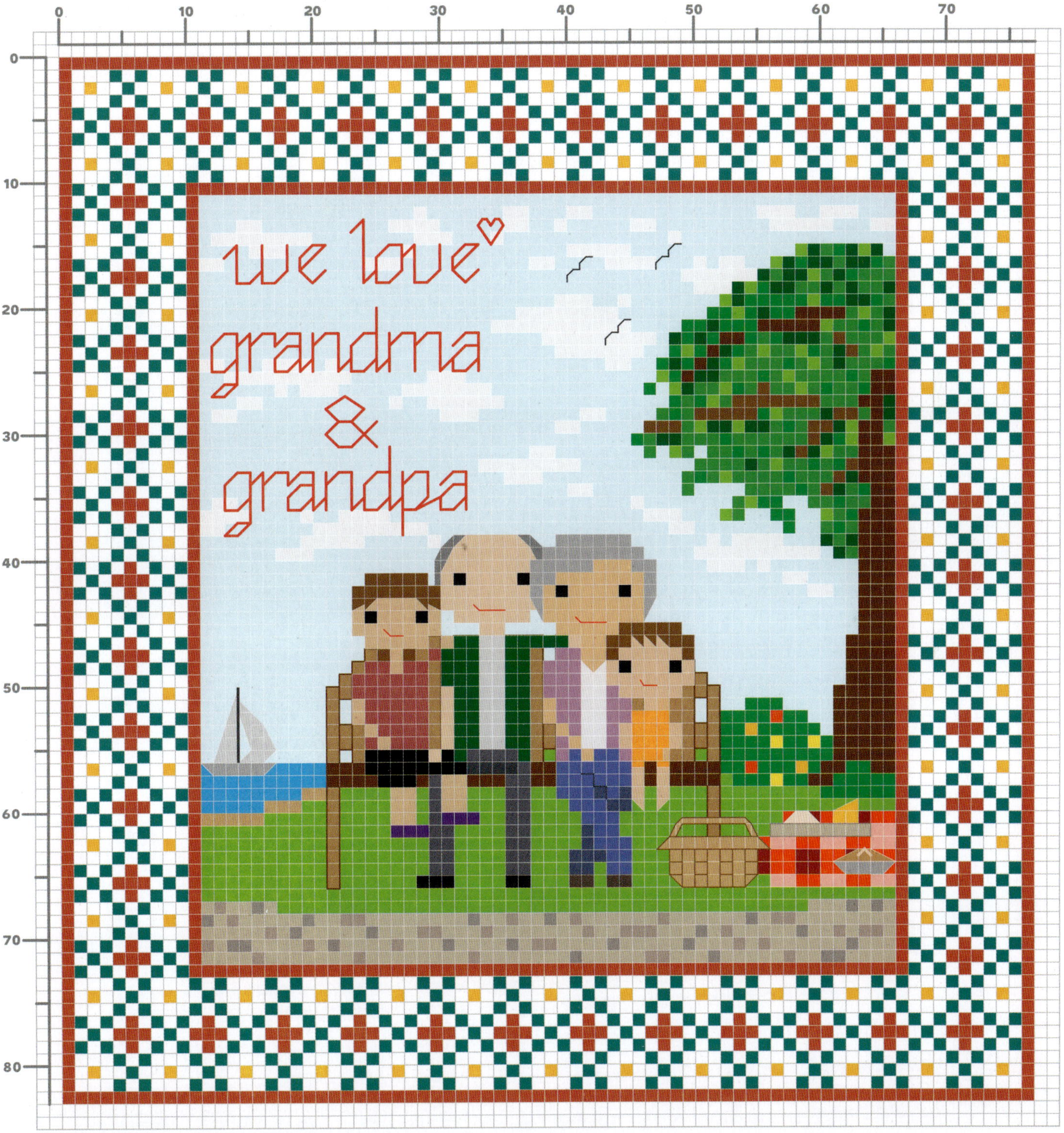

0
10
20
30
40
50
60
70
we love
grandma
&
grandpa

GRANDPARENT APPRECIATION *individuals*

IF ADJUSTING THE FULL PATTERN IS TOO COMPLICATED, OR IF A GRANDPARENT IS SINGLE OR WIDOWED, TRY STITCHING UP ONE OF THESE SMALLER PATTERNS OF APPRECIATION.

CIRCLE BORDER

Pattern Dimensions:

44 squares wide
x 44 squares high

Finished Dimensions on Size 14 Aida Fabric:

3.1" x 3.1"
(8 cm x 8 cm)

BERRY BORDER

Pattern Dimensions:

41 squares wide
x 45 squares high

Finished Dimensions on Size 14 Aida Fabric:

2.9" x 3.2"
(7.5 cm x 8.25 cm)

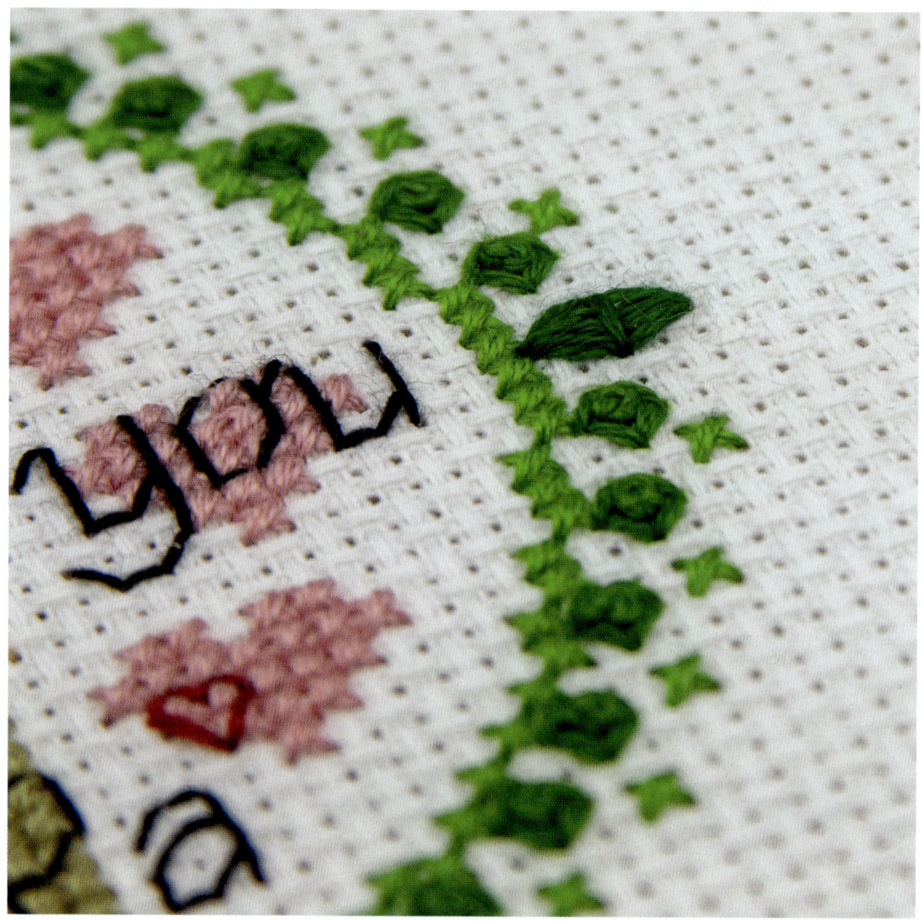

INSTRUCTIONS

1 Cut the fabric 7" x 7" (18 cm x 18 cm), mark the center point, and secure it in the center of an embroidery hoop. Customize the pattern.

These portraits were lovingly stitched by Hillary Nestrick! Follow her on Instagram @keystonecrossstitch.

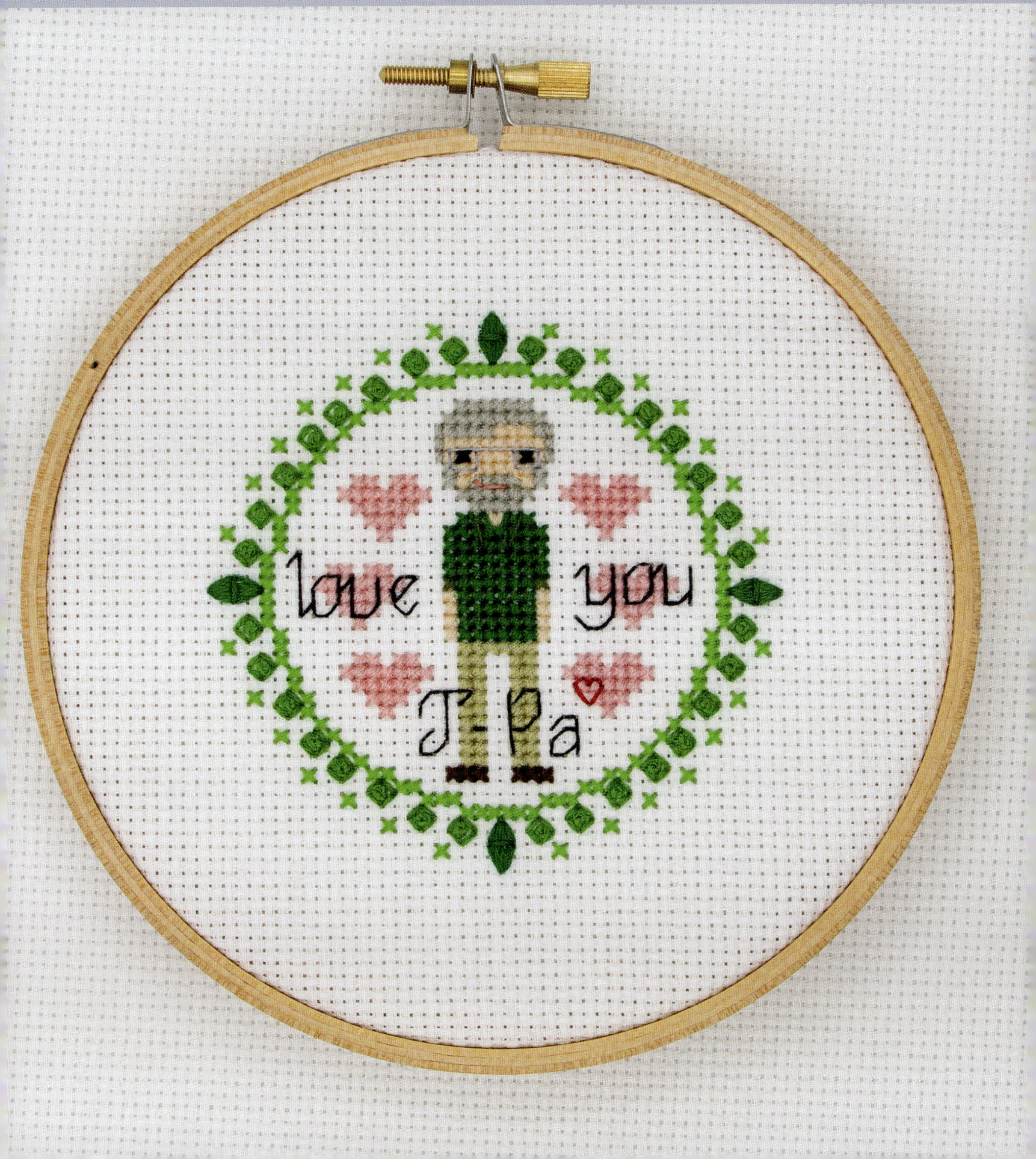
love you
J-Pa

2 Choose a border and a grandma or grandpa character.

3 Notice how Grammy's hair isn't one solid color? Since the recommended number of threads for cross-stitching is 3, you can choose to combine up to 3 single threads of 3 different colors to create a more dynamic-looking head of hair!

4 Change the hairstyle if needed, and make width adjustments if you'd like to. Since this is an individual character the height is not relative to anyone else and can remain unchanged.

5 The text is optional and you may cross-stitch the hearts without the text overlay.

6 Using the alphabets at the back of the book (see page 106), you can create your own words, or simply stitch "Love You" with one word on either side of the character.

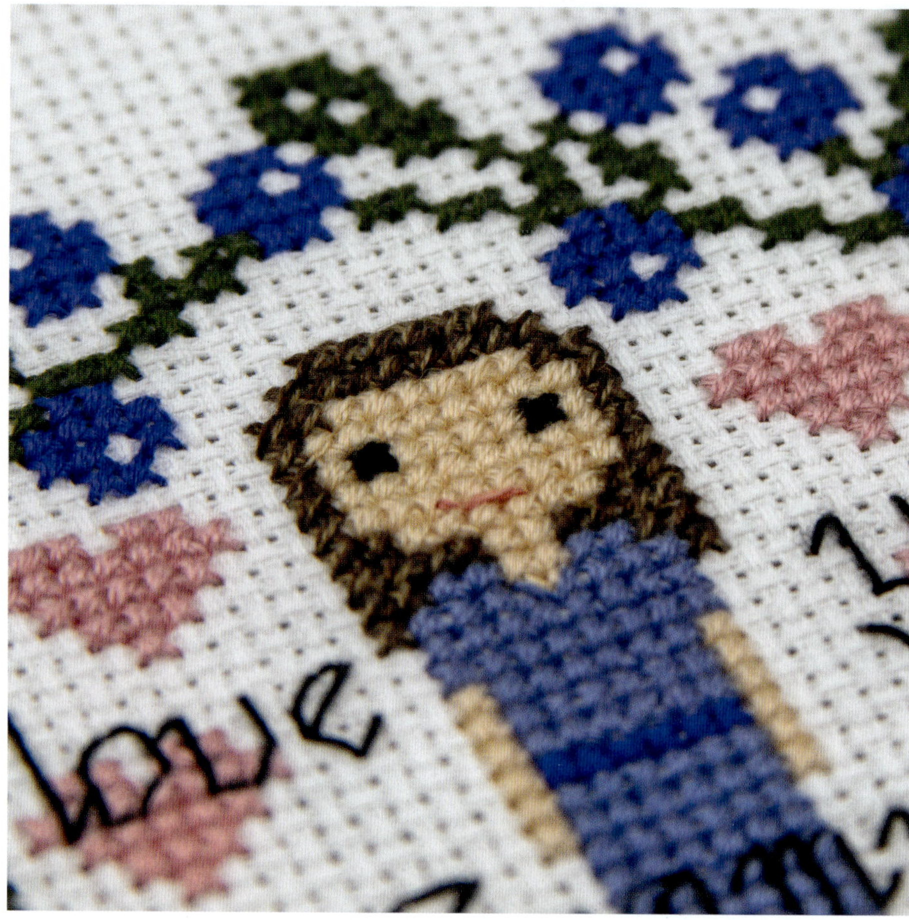

7 Choose floss colors for the character's skin tone and hair color (see page 38).

8 Use 3 strands of floss to cross-stitch each square in the pattern.

9 Use 1 strand of floss to backstitch all linear details, except use 2 threads for the mouths and text.

customization tip!

Remember you can swap the grandma character for the grandpa character if you prefer this border!

Feel free to get creative with your borders and details! The larger leaves at the top, bottom, left, and right of this portrait are stitched with groups of parallel straight stitches, and the smaller leaves are filled in with French knots instead of cross-stitches.

tip

Check out the other alphabet styles on pages 47-48, and use the graph paper on page 109 to work out the perfect message for your portrait.

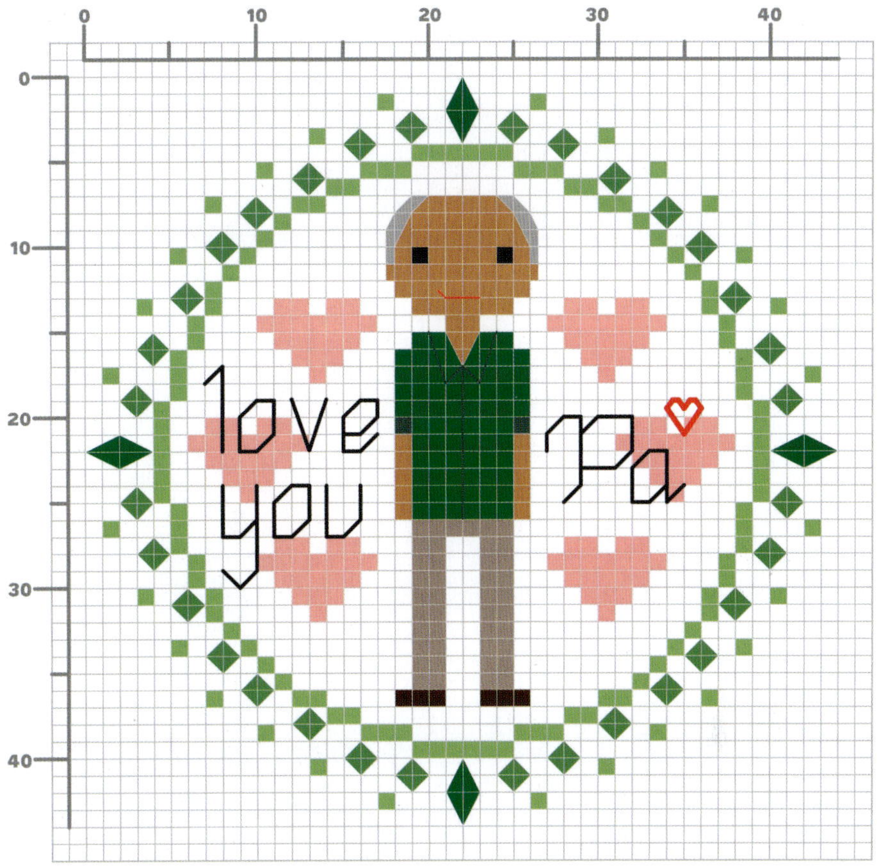

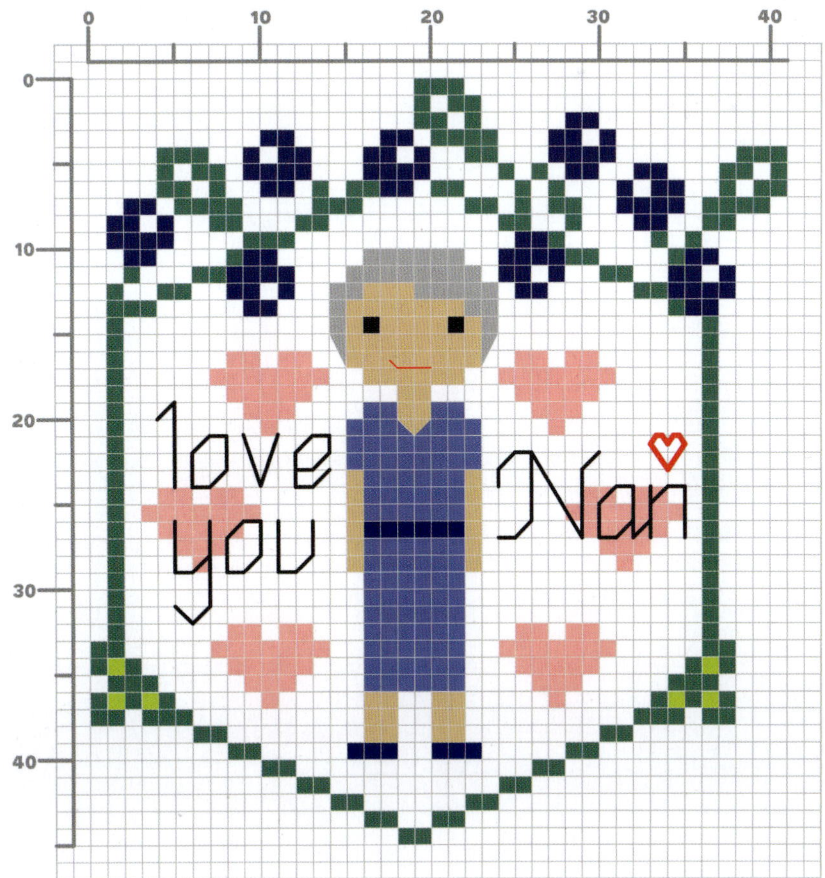

coffee break

WHO DOESN'T LIKE TO MEET UP WITH FRIENDS AT A FAVORITE COFFEE SHOP FOR A WARM BEVVIE?

Pattern Dimensions:
92 squares wide
x 68 squares high

Finished Dimensions on Size 14 Aida Fabric:
6.6" x 4.9"
(17 cm x 12.5 cm)

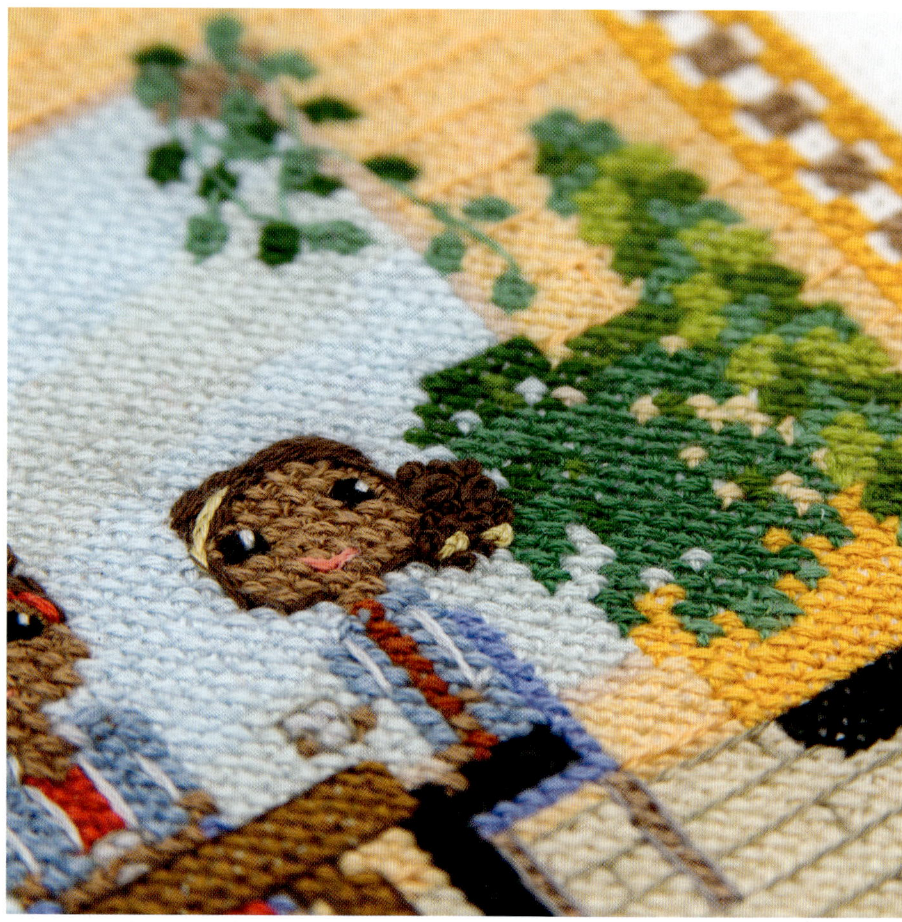

INSTRUCTIONS

1 Cut the fabric 11" x 9" (28 cm x 23 cm), mark the center point, and secure it in the center of an embroidery hoop. Customize the pattern as needed.

2 Change the hairstyles if you'd like, and make any height or width adjustments to the characters in the pattern (see page 42).

3 Decide if you'd like to make other pattern adjustments to the pattern, like removing or changing the border for a different one in the book, or adjusting the pattern's dimensions by removing columns or rows.

4 Choose floss colors for each character's skin tone, hair color, and clothing (see page 38).

This portrait was lovingly stitched by Naya Janae Johnson! Follow her on Instagram @nayajanaecreates.

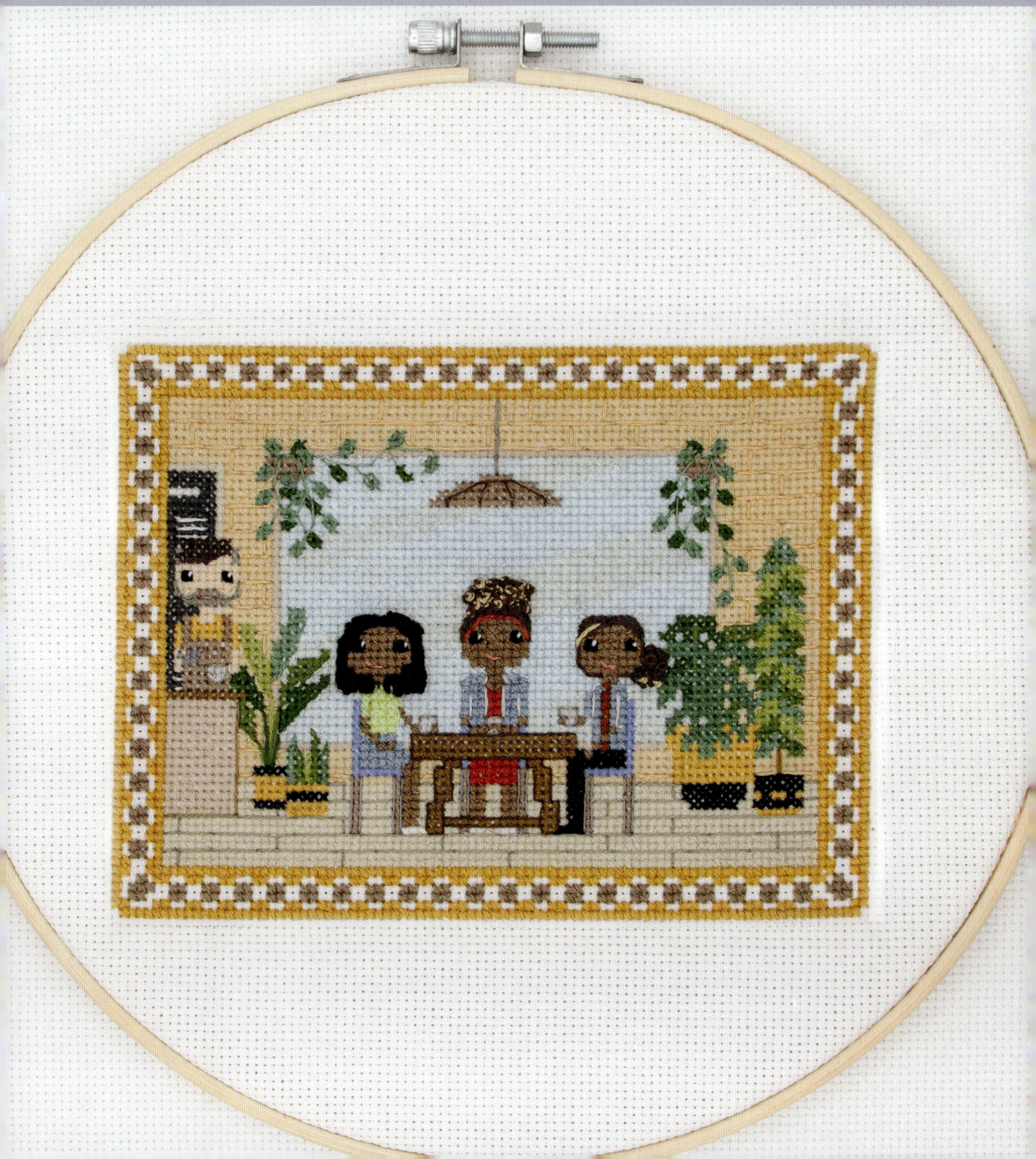

5 Choose floss colors for the scenery.

6 Use 3 strands of floss to cross-stitch each square in the pattern.

7 Use 1 strand of floss to backstitch all linear details, except use 2 threads for the mouths.

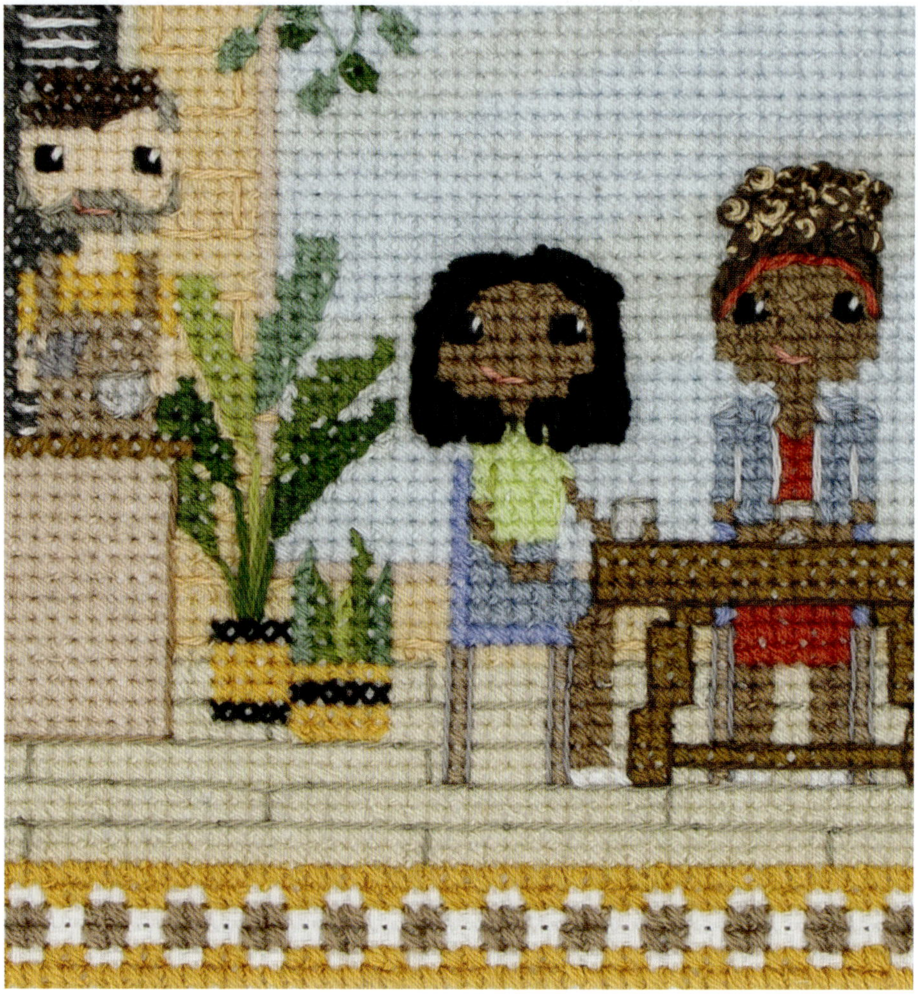

Do you have a favorite barista? Stitching a scene like this could make for a perfect gift!

customization tip!

Little details, big wow! This portrait shows the sweet impact of choosing the sparkly eyes effect for its characters, adding just a dash of white to each of the eyes with a straight stitch. Additionally, all the linear details in the walls, flooring, clothing, and greenery are stitched as long, easy straight stitches. The choices are simple but the impact is huge! The hairstyles in this portrait also display how effective it can be to use more than one color for the style.

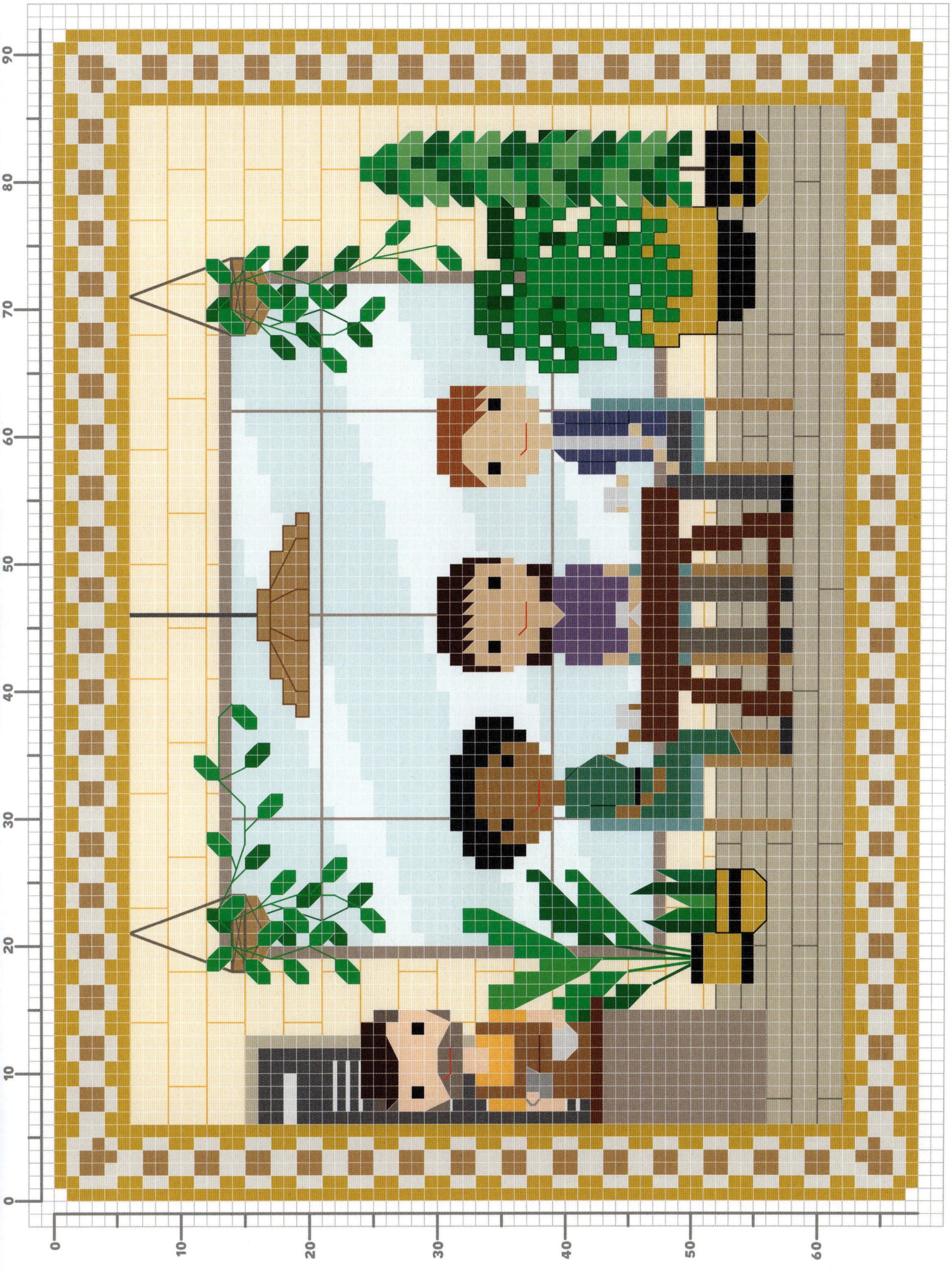

wintertime fun

TAKING ADVANTAGE OF FRESHLY FALLEN SNOW IS SOME OF THE BEST (AND MOST FUN) PART OF WINTER!

Pattern Dimensions:
67 squares wide
x 83 squares high

Finished Dimensions on Size 14 Aida Fabric:
4.8" x 5.9"
(12.25 cm x 15 cm)

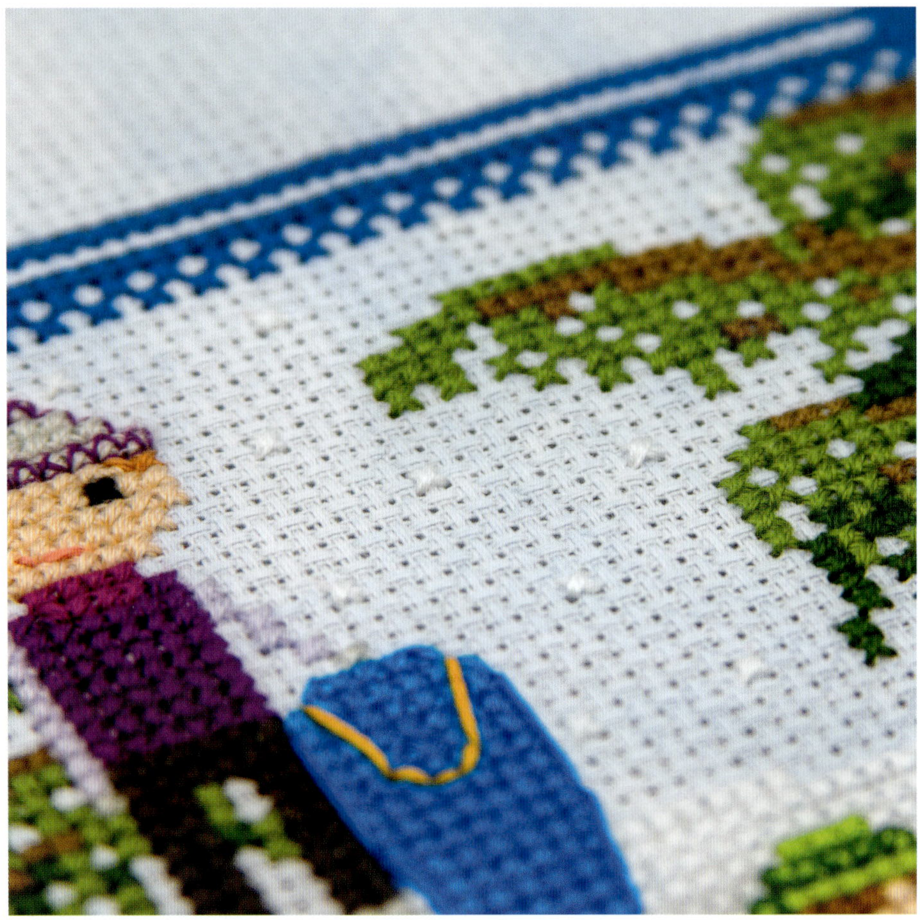

INSTRUCTIONS

1 Cut the fabric to 9" x 10" (23 cm x 26 cm), mark the center point, and secure it in the center of an embroidery hoop. Customize the pattern as needed.

2 Since most characters are in hats in this pattern, changing hairstyles may not be as necessary, but consider if bangs need to be added or removed, etc.

3 If needed, make any height or width adjustments to the characters in the pattern.

4 Decide if you'd like to make other pattern adjustments to the pattern, like removing or changing the border or adjusting the pattern's dimensions by removing columns or rows.

This portrait was lovingly stitched by Hillary Nestrick! Follow her on Instagram @keystonecrossstitch.

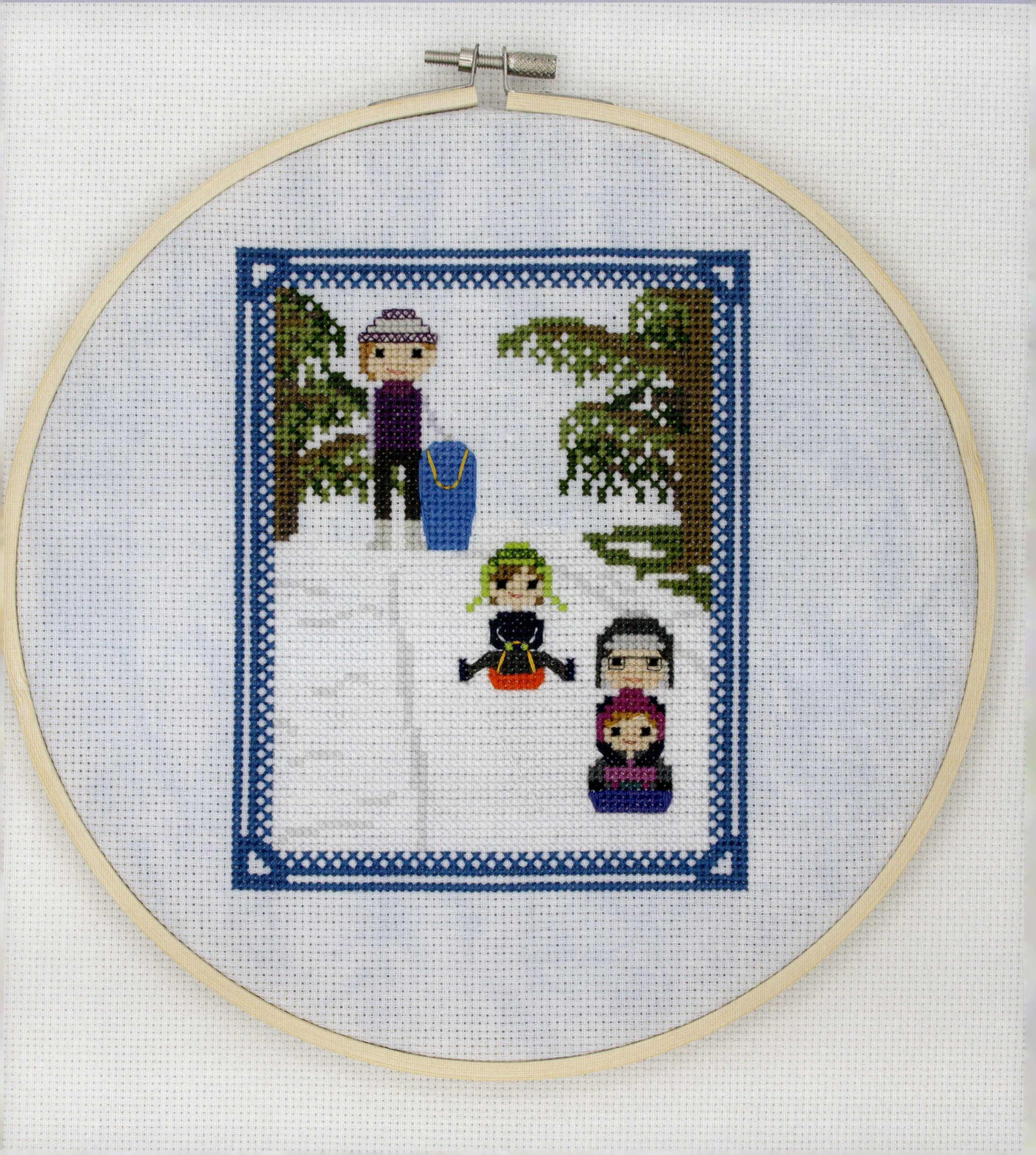

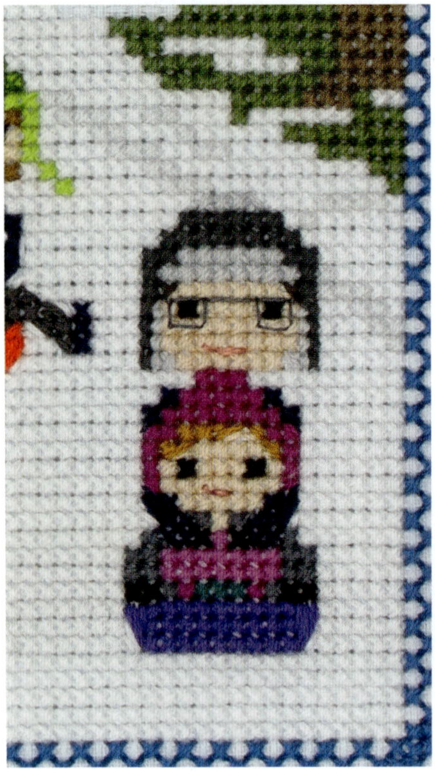

Glasses are the perfect time to "think outside the box" in a very literal way! Stabbing your needle through your work outside the holes of the Aida fabric may be just the thing to ensure an accessory, like eyeglasses, sits in the perfect spot.

5 There is room to stitch one or two more sledding children in the open snow space of the pattern if more are needed. Use the same pattern of the solo sledding child as a starting point. (You could also add a furry friend (see page 108)! Reference "Family Night In" (page 52) or "Autumn Fun" (page 96) for a dog or cat).

6 Choose floss colors for each character's skin tone, hair color, and clothing (see page 38).

7 Choose floss colors for the scenery.

note

The children in this pattern can represent a wide range, from around ages five to ten and one to four, respectively.

8 Use 3 strands of floss to cross-stitch each square in the pattern.

9 Use 1 strand of floss to backstitch all linear details, except use 2 threads for the mouths.

customization tip!

Check out the fabric! An easy way to give your portrait a sense of place is to choose a specific type of Aida fabric to support it. In this case, a chilly, light tie-dye blue creates a beautiful backdrop, and replaces the need to cross-stitch a sky background.

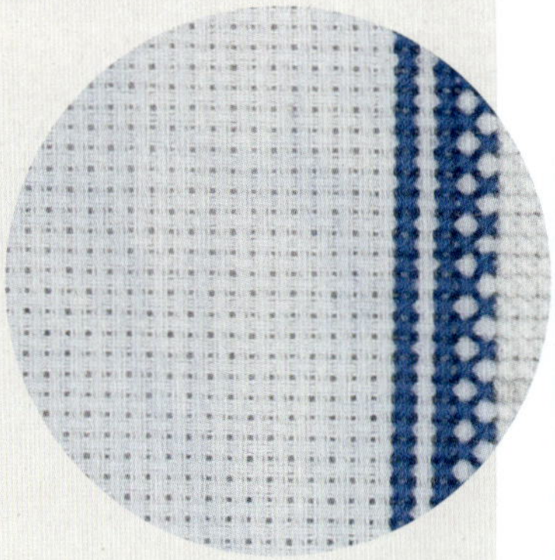

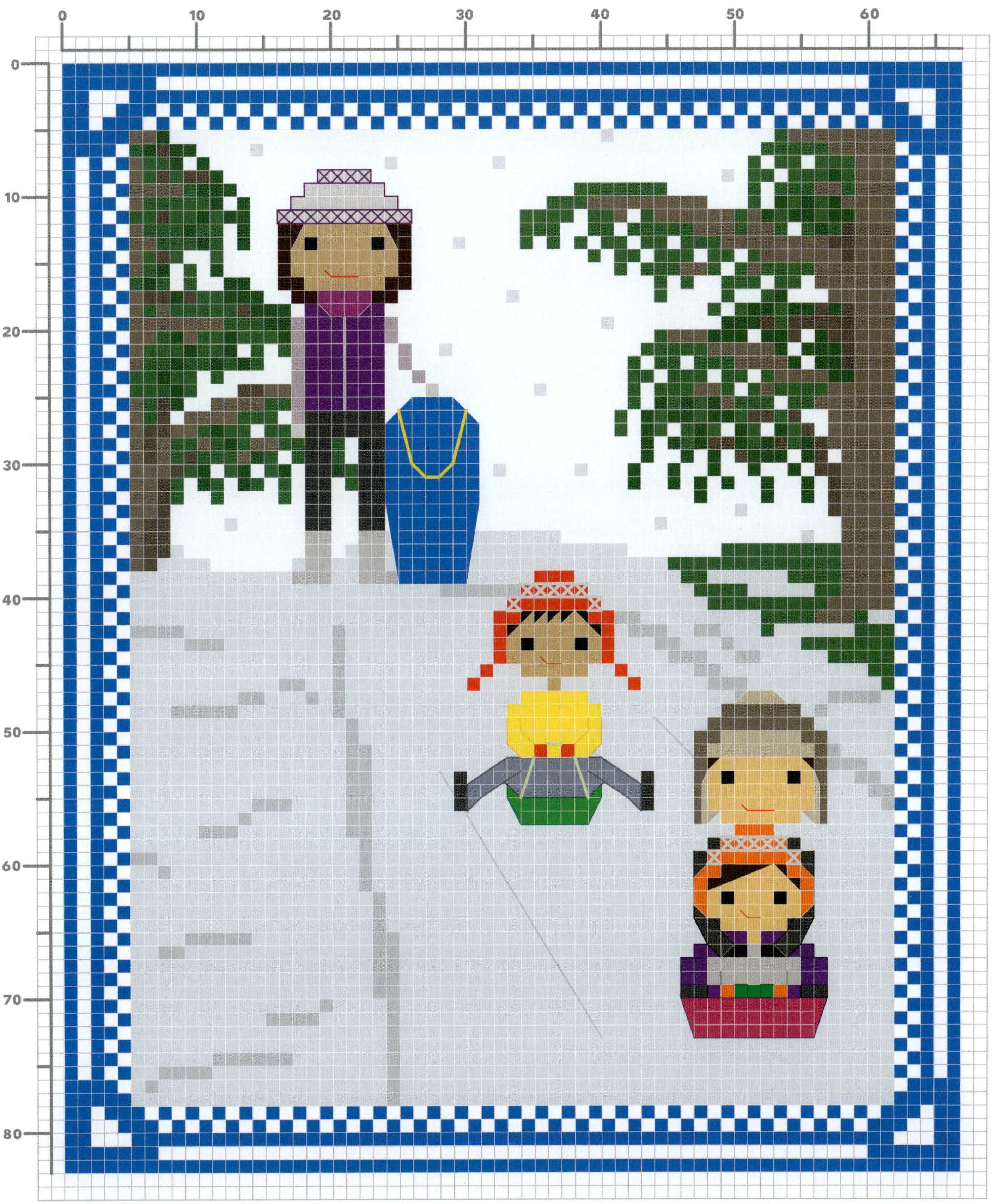

springtime fun

APRIL SHOWERS BRING MAY FLOWERS—AND FEED OUR VEGETABLE GARDENS, TOO! THE REFRESHING ENERGY OF SPRING IS A JOY TO EXPERIENCE ALONGSIDE OUR NEAREST AND DEAREST.

Pattern Dimensions:
80 squares wide
x 63 squares high

Finished Dimensions on Size 14 Aida Fabric:
5.7" x 4.5"
(14.5 cm x 11.5 cm)

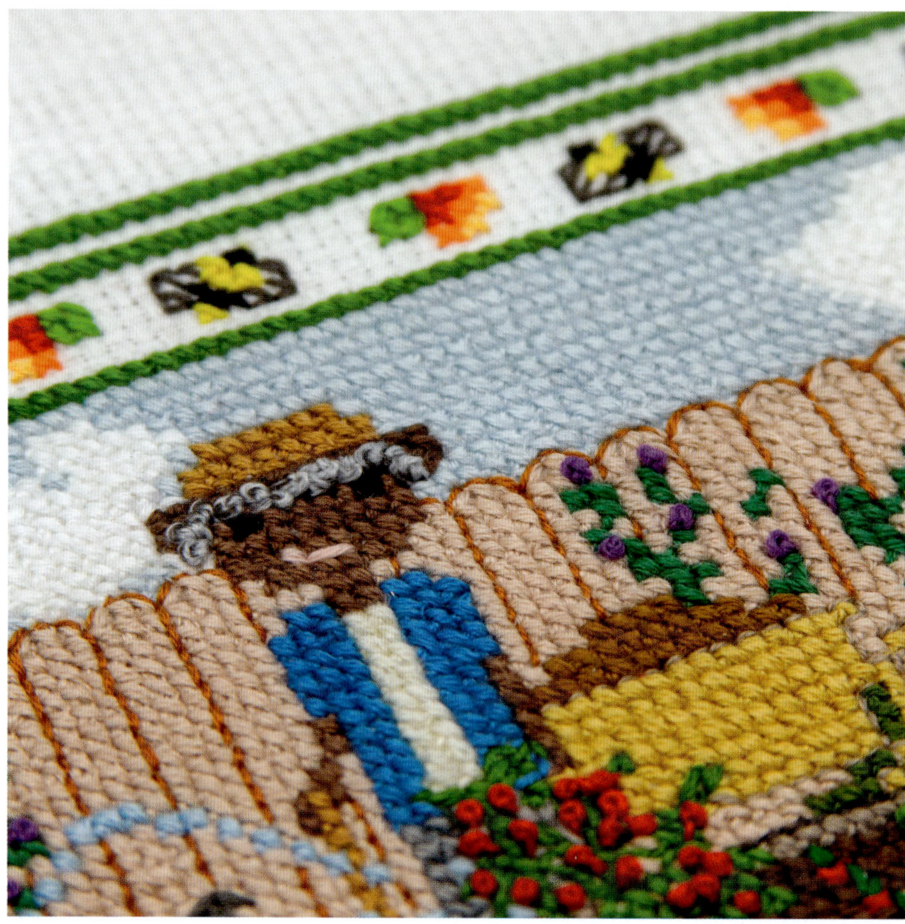

INSTRUCTIONS

1 Cut the fabric to 10" x 8" (26 cm x 21 cm), mark the center point, and secure it in the center of an embroidery hoop. Customize the pattern as needed.

2 Swap any hairstyles you'd like with examples from the front of the book (see page 44).

3 If needed, make any height or width adjustments to the characters in the pattern.

This portrait was lovingly stitched by Natalie Bryant! Follow her on Instagram @sunflowerstitchseasons.

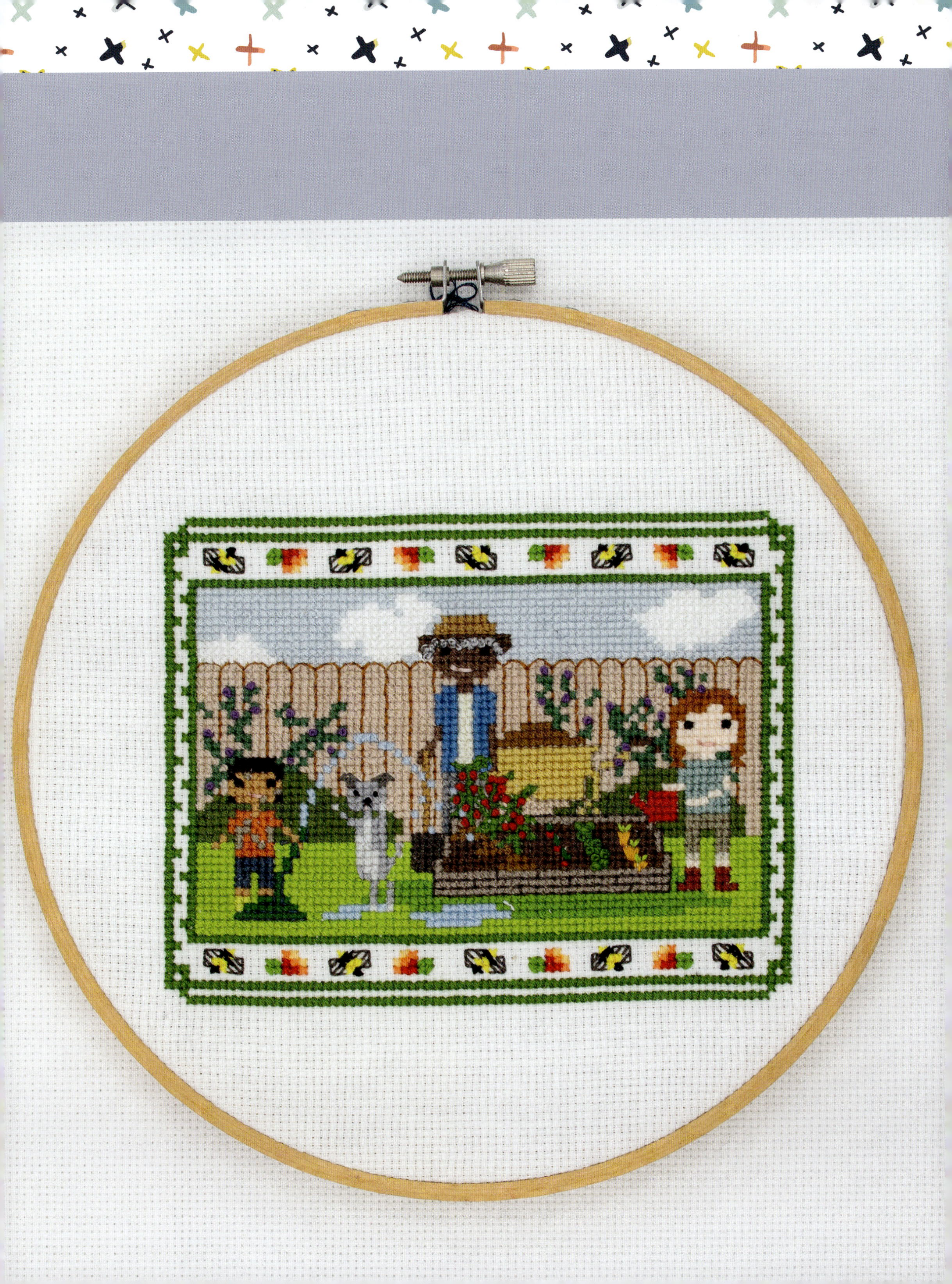

note

The child in this pattern could represent a child from three to six years old.

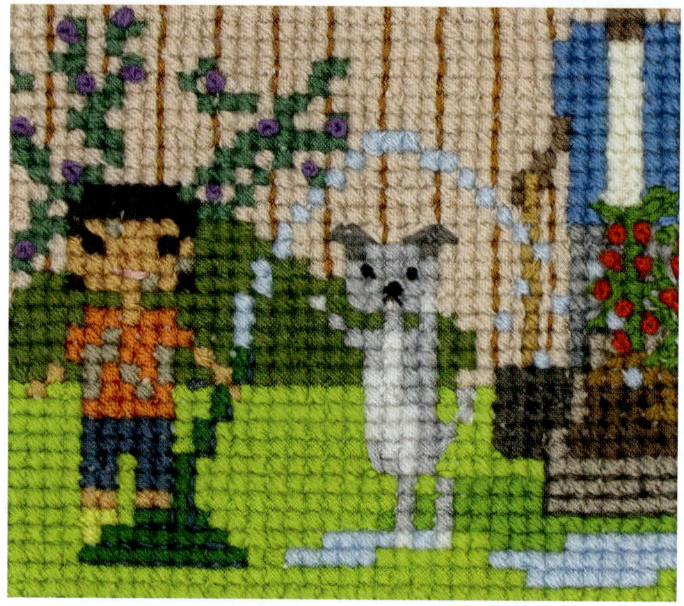

Woof woof! Does your dog chomp at the hose or sprinkler water too? If not, consider swapping the dog's pose with one of the other pet pattern options at the end of the book.

4 Decide if you'd like to make other pattern adjustments to the pattern, like removing or changing the border, adjusting the pattern's dimensions by removing columns or rows of the pattern, or copying the child portion of the pattern to place near the female in the pattern if more kids are needed.

5 Choose floss colors (see page 38) for each character's skin tone, hair color, and clothing, as well as the dog's fur.

6 Choose floss colors for the scenery. Choosing someone's favorite colors to represent the flowers in the background is an easy, thoughtful way to show them you care!

7 Use 3 strands of floss to cross-stitch each square in the pattern.

8 Use 1 strand of floss to backstitch all linear details, except the mouths.

9 Use 2 strands of floss to stitch the mouths and all circular elements (flowers, tomatoes) as French knots.

customization tip!

A bright color palette has been chosen to gorgeously convey the spirit of spring, and the hair colors and skin tones have been chosen to reflect specific individuals. Notice the clever use of French knots throughout! From the flowers, to the tomatoes, to the curls of hair, French knots can be a versatile tool in your portrait-making.

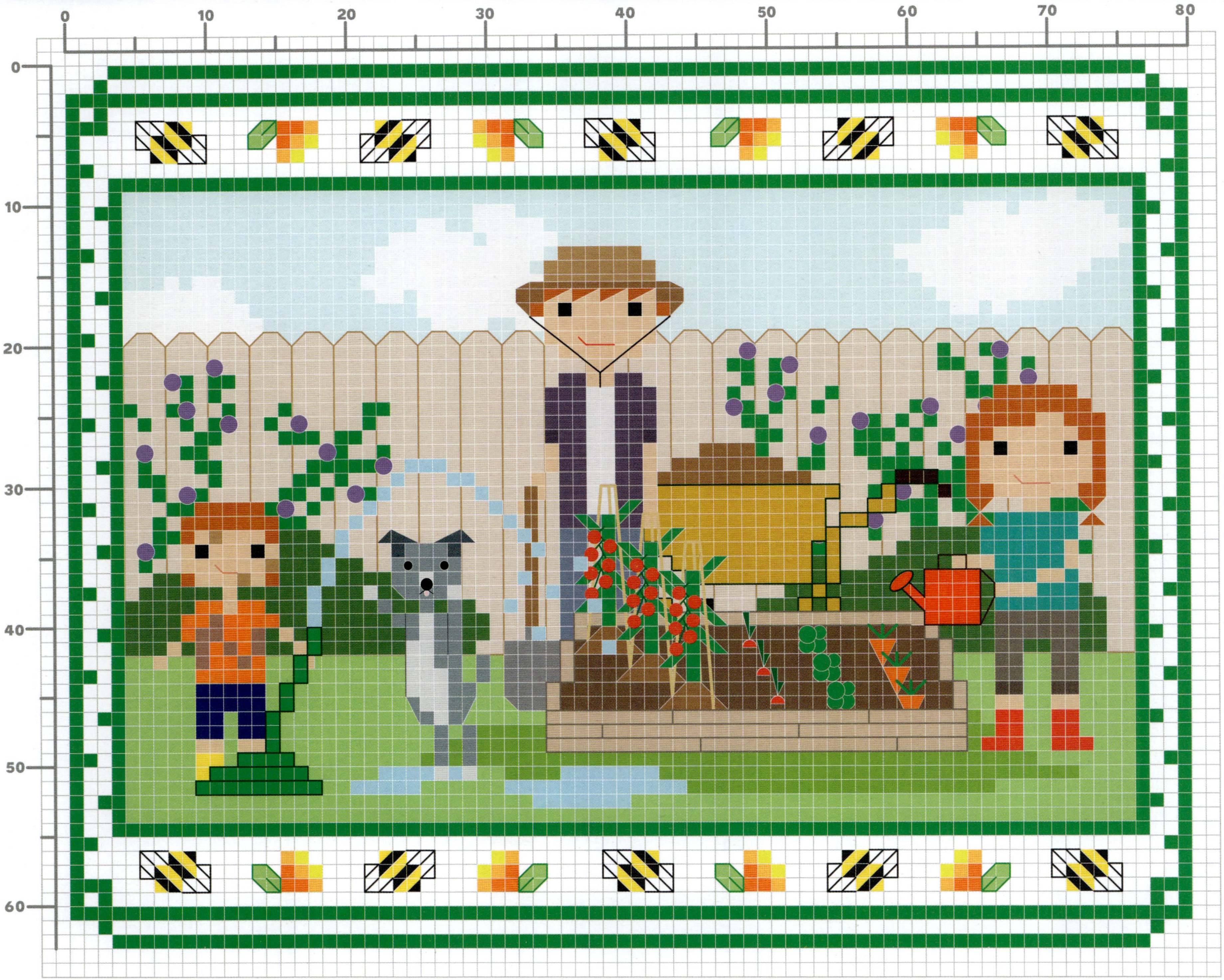

0
10
20
30
40
50
60
70
80

summertime fun

IT'S A POOL PARTY FOR THE WHOLE FAMILY TO ENJOY!

Pattern Dimensions:
76 squares wide
x 80 squares high

Finished Dimensions on Size 14 Aida Fabric:
5.4" x 5.7"
(14 cm x 14.5 cm)

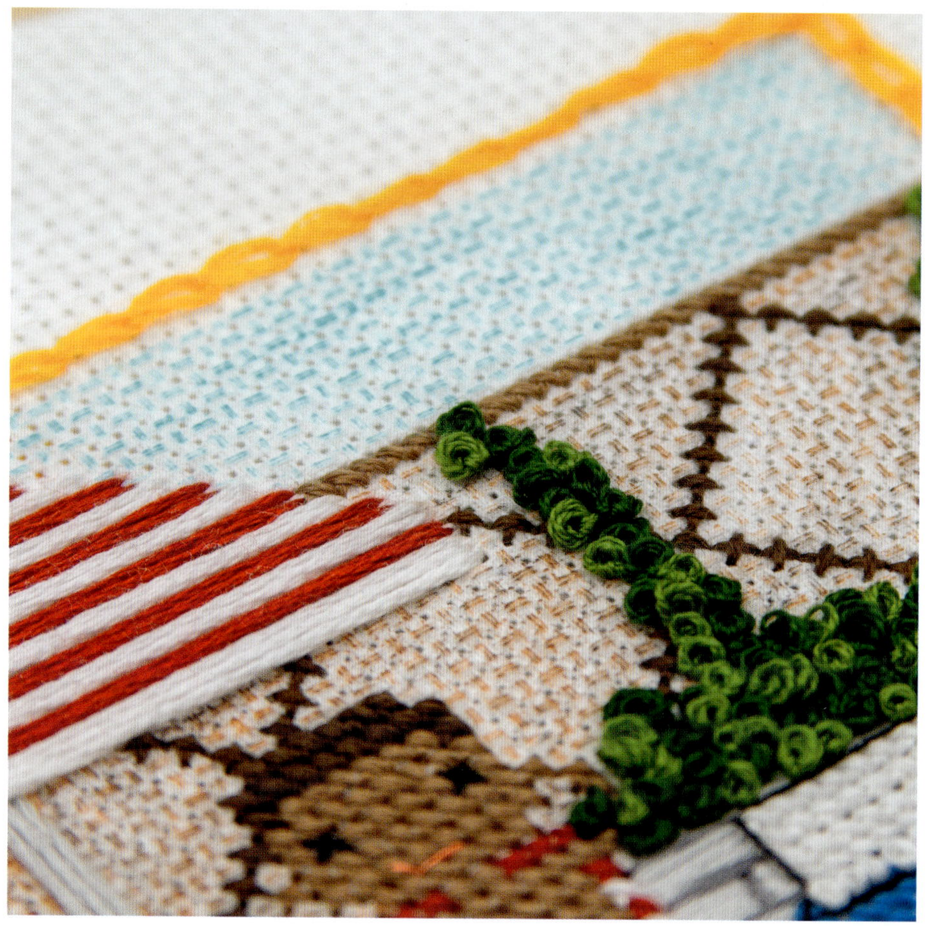

This portrait was lovingly stitched by Amanda Irvin. Follow her on Instagram @erinandelizabeth.

INSTRUCTIONS

1 Cut the fabric to 9" x 9" (23 cm x 23 cm), mark the center point, and secure it in the center of an embroidery hoop. Customize the pattern as needed.

2 Swap any hairstyles you'd like with examples from the front of the book (see page 44).

3 If needed, make any height or width adjustments to the characters in the pattern. The children in this pattern can most easily represent a three- to six-year-old and two seven- to twelve-year-olds, left to right.

4 Decide if you'd like to make other pattern adjustments, like removing or changing the border, adjusting the pattern's dimensions, or by removing columns or rows of the pattern. I recommend not removing more than two columns from each side of the pattern (four columns total).

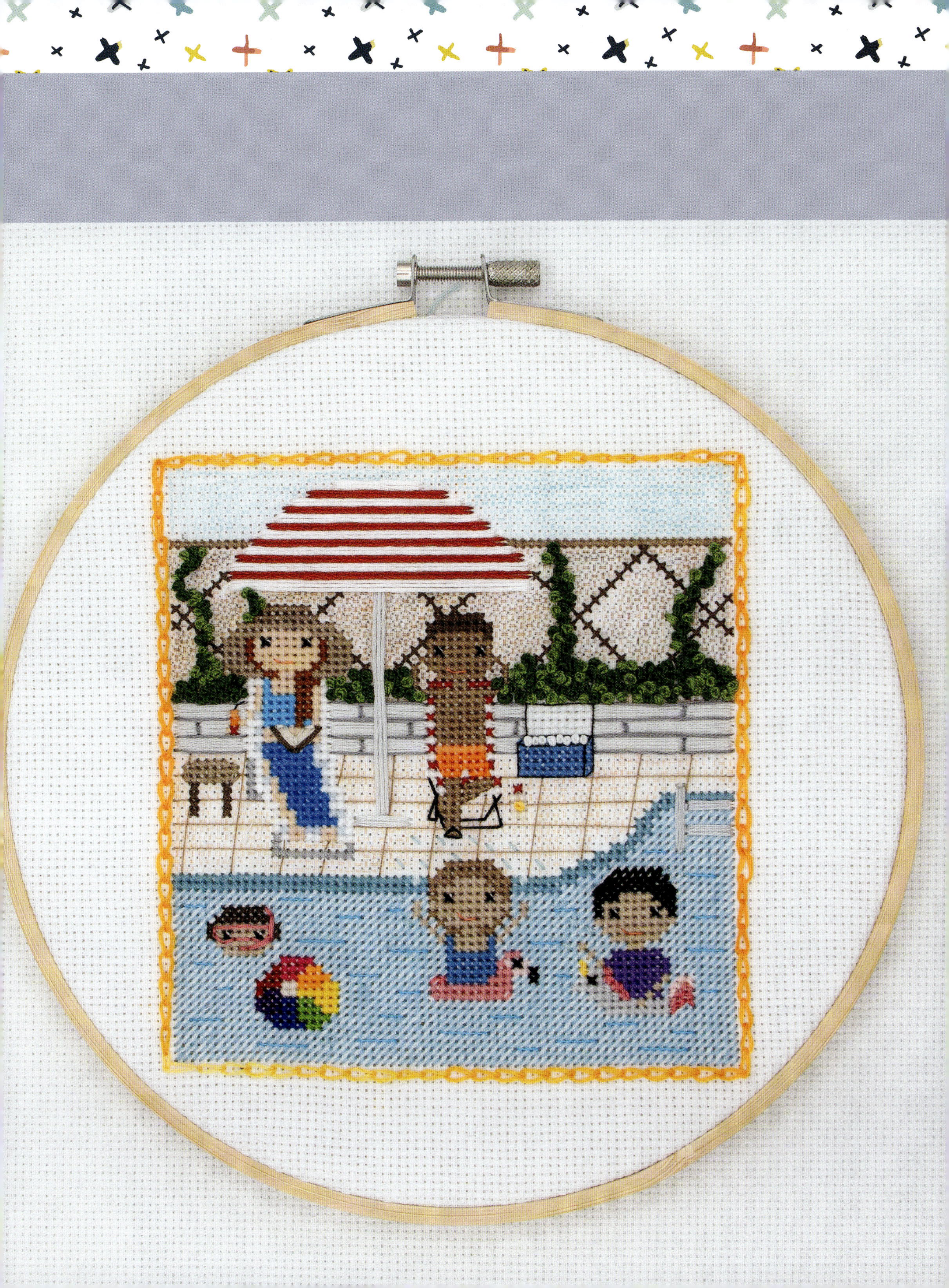

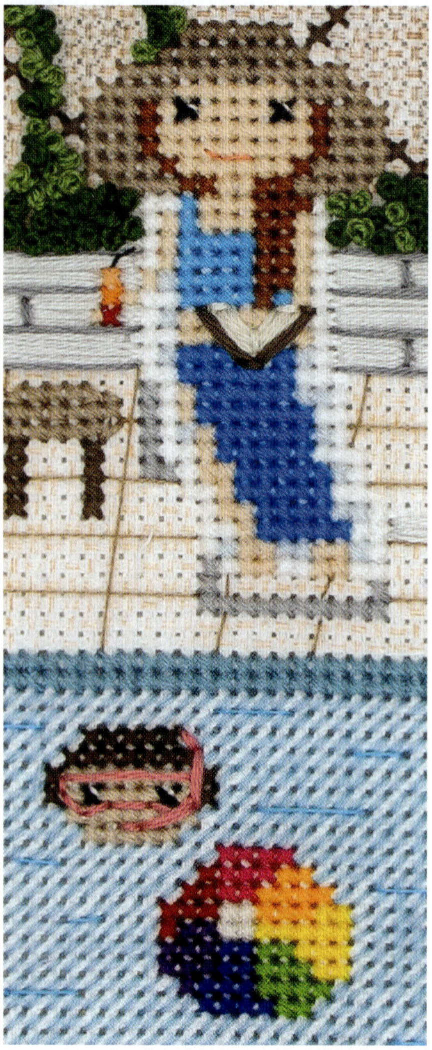

Time-saving stitches: Long straight stitches, long satin stitches, and coloring in an area with a fabric marker are ways to cut back on stitching time if you're in a pinch!

5 Choose floss colors for each character's skin tone, hair color, and attire (see page 38).

6 Choose floss colors for the scenery.

7 Use 3 strands of floss to cross-stitch each square in the pattern.

8 Use 1 strand of floss to backstitch all linear details, except use 2 strands for the mouths.

tip

The pool's water is stitched with diagonal half stitches. The umbrella and retaining wall were created with long, parallel straight stitches, or satin stitches. The greenery uses two different colors of green French knots, and the simple border is a daisy chain stitch.

customization tip!

This portrait's techniques create dimension and save time. The sky, lattice fence, and concrete are colored in. That's right, many stitchers like to utilize permanent fabric markers or even watercolor paints to help fill in large sections of a pattern. (Try them out on a spare scrap of fabric before you use it directly on your project so you can get the hang of it!)

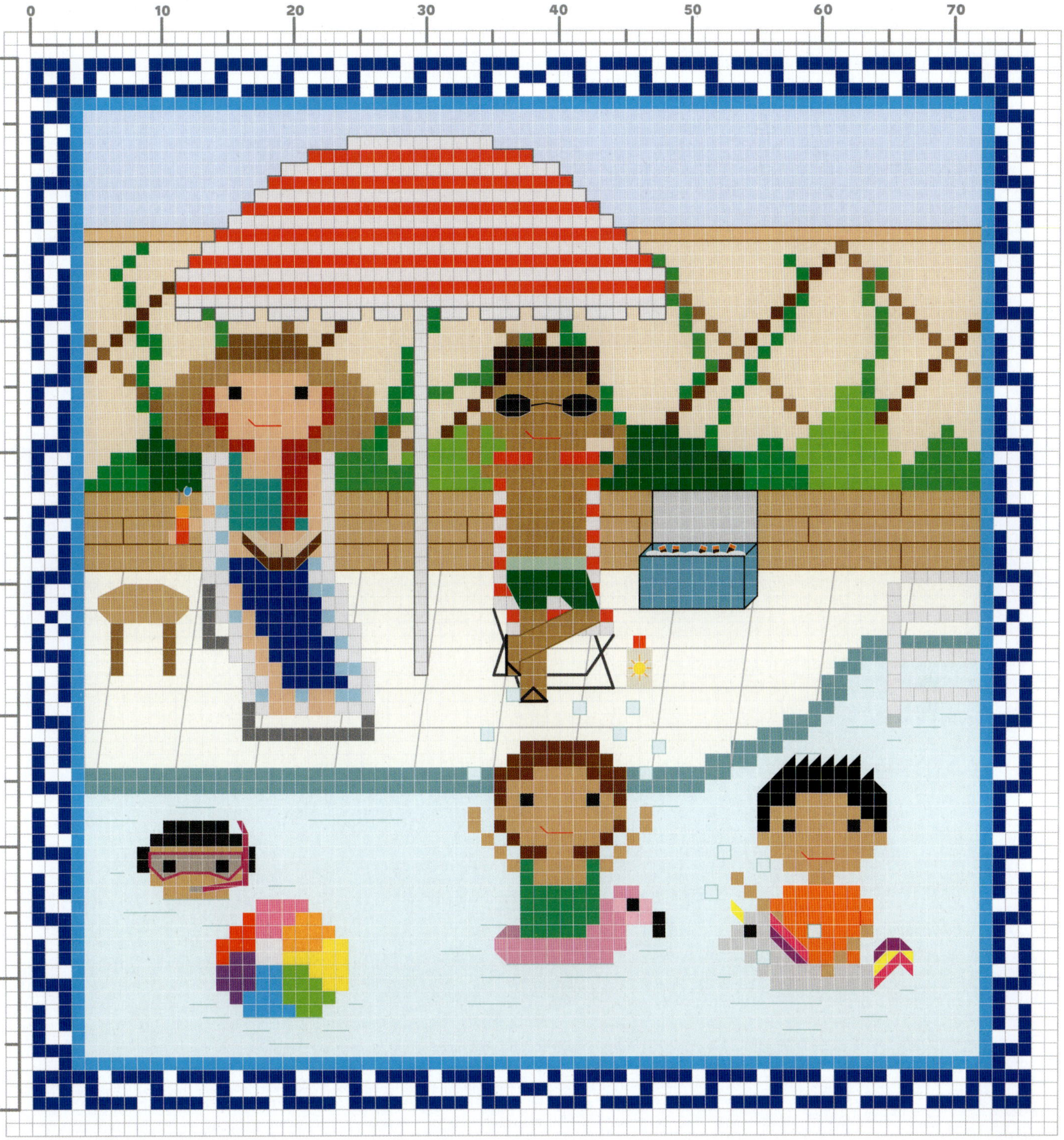

0
10
20
30
40
50
60
70
0
10
20
30
40
50
60
70
80

autumn fun

IF IT ISN'T AUTUMN'S SCENTS OF BRAND-NEW SCHOOL SUPPLIES OR THE FLAVORS OF APPLE AND PUMPKIN THAT ENTICE YOU, IT MUST BE THE CRISP, COOL AIR AND THE SOUND OF CRUNCHING LEAVES!

Pattern Dimensions:
60 squares wide
x 72 squares high

Finished Dimensions on Size 14 Aida Fabric:
4.3" x 5.1"
(11 cm x 13 cm)

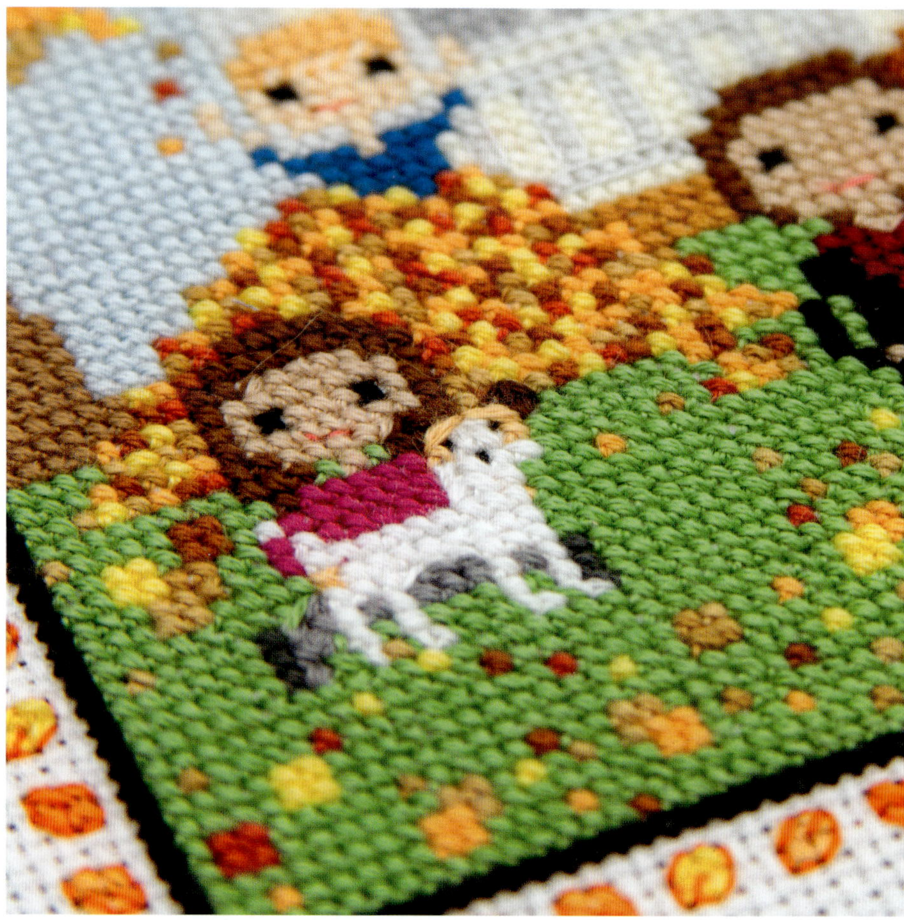

INSTRUCTIONS

1 Cut the fabric to 8.5" x 9" (22 cm x 23 cm), mark the center point, and secure it in the center of an embroidery hoop. Customize the pattern as needed.

2 Replace any hairstyles you'd like with examples from the front of the book (see page 44).

3 If needed, make any height or width adjustments to the characters in the pattern.

This portrait was lovingly stitched by Kayla Rosenthal! Follow her on Instagram @kaylasstitches.

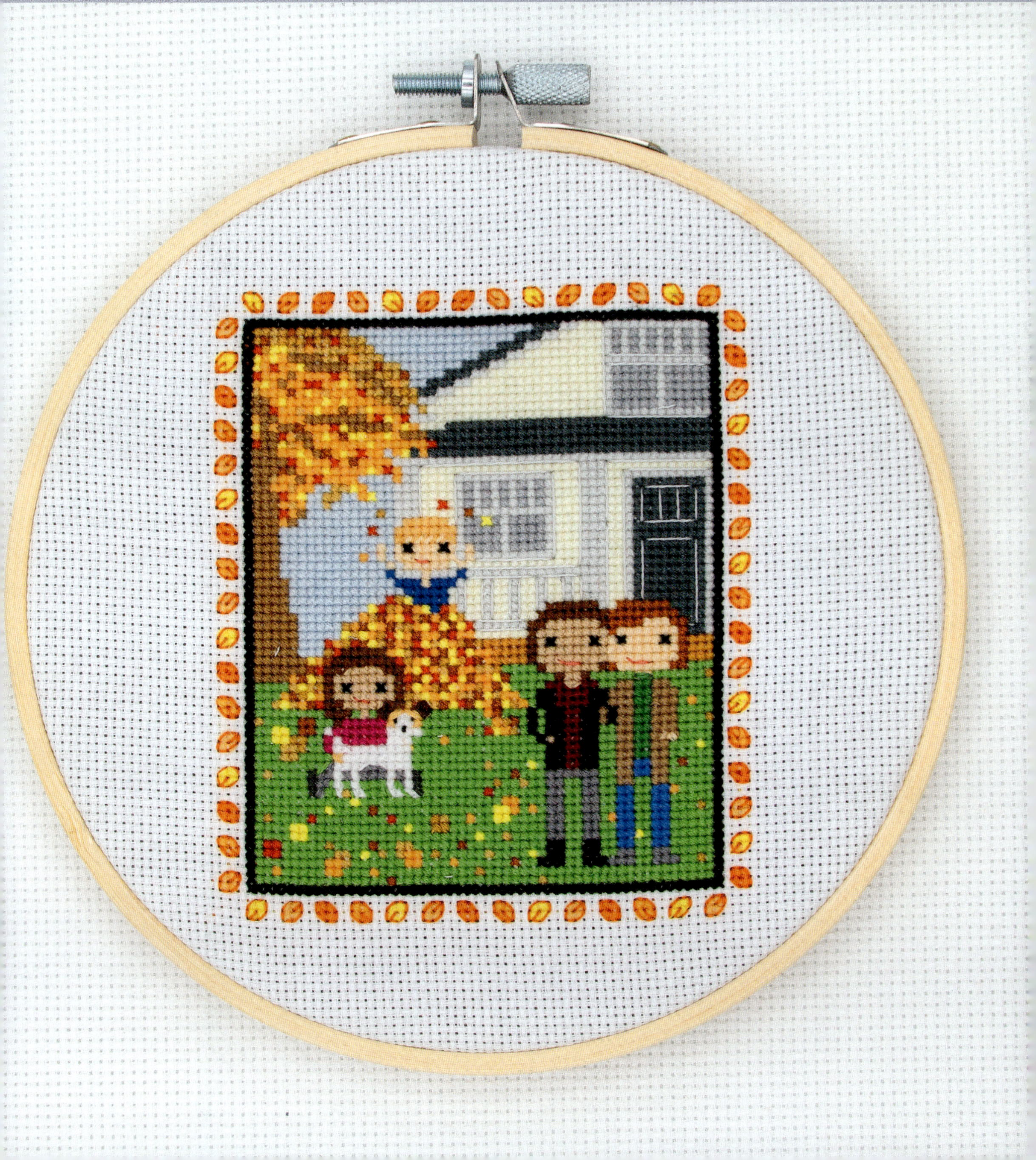

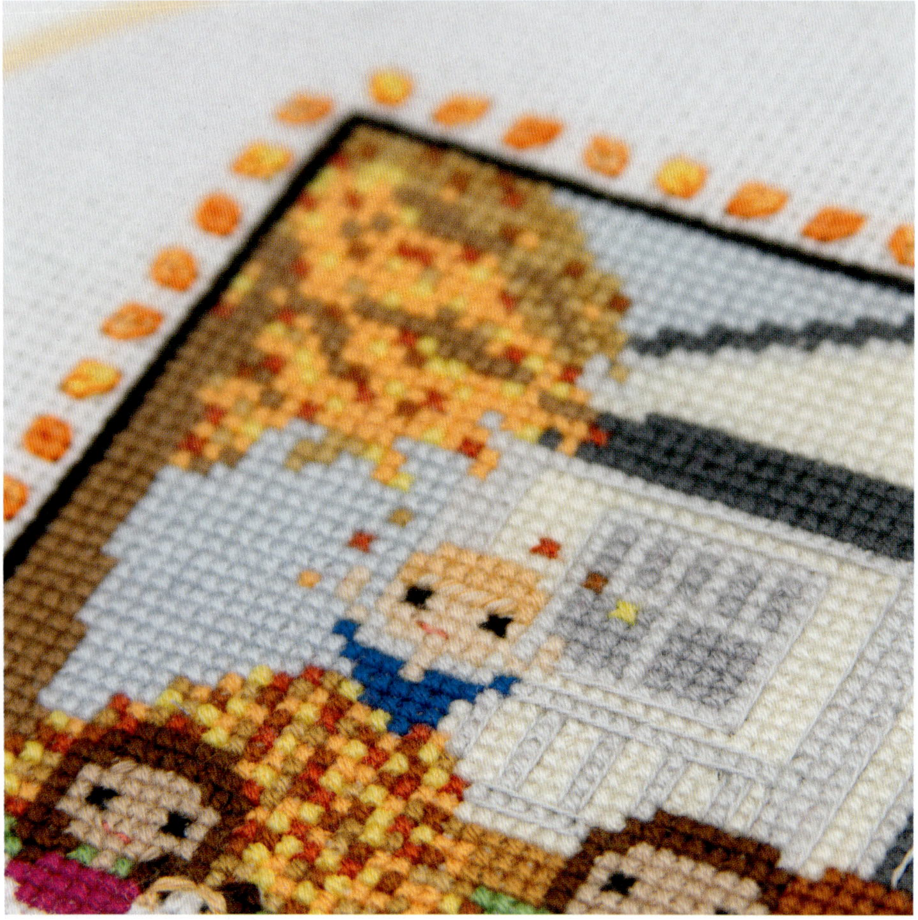

note

The children in this pattern can represent the range of five to ten years old.

4 Decide if you'd like to make other adjustments to the pattern, like removing or changing the border, adjusting the pattern's dimensions, or by removing columns or rows of the pattern. Due to the nature of this pattern, I recommend removing no more than 2 columns from the right side, but up to 4 columns on the left side will work fine.

5 Choose floss colors for each character's skin tone, hair color, and attire (see page 38).

6 Choose floss colors for the scenery and home in the background.

7 Use 3 strands of floss to cross-stitch each square in the pattern.

8 Use 1 strand of floss to backstitch all linear details, except use 2 strands for the mouths.

9 Use French knots to stitch the circles of the dog's face, with 2 threads for the eyes and 3 threads for the nose (see page 30).

customization tip!

Notice how the use of simple straight stitching in this portrait helps amp up the details! The leaves are outlined in small straight stitches. The details of the home's doors, windows, and moldings are accentuated with long straight stitches. And the tiniest straight stitches of all fill in the eyes and nose of the dog's face.

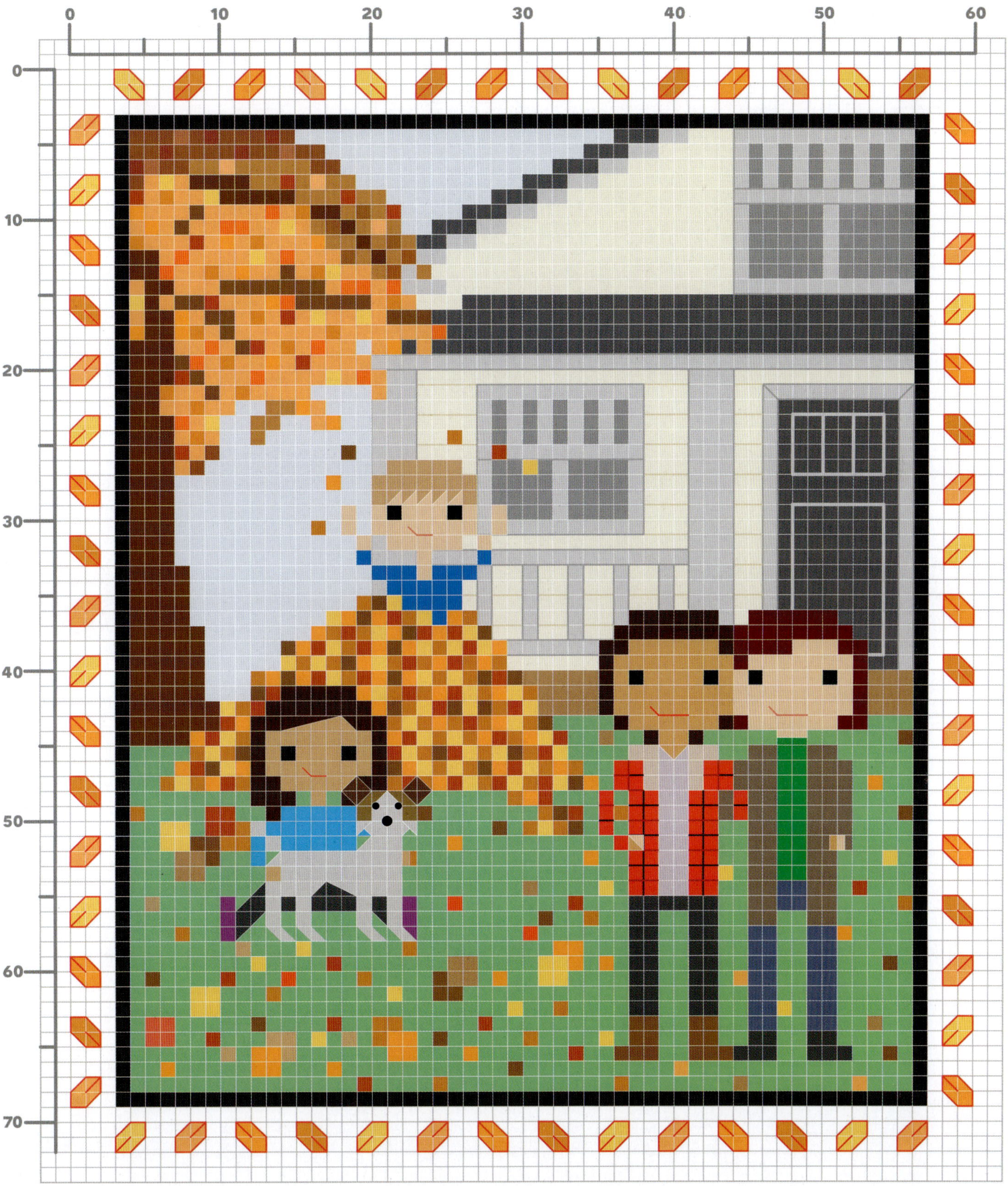
0
10
20
30
40
50
60
0
10
20
30
40
50
60
70

finishing a portrait in a hoop

TO GIVE YOUR PIECE A NICE FINISH IN ITS HOOP, FOLLOW THE INSTRUCTIONS HERE.

I suggest using felt to finish the back side, since it's inexpensive and easy to work with, but theoretically any fabric should do. Just be aware the thinner the fabric, the more any gathers in the Aida fabric may affect how smooth the fabric looks.

You may also finish the back using a decorative, heavyweight cardstock. Instead of sewing it on, use a few dabs of very strong, fabric-friendly glue.

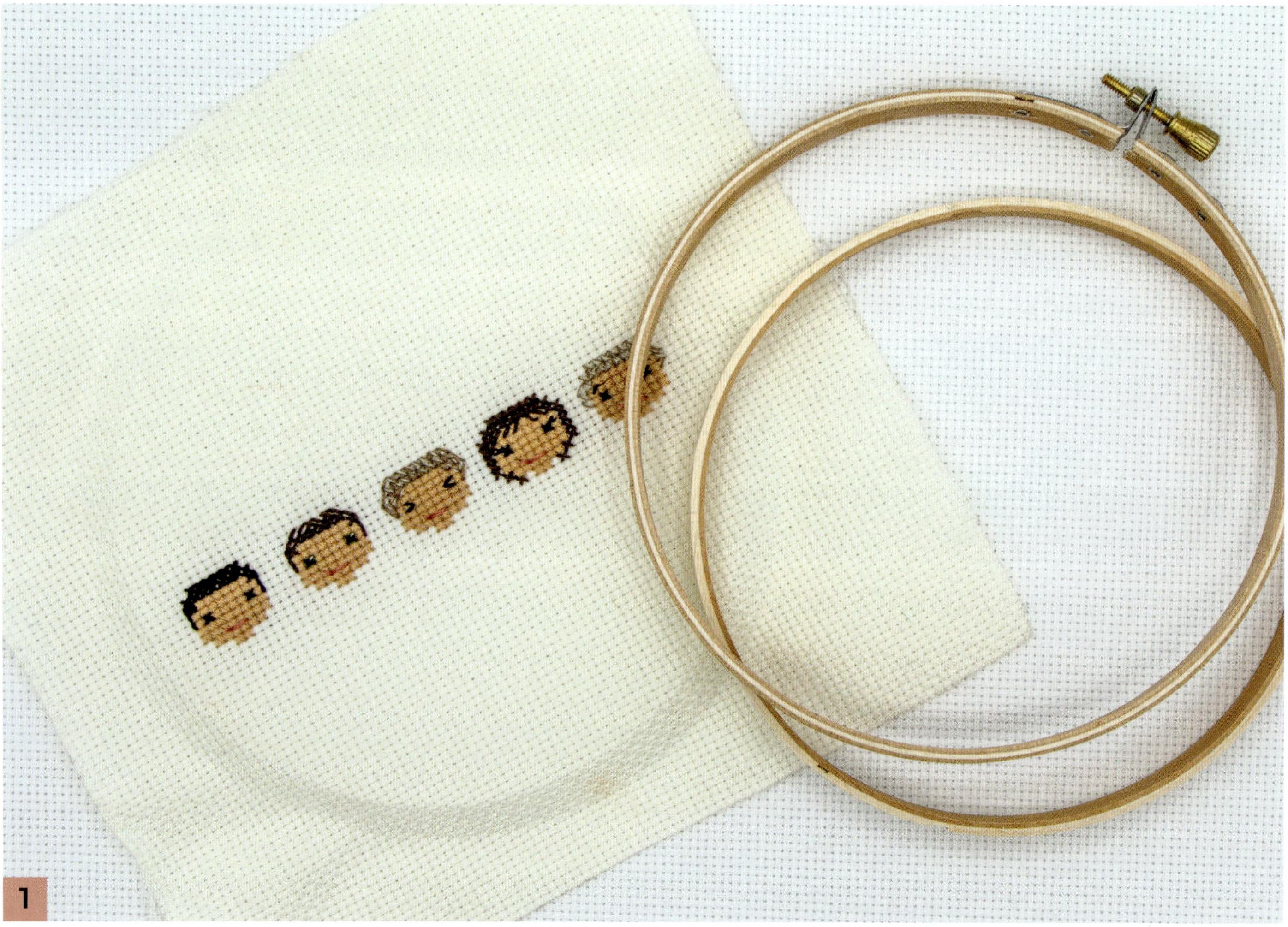

1

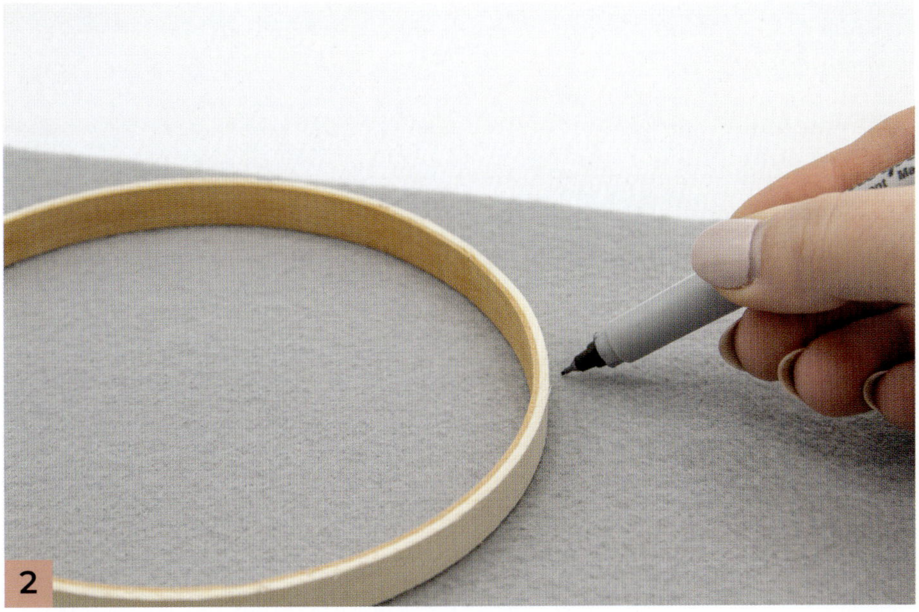

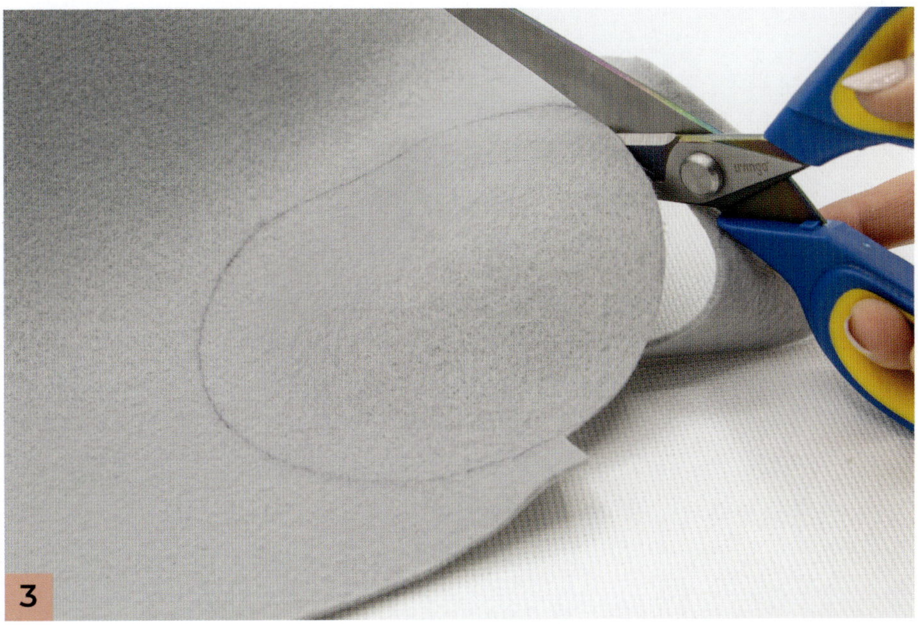

1 Oftentimes you'll find you have to re-center a finished piece in the hoop—that's totally normal. Remove your work and set aside the inner, smaller hoop.

2 Trace the inner hoop on a piece of felt with a fabric pen or permanent marker.

3 Cut out the circle, right along the traced line.

4 Remount your work in the hoop, making sure it's centered. You may have to work against some preexisting ridges, which will usually smooth out as you remount. If, however, they are visible when you center your pattern, you can simply remove your work again and steam the ridges out with a steamer or iron, then remount/re-center once more.

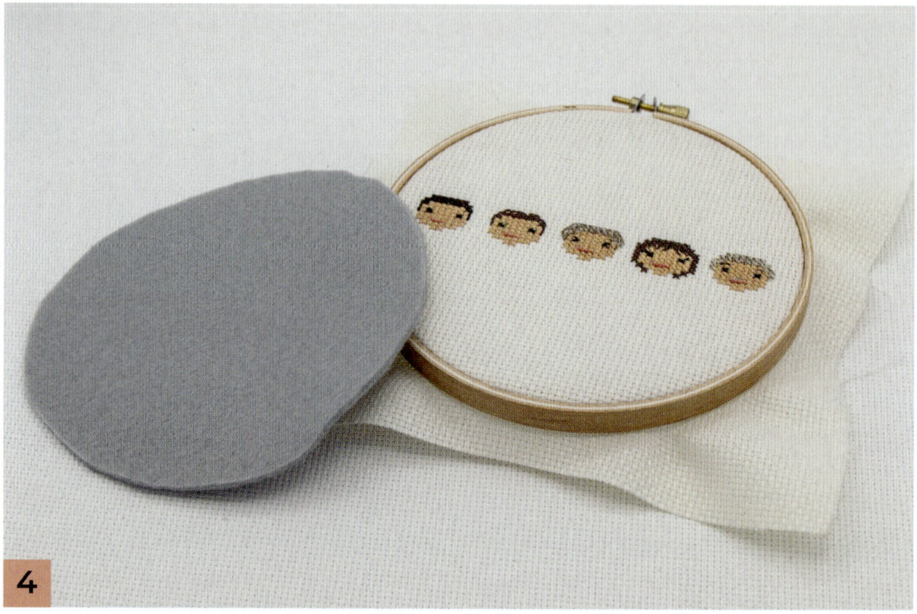
4

5 Trim the excess fabric from around your work. It does not have to be perfectly even all the way around, but be sure to leave absolutely no less than a ½ inch (1.25 cm), and no more than 1.5 to 2 inches (3.8 cm to 5 cm). A larger hoop (8-inch or 20 cm and more) should have closer to 2 inches (5 cm) all the way around.

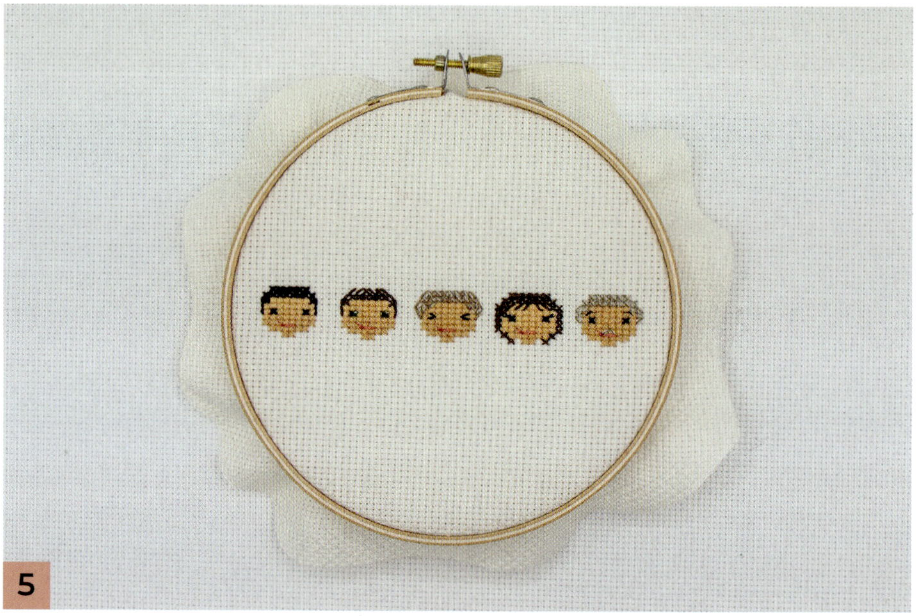
5

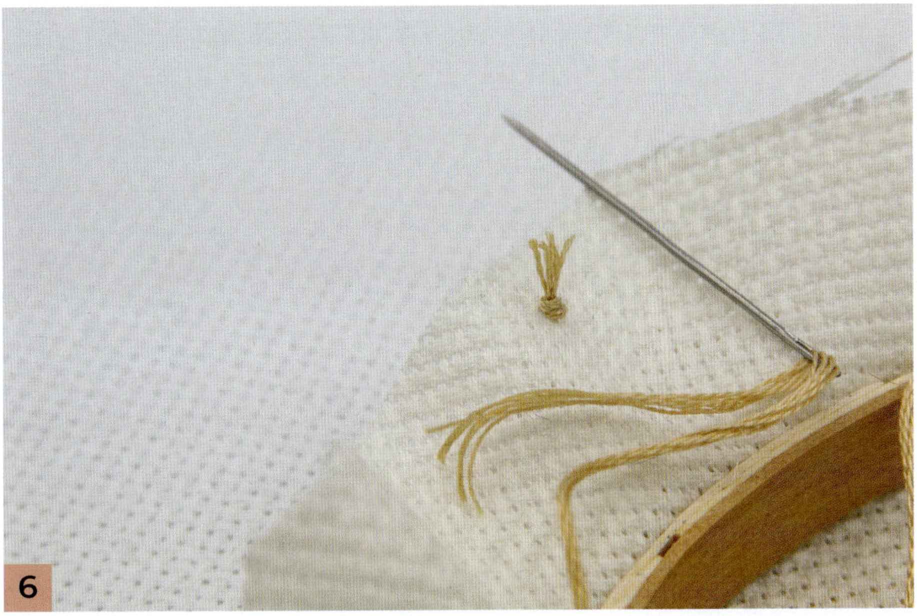

6

6 Cut a length of floss that's at least as long as the total circumference of your hoop. Thread a needle with all 6 strands. Go ahead and tie a double knot in the end for good measure, and in the excess rim of your Aida fabric outside the hoop, bring your needle and floss through from the back to the front—aiming outside the holes of the Aida fabric for extra security. Be sure to leave a minimum of around ¼ inch (0.6 cm) between your needle's placement and the outermost edge to prevent fraying.

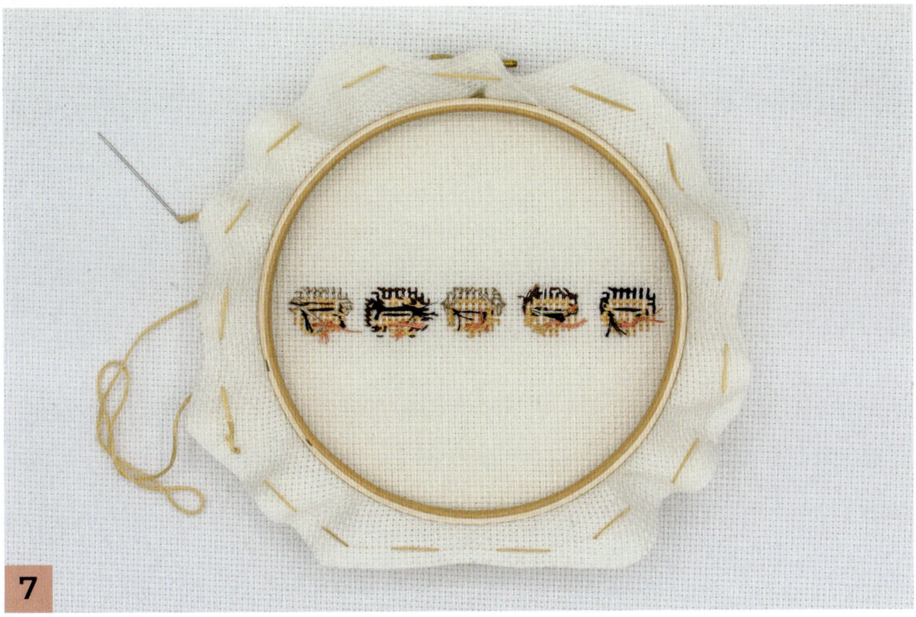

7

7 Work your way around the outside edge of your fabric with a long, relatively consistent running stitch. It does not have to be perfect and it doesn't matter if you aim inside or outside the holes of the Aida fabric. Remember to keep your needle at least ¼ inch (0.6 cm) from the outer edge to prevent fraying.

8 When you get back to your starting point, pull very, very tightly so that the edges of the Aida fabric scrunch in toward the center. You may have to work with the floss a bit to be sure the tension is consistent all the way around, and that the Aida fabric ruffles or pleats together evenly.

9 Keeping the tension very tight, secure the floss. This can be done in a number of ways. I typically just run my needle and floss around and around the edge many times, looping under itself, until I feel confident the floss won't slide or catch.

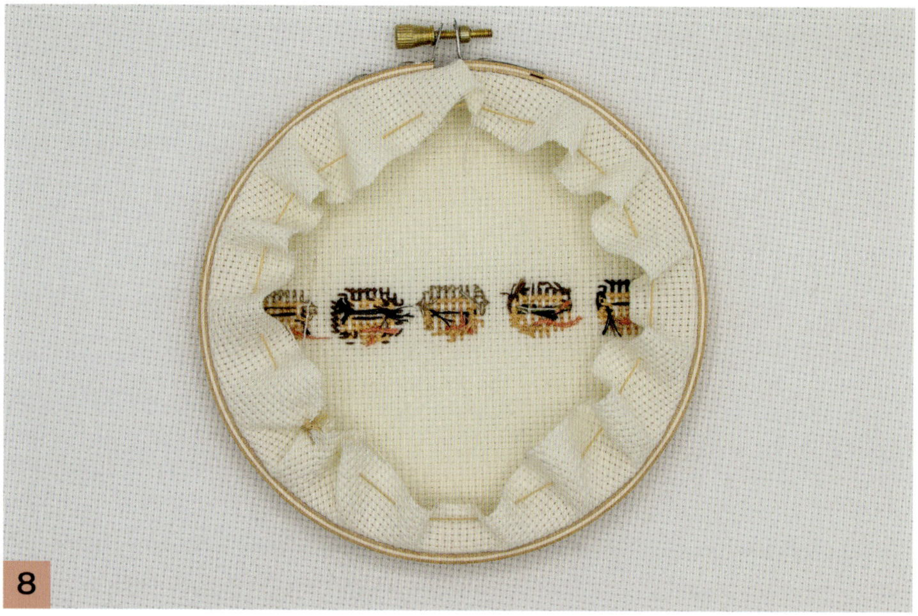
8

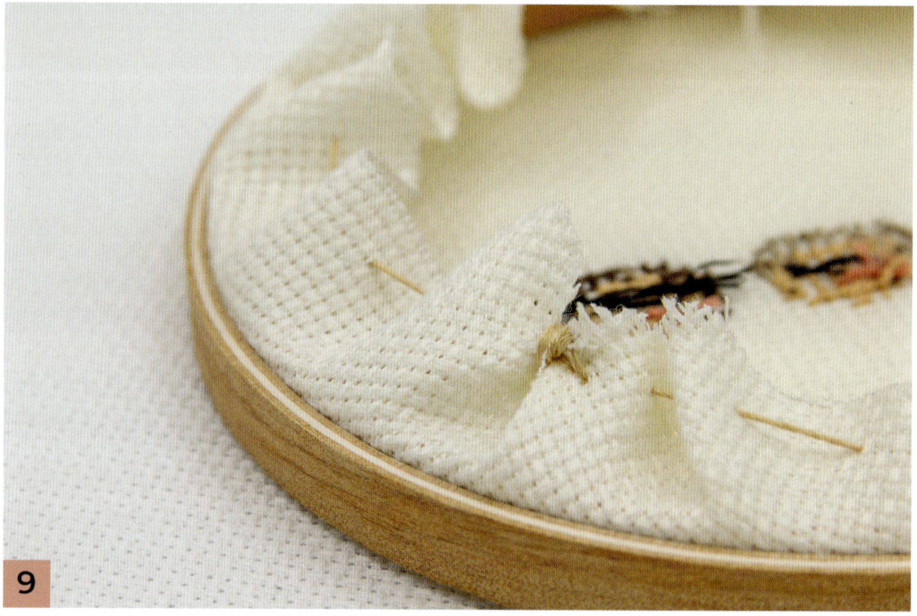
9

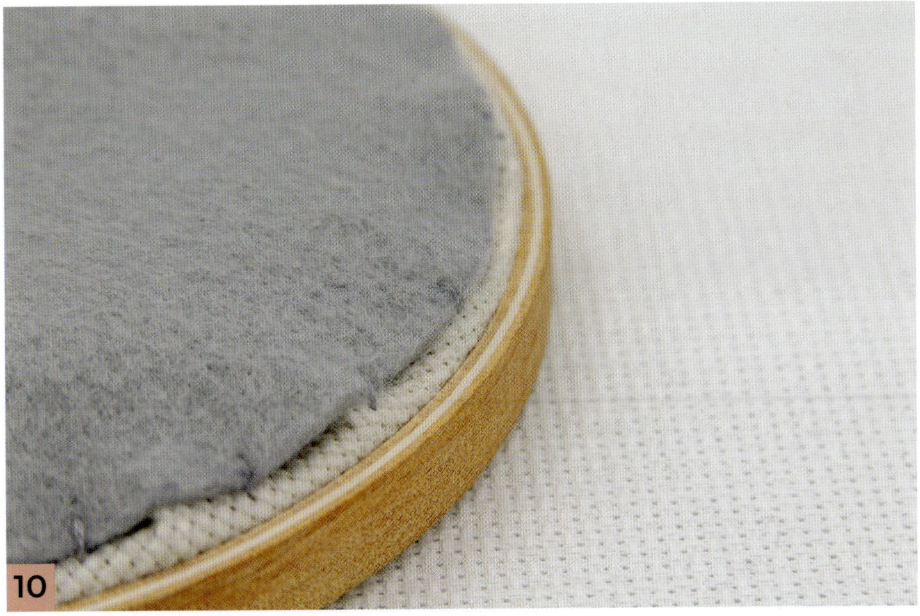

10

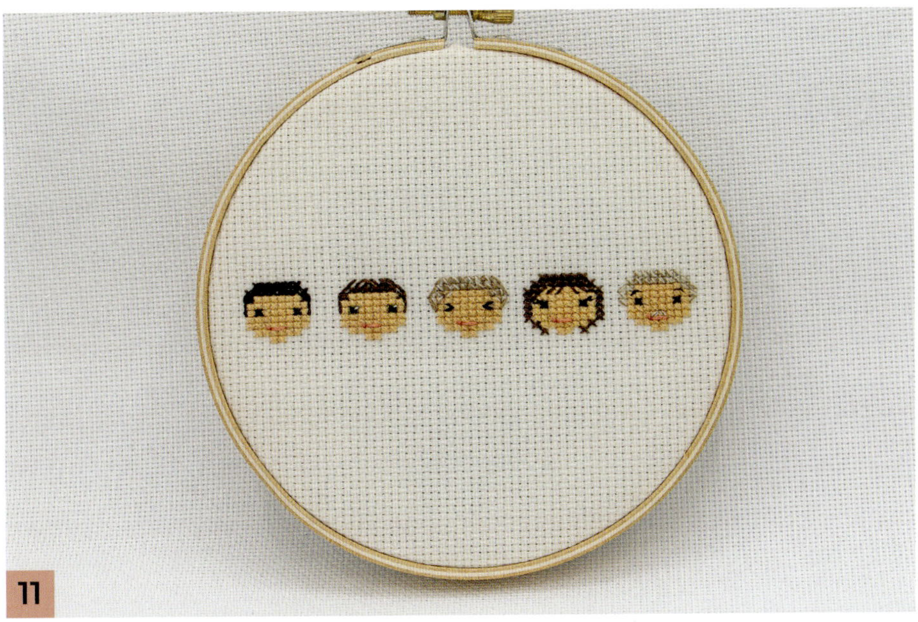

11

10 Lay your felt circle atop the back side of your finished work (traced side facing down in case any of the outline is still visible), and stitch the edge of the felt to the edge of the Aida fabric using floss of a similar color. Any kind of securing stitch you like will do, as long as the stitches are consistent and do the job of securing the backing to the Aida. Patience is key here!

11 When finished, the back of your hoop will look neat and tidy and the front will show no signs of any unsightly, fraying edges! Well done!

resources

THESE ADDITIONAL RESOURCES CAN HELP YOU FURTHER ADJUST, CUSTOMIZE, AND PERSONALIZE THE PATTERNS FOUND IN THIS BOOK.

BORDERS & ALPHABETS

Don't forget that the best thing you can do is take a deep breath and dive in! There is no "wrong" choice when it comes to your creativity. If you try something and don't like it, you can always change it or start over. No big deal!

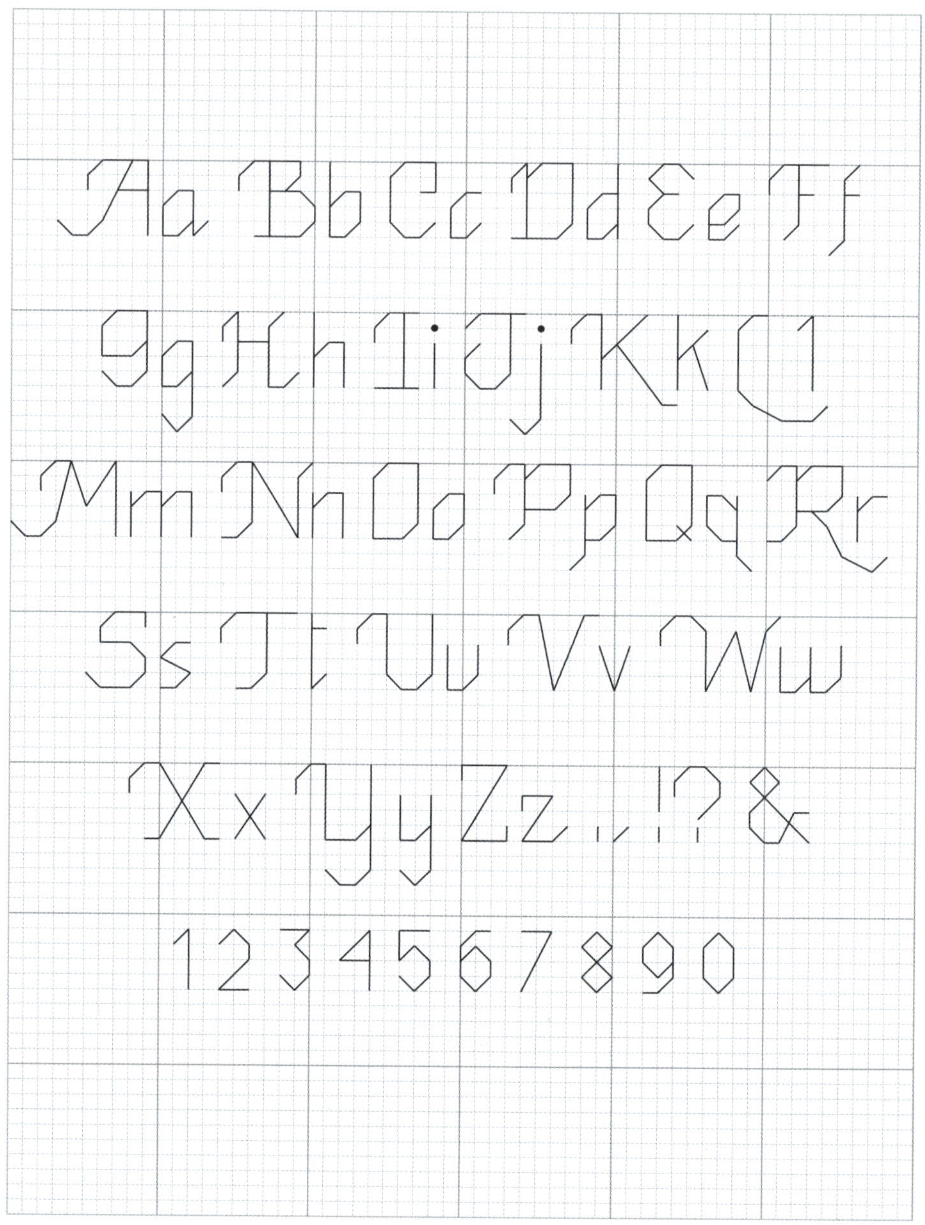

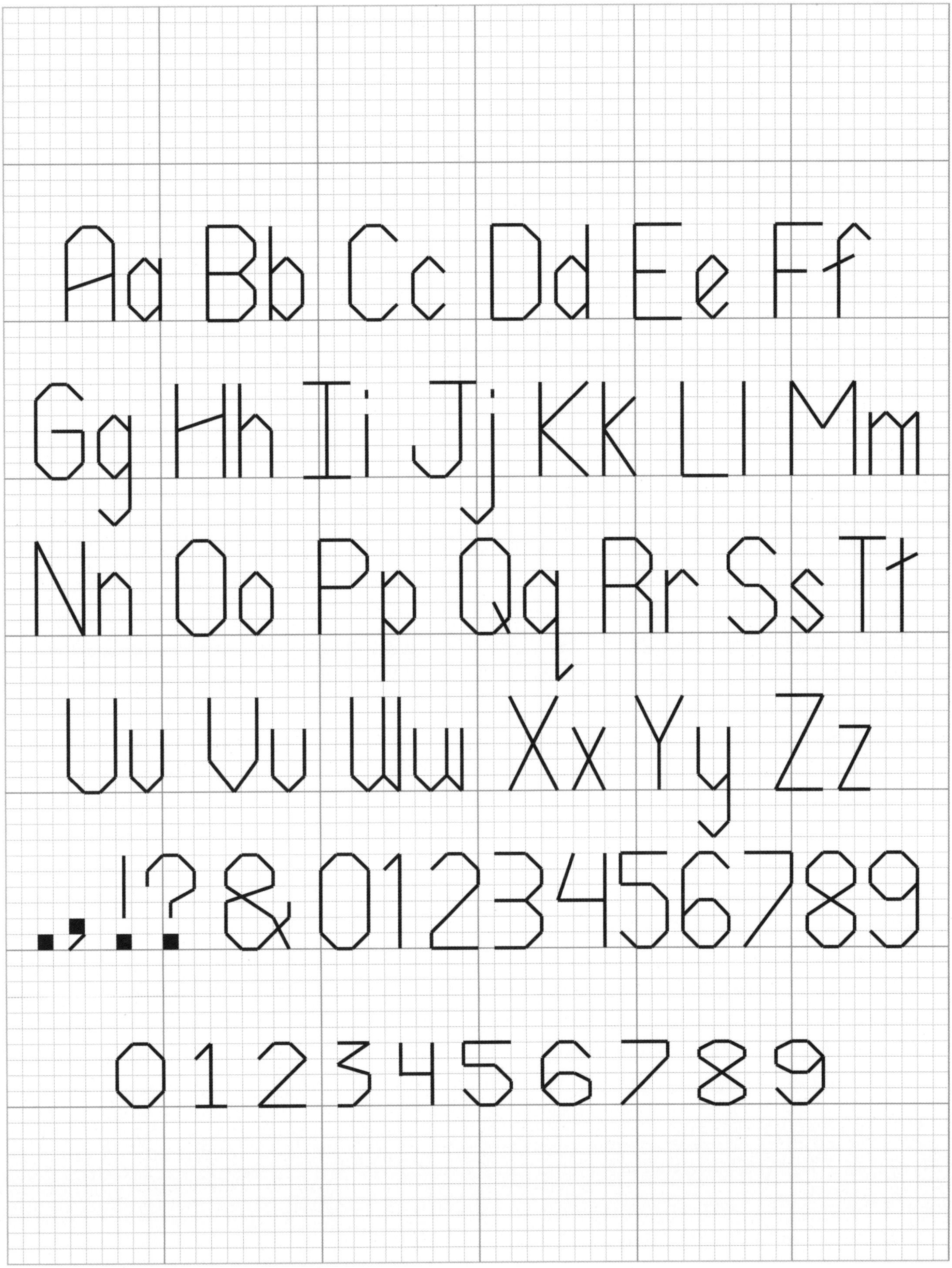
Aa Bb Cc Dd Ee Ff
Gg Hh Ii Jj Kk Ll Mm
Nn Oo Pp Qq Rr Ss Tt
Uu Vv Ww Xx Yy Zz
.,!?&0123456789
0123456789

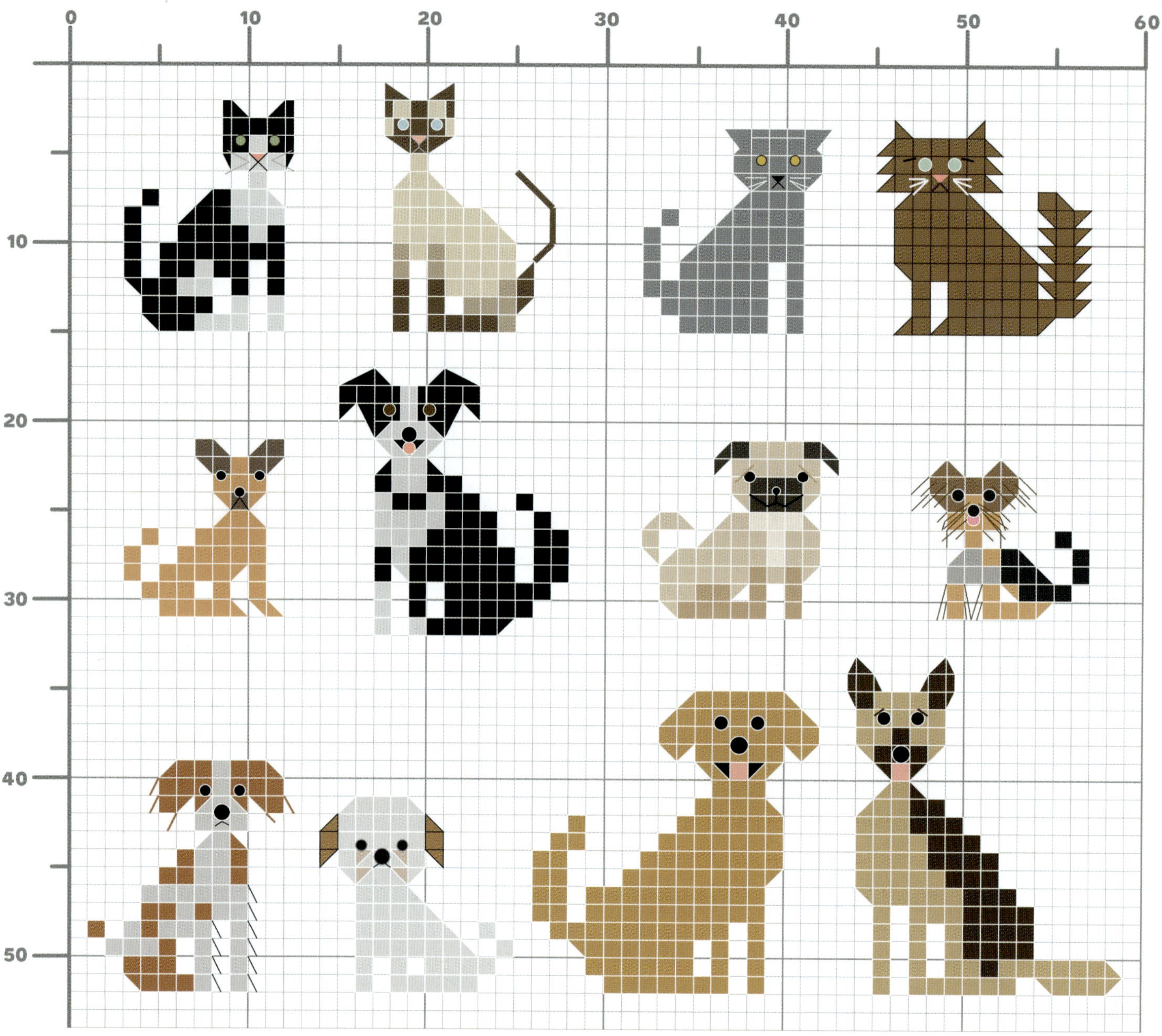

PATTERNS FOR DOGS & CATS

If you'd like to add a furry friend to your scene, or replace an existing pet with a different one, here are a selection of dog and cat patterns you can use for your customization needs!

Since each and every furry friend is uniquely colored and patterned, look closely at the pet you're re-creating, and choose as many floss colors as you need to get it just right. Keep in mind you can combine floss colors (using 1 to 3 threads of 1 to 3 different colors), or simply change floss colors as many times as you need while you stitch.

GRAPH PAPER

Blank graph paper has many uses when customizing your cross-stitch patterns. Make a copy of this before using it so you can utilize this blank page again and again!

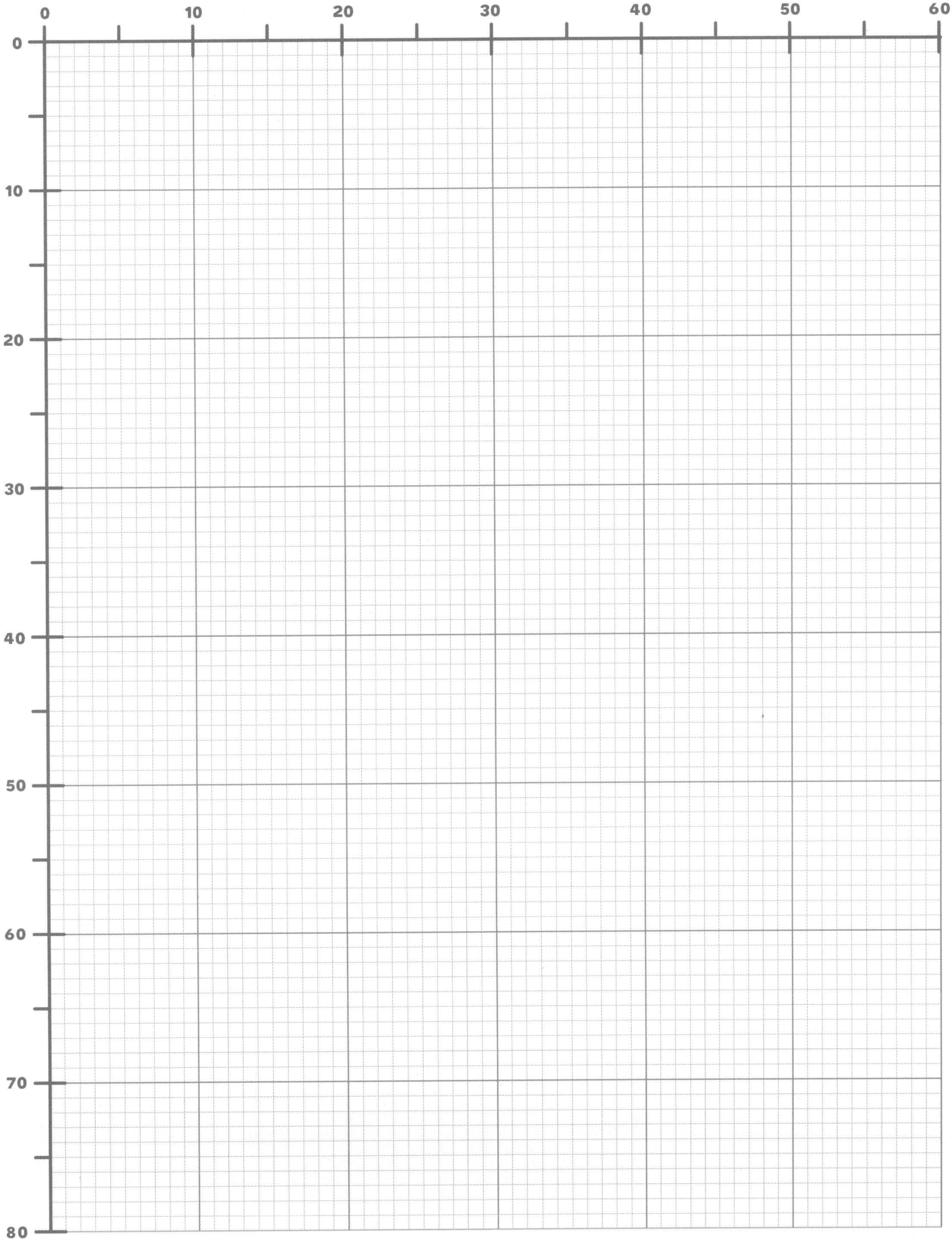
0
10
20
30
40
50
60
0
10
20
30
40
50
60
70
80

about stitch people + the author

STITCH PEOPLE WAS FOUNDED IN 2012 BY LIZZY DABCZYNSKI-BEAN AND SPENCER BEAN.

What started as a small, customized, cross-stitched family portrait-making service has expanded into a thriving community of tens of thousands of creative and inspiring stitchers around the world. In addition to custom portraits and custom portrait patterns, Stitch People now offers a vast library of hundreds of mix-and-match, totally customizable cross-stitch family portrait patterns, which are available both in physical book form and digital download. Follow us @stitchpeople or visit us at stitchpeople.com.

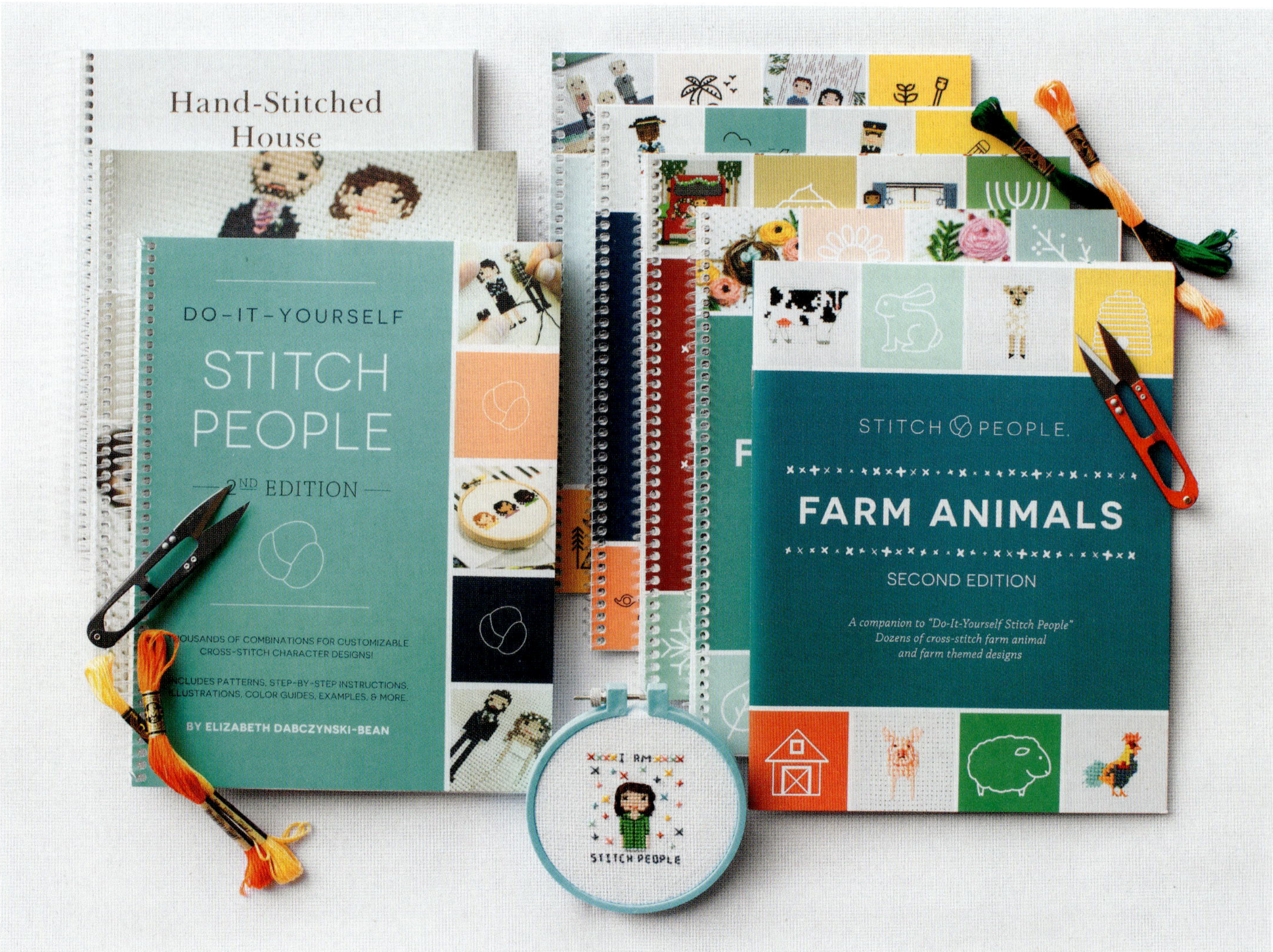

STITCH PEOPLE WOULD BE NOTHING WITHOUT OUR SMALL-BUT-MIGHTY TEAM AND SUPPORTIVE COMMUNITY:

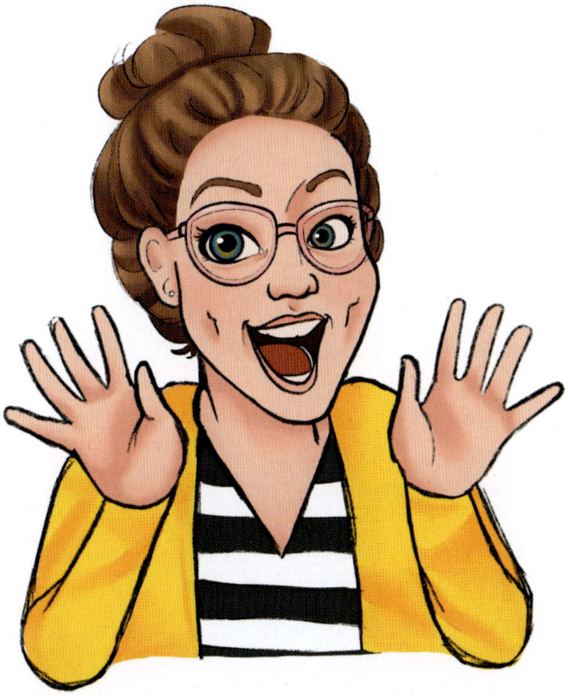

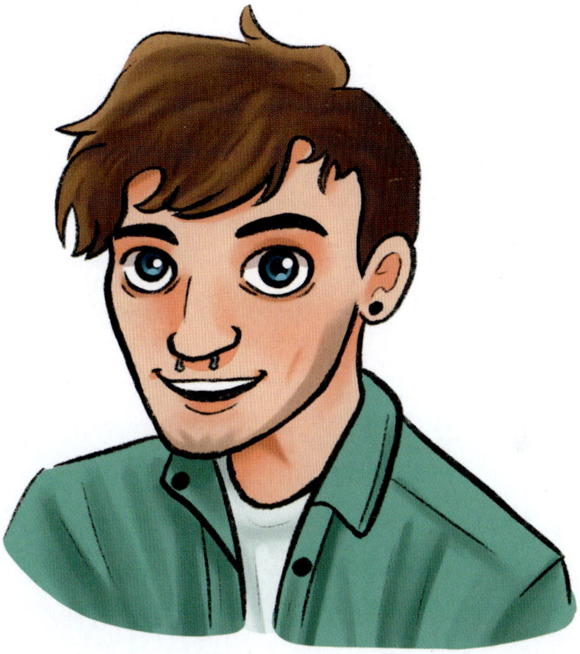

LIZZY BEAN

Raised via East Coast, USA, and now living in the Intermountain West, Lizzy is a full-time creative, life enthusiast, and classic jack-of-all-trades. Lizzy has been the face of and Principal Designer for Stitch People for the last ten years, during which time she has also worked professionally across a broad spectrum of professional industries, her favorite of which being producing, writing, directing, or acting in TV and film productions. She loves laughing, learning new things, loving on rescue dogs, and helping people make their dreams come true. Follow her @lizzydbean or visit lizzydbean.com.

JULIAN ODESSA

Julian is Design Lead and resident Australian at Stitch People. His tale is a common one—boy starts out as a musician, becomes a cancer researcher, then returns to the arts to work from home in his comfy pants, helping cross-stitchers reconnect with their creativity. Classic. He writes for *CrossStitcher Magazine UK*, exploring the relationship between art and mindfulness. In his downtime, Julian enjoys being a foliage wizard and tending to his ever-growing plant brood, playing and writing music, performing in local theater, and getting out into nature as often as possible. Follow Julian on Instagram @jojodessa.

stitchers

The beautiful portraits in this book were lovingly stitched by the following extraordinary stitchers:

Amanda Irvin @erinandelizabeth

Andrea Emslie @stitchyandrea

Christy Pawloski @sunlightstitchery

Erika Cota @arkacota

Hillary Nestrick @keystonecrossstitch

Natalie Bryant @sunflowerstitchseasons

Kaya Rosenthal Happily offline

Naya Janae Johnson @nayajanaecreates

Teresa Victor Happily offline

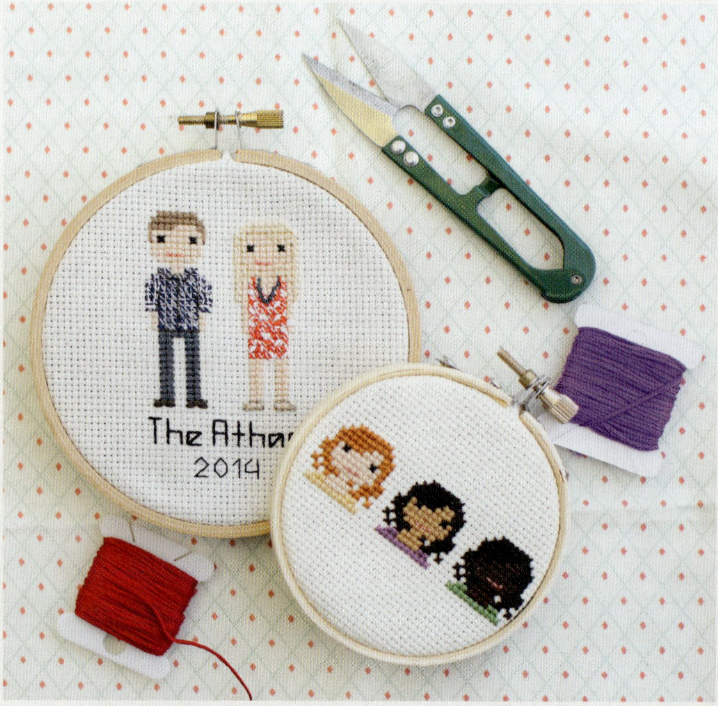